THE SEARCH FOR THE RELIGIOUS IDEAL IN SELECTED WORKS OF JOSÉ CASTILLO-PUCHE

Front Cover:

Cover photograph courtesy of the Cistercian Community of El Poblet, Tarragona, Spain.

José Luis Castillo-Puche. Born 1919.

THE SEARCH FOR THE RELIGIOUS IDEAL IN SELECTED WORKS OF JOSÉ CASTILLO-PUCHE

Martin Farrell

Studies in Art and Religious Interpretation
Volume 26

The Edwin Mellen Press
Lewiston•Queenston•Lampeter

Library of Congress Cataloging-in-Publication Data

Farrell, Martin.
  The search for the religious ideal in selected works of José Luis Castillo-Puche /
Martin Farrell.
      cm. -- (Studies in art and religious interpretation ; v. 26)
  Includes bibliographical references and index.
  ISBN 0-7734-7864-7
  1. Castillo Puche, Josâ Luis--Criticism and interpretation. 2. Christian life in literature.
  3. Vocation in literature. I. Title. II. Series.

  PQ6605.A857 Z64 2000
  863'.64--dc21
                                                                          99-053189

This is volume 26 in the continuing series
Studies in Art and Religious Interpretation
Volume 26 ISBN 0-7734-7864-7
SARI Series ISBN 0-88946-956-3

A CIP catalog record for this book is available from the British Library.

The Edwin Mellen Press   The Edwin Mellen Press
Box 450   Box 67
Lewiston, New York   Queenston, Ontario
USA 14092-0450   CANADA L0S 1L0

The Edwin Mellen Press, Ltd.
Lampeter, Ceredigion, Wales
UNITED KINGDOM SA48 8LT

Printed in the United States of America

With gratitude to José Luis Castillo-Puche without whose generosity and cooperation this study would not have been possible.

Table of Contents

Preface   ix

Chapter 1 Introduction   1

Chapter 2 Sin camino   9

    A. The Seminary Environment   12

    B. Attraction to the World   16

    C. Indecision   33

Chapter 3 Como ovejas al matadero   49

    A. Social Justice   51

    B. Sacrifice   62

    C. Sexual Repression   65

Chapter 4 Trilogía de la liberación: Introduction   93

    A. Life and Literature   95

    B. Narrative   108

Chapter 5 El libro de las visiones y las apariciones   117

    A. Symbols of Oppression   119

        1. Hécula   120

        2. Death   125

        3. Cirilo and Cayetano   134

    B. Symbols of Liberation   140

        1. Water   144

        2. The Mother   147

Chapter 6 El amargo sabor de la retama   155

    A. Thirst   160

B. Guilt   169

    1. The Revolution   172

    2. Sexuality   179

    3. The Vocation   183

C. Happiness   188

D. Depression   194

Chapter 7 Conocerás el poso de la nada   201

A. The Ideal   205

B. The Reality   213

C. The Ideal Abandoned   221

    1. The Loss of Identity   223

    2. The Death of the Mother   227

D. Reactions   231

Chapter 8 Conclusion   245

Bibliography   253

Index   259

Preface

El profesor Martín Farrell, con una técnica de análisis profundo de las motivaciones vocacionales, concretamente de la vocación sacerdotal en la España de la posguerra civil, ha hecho un trabajo admirable y exigente sobre aquellas novelas mías que se refieren a estos temas, enfocándolos en un estudio global asociado a mi propia personalidad de aspirante al sacerdocio y trasladando mis propias vivencias personales a todos los niveles y matices de los textos analizados. Ordenando con gran sentido categórico toda la problemática del ideal religioso y moral, el autor de este excelente trabajo lleva a cabo además de una exploración y análisis sicológico de los personajes una auténtica pregrinación cronológica de los mismos y sus circunstancias espirituales. Lo que permanece tras el examen crítico del profesor Farrell es el contenido y el desarrollo vital de una existencia azarosa, rebelde, dubitativa, soñadora por un lado y truncada o fracasada por el otro, dilema angustioso entre la voluntad de querer ser sacerdote y las contingencias de la vida, los altibajos de la conciencia y el desacuerdo conciertas prácticas, conductas se incluso enseñanzas, de tal modo que los protagonistas navegan desde el idealismo religioso y hasta misionero más exaltado hasta las privadísimas razones particulares controvertidas y prácticamente inconfesables.

Con gran acierto, el profesor Farrell concentra el análisis de las novelas elegidas para su estudio en unos temas fundamentales, como son la vocación, la sexualidad, la culpa, la muerte, la identidad y la liberación, temas que, al margen de lo religioso han sido siempre recurrentes en mis novelas y puede decirse que han sido mi gran preocupación de narrador. Se nace con la sensación opresora del imperio de la carne y la lucha para encontrar el testimonio adecuado a esta opresión, puede ser para el escritor incluso torturante. Luego, las lecturas y las experiencias vitales entran en confrontación con las experiencias en los seminarios, sobre todo si hablamos de los seminarios españoles anteriores al Concilio Vaticano II, experiencias que suscitan en los ordenandos dudas, desconfianzas y hasta cierta incredulidad destructora, casi siempre motivada por las conductas de los superiores de alta jerarquía espiritual que a veces confunden y pervierten las intenciones vocacionales más puras a base de malos ejemplos se hipocresías, y algunas de mis novelas aluden concretamente a estas nefastas influencias. El hombre es débil, pero no se puede edificar un sacerdocio íntegro y evangelizador sobre la aceptación sin más de esta debilidad. Justamente el Evangelio se tenía muy poco en cuenta en la educación teológica en aquellos años de la posguerra española, cuando lo que abundaba era la casuística escolástica y las teorizaciones abstractas, lejos de los compromisos morales más acuciantes.

El secretismo del sexo, por ejemplo, era en aquellos tiempos prácticamente aberrante, hasta llegar a su eliminación física del cuerpo humano en las imágenes; los silencios, las persecuciones de maestros, sacerdotes, incluso de médicos, fomentaban la capacidad de fingimiento, reserva y falsedad de las conductas, perturbaban la conciencia de los jóvenes educandos y alteraban su sensibilidad. Todo se ocultaba, se prohibía, se perseguía, y de esta manera era cómo surgían las amistades más peligrosas y se creaba una moral falseada de tergiversaciones y ocultamientos desquiciadores para cualquier sensibilidad que aspirase a un ideal puro y sincero. En relación con la sexualidad aparece a menudo la culpabilidad. No nacemos culpables sino culpados, previamente a toda acción de la voluntad humana. Esta es la culpa que, según el cristianismo, se borra con el bautismo. Pero hay otra culpa, la culpa del propio existir, la consecuencia prematura de la disconformidad con lo establecido, la rebeldía contra el destino impuesto por medio de tabúes, dogmas, doctrinas, costumbres. En este sentido es difícil admitir que somos culpables, pero lo somos. Porque la culpa no brota de los vicios o los placeres prohibidos, salvo que sean contra natura o contra la humanidad. La culpa nos acecha desde pequeños en forma de pequeñas transgresiones que a unos afectan más que a otros. Depende de la sensibilidad. Este sentimiento de culpa busca precisamente la libertad que puede ser encontrada por vía del arte, o incluso de la locura, una enajenación o supresión de las ataduras, sumisiones, disciplinas o penitencias, todo lo que se opone al libre albedrío del hombre en porfía cotidiana. La sensacón física y moral de la culpa está en la raíz de la vida, es congénita y acusatoria, es un lastre del nacer y del vivir, un peso hredado que la mente compulsa a diario y que se confirma con desastres, calamidades, injusticias, mentiras. Todo lo que nos rodea es culpa o lamentación y el hombre siente la necesidad de la inocencia y de la expiación, y busca la paz y la aceptación de os planes de Dios creador y redentor. Pero en cambio se encuentra con que a su alrededor todo es mandato, confusión, amenaza, y piensa que estos no son los planes del Dios misericordioso. Entonces nace la rebeldía. La culpa busca su propia redención en el interior del hombre, sin intervención sacerdotal, sin amenazas, sin consejos ni absoluciones. El hombre en este caso se convierte en ministro-sagrado-religioso o laico de la propia personalidad espiritual y el hombre caído puede ser y aspira a ser su propio salvador, siempre que tenga fe profunda y siga los mandamientos de la voluntad divina, pero sin accesorios mediáticos, sin represiones fanáticas o coercitivas. El hombre lleva en sí mismo la posibilidad de redención y de perdón. El Evangelio del amor y del perdón siempre ocupará el vacío humano y divino que Cristo vino a colmar.

La contradicción entre la atracción de lo hermoso de la vida y la as piración al abandono de lo mundano forma parte de la luche vocacional. El fenómeno de la vida, desde el comienzo, es un fenómeno medio triste medio gozoso, desde la atracción del mundo al misterio de la realidad circundante, se choca con la reserva de que el vivir es un misterio incomunicable; lo que se vive no sólo es una realidad atractiva y hermosa sino que es a la vez un miedo, una peligrosidad acechante, una contradicción entre lo que se percibe y lo que no es posible captar pero se intuye. La vida es una tentación, más que una diversión, es un ciudado, una soledad, una rara ensoñación de fascinantes colores y movimientos que en un momento dado puede esfumarse, como un suspiro en el aire, entre el verdor de los árboles, la ráfaga del viento y la fuerza cegadora del sol.

En cuanto a la identidad consiste en el concimiento de uno mismo. ¿Quién soy? ¿Dónde estoy? ¿Para qué?... Pero la identidad puede perderse precisamente por los sentimientos de culpa, abandono, pérdida de la memoria, frustraciones, y también por la contradicción entre el sentimiento propio y las imposiciones o las opresiones incomprendidas. De ahí que la identidad se recupere por la memoria, haciendo un gran esfuerzo por coordinar los recuerdos del pasado con el presente, es decir, asumiendo la propia personalidad a través de los recuerdos se integrándolos en el presente, sea este cual sea. La identidad así alcanzada es aceptarse uno a sí mismo, asumiendo la imperfección pero creando a la vez la posibilidad de la propia corrección, en una aspiración ascendente de perfección. Lograr la identificación de la propia personalidad con la realidad ambiental, social y moral, sin dejar de ser uno mismo, sin perder el ansia de plenitud en medio incluso de la incomprensión y de la injusticia, es una virtud a menudo difícil de lograr, pero cuando se logra es fuente de serenidad y de paz espiritual.

La pérdida de la identidad es algo grave en la persona humana, algo que a menudo conduce a la Siquiatría; pero yo escribí la *Trilogía de la liberación* precisamente como un ejemplo de recuperación de la identidad y de la inocencia a base de recorrer la infancia opresiva y la juventud frustrada a través de los recuerdos. La liberación se logra por la sinceridad, reconociendo y aceptando todo lo que han sido errores, falsedades, hipocresías, buscando la verdad desnuda y la libertad interior (fundamento de la confesión y penitencia católicas), oponiendo la libertad personal frente a las imposiciones falsas y opresivas. La liberación, pues, en la obra de arte exige una técnica de renuncia y extirpación, el autor tiene que ir derribando todas las barreras de su propia moral conservadora para llegar al fondo de la denuncia de falsos ídolos, pantallas, refugios, trucos y toda clase de cortinajes que el ser humano puede implantar para protegerse. La liberación así es renuncia total y búsqueda de la verdad por dura que sea. El auto se declara en desnudez y simplicidad totales sin dejar de ejercer la protesta y la rebeldía.

Se ha dicho, y el profesor Farrell lo acepta incluso documentado, que la *Trilogía de la liberación* es totalmente autobiográfica. Realmente, estas tres obras, como otras mías, están hechas de mis vivencias y experiencias, pero no de mi biografía, que son cosas distintas. En mis novelas están mis vivencias, hasta puede decirse que está lo vivido por mí, pero no mi biografía, que siempre aparece muy alterada en la obra de arte. Otra cosa sería una historia, no una novela. Un ejemplo clarísimo está en la muerte de la madre, uno de los episodios más resaltados y más elogiados de *Conocerás el poso de la nada*, y sin embargo totalmente inventada, ya que mi madre falleció en circunstancias muy distintas y ni siquiera estuve a su lado cuando murió. ¿Que quise compensar quizás el fallo de mi ausencia en la muerte de mi madre con un episodio altamente dramático y sentimental? Pudiera ser desde el mismo subconsciente del narrador.

Finalmente, quiero agradecer al profesor Farrell la objetividad y la independencia de juicio con que trata estas obras mías tan conflictivas. De ellas se desprende sin duda que el autor ha vivido siempre dentro del cristianismo, pero con una fe, aunque inquebrantable, un tanto indisciplinada y respondona. Mi instinto espirtual y mi ansia de justicia y de verdad me han llevado a menudo a concebir sueños de reformas - algunas se han cumplido - y de mayor sinceridad y libertad dentro de la Iglesia. He creído y agradecido en muy pródigas ocasiones el premio de la Gracia no merecida, pero quizás mi amor a la belleza, al orden y a la perfección me han conducido en ocasiones a la tentación de la rebeldía y de la indisciplina. Fui, por lo tanto, poco consecuente con los dones recibidos, pero por fortuna nunca me faltó el sentido cristiano de la vida y de la muerte.

JOSE LUIS CASTILLO-PUCHE

CHAPTER 1
Introduction

It could be said that the literary career of Castillo-Puche began in 1943 with his short story *Bienaventurados los que sueñan* published in serial form in *La Verdad* of Murcia.[1] However, it was 1947 before the author had completed his first major novel entitled *Sin camino*, regarded as a powerful testimony to his own experience of the religious seminary of Comillas in northern Spain. As the author's literary career progressed with the publication of *Con la muerte al hombro* in 1954, *El vengador* in 1956, *Hicieron partes* in 1957 and *Paralelo 40* in 1963, it became increasingly clear that his literary creation was fundamentally related to real situations in the author's own experiences. This relationship between life and literature is equally evident in the later works from *Como ovejas al matadero* in 1971 to *Conocerás el poso de la nada* in 1982 and has led to a tendency among critics such as Sobejano and Peñuelas to regard them as both realistic and autobiographical.[2] A similar observation has also been made by Ramón Jiménez Madrid while commenting on *El libro de las visiones y las apariciones*, the first part of the so-called *Trilogía de la liberación*, where he indicates the themes which appear to be of most concern to the author:

> Como en casi todas sus novelas, vuelve Castillo-Puche a reincidir en su problemática y lacerada autobiografía ... Los conceptos de amor y odio, vida y muerte, guerra civil con dos bandos antagónicos, la Iglesia eterna frente a la de rostro o dimensión humana, las imposiciones de la sociedad estratificada y convencional frente al individuo, el autoritarismo ciego y fanático frente a la conciencia personal o la libertad, son elementos que se disuelven constantemente o se diluyen por la totalidad de su obra.[3]

All these elements form part of a reality personally experienced by the author during a specific historical period and in particular geographical areas of Spain. These notions of time and place, along with the social environment, are, for Emilio González-Grano de Oro in his study of the *Trilogía de la liberación*, the fundamental dimensions on which the transmission of that reality is based:

> La realidad de Castillo-Puche se encuentra primeramente en el espacio de tiempo por él acotado. De toda su obra narrativa, incluida la extranovelística, puede afirmarse que está referida a un tiempo cuyos límites enmarcan el presente histórico y vital de su autor. También a esa realidad se la encuentra en el lugar en que discurre el relato de ese tiempo como parte de una realidad geográfica conocida directamente o visitada por él. La encontramos, por último en la circunstancia cultural, social e histórica reflejada por el autor y tan íntimamente a él unida.[4]

The stages of life depicted in the novels range from childhood and adolescence to youth and manhood with each stage associated with a particular set of conflicts. The geographical situation is variable although a great deal of reference is made to the author's native town of Yecla, transformed into Hécula in the novels. Apart from Hécula, other locations in the novels include Santander, the Basque region, Madrid and Murcia, all of which are familiar to the author. The Civil War is the central historical event to pervade most of his novels; nevertheless, there are also many references to both the period of the Second Republic and the post-Civil War era.

In a later chapter the question of life and literature will be discussed in more detail when both characters and elements from the *Trilogía de la liberación* will be related to the people and events in the author's own experience. It will also be seen how, while admitting that his novels contain many elements from reality, Castillo-Puche rejects the allegation of being autobiographical or a realist since he claims that literary creation is quite distinct from mere biography:

> Diría que la novela es la vida misma, pero una vida transfundida al plano de la creación, nada de realismo, nada de imitación de la realidad, porque tampoco la vida es la realidad que vemos, como muchas veces se ha creído. La novela es una realidad y es vida, pero vida y realidad distintas, nuevas, situadas en otro plano. Es una realidad hecha de palabras, de imágenes, hecha, en una palabra, arte literario.[5]

In other words, no matter how much personal experience is included in the novel, there will always be fantasy or invention to alter and transform that experience into another reality, a literary reality. Furthermore, he believes that what matters most in the novel is not the external or social reality but rather the plight of the protagonist as a human being:

> Tengo que decir que no creo que existan novelas autobiográficas; existen novelas del hombre, de un hombre o una mujer, que puede ser el propio novelista o la novelista, o puede ser otro hombre. Si es una buena novela será la novela de cualquier hombre o por lo menos de muchos hombres.[6]

There is an experience included in the novels, however, that is common only to a limited number in society but which, in my view, is crucial to the understanding of the author and his work, and it is his experience of seminary life. In reality, Castillo-Puche spent eleven years of his early life in a religious establishment which included a period in Murcia from the age of ten to seventeen before the Civil War and a period in Comillas after the Civil War from the age of twenty to twenty-four.

With so much of his youth spent within the seminary, it is inevitable that such an element of reality should form the raw material of the novels. While much of his work has some sort of reference to the religious education, only a limited number actually have the vocation as one of the principal themes, namely, *Sin camino, Como ovejas al matadero*, and the three novels of the *Trilogía de la liberación*: *El libro de las visiones y las apariciones*, *El amargo sabor de la retama* and *Conocerás el poso de la nada*. In the trilogy the seminary experience is recounted in the third novel but many of the elements in the two preceding novels are connected to the notion of the religious vocation.

These novels, however, could not be considered to be religious works or Catholic novels as they are not concerned with the questions of faith or doctrines. Instead, these novels are mainly involved with human experience and can appeal to any individual who has ever experienced a personal ideal or an oppressive upbringing or a sense of anxiety and uncertainty. In this sense, my study is not so much an analysis of Catholic tradition and practice, but rather an attempt to clarify the major issues confronting those characters in the novels who embark upon a religious career. Consequently, my study will be particularly concerned with the concept of the religious ideal in the face of family pressure, an oppressive environment, sexuality and the sense of identity. By embracing all the factors and forces surrounding the religious ideal, I hope to distinguish between how much the vocation is to do with personal choice and how much can be attributed to external influence and circumstances. Also, as the earlier reference to autobiography suggests, I will attempt to show the connection between the experiences of the characters in the novels and the personal experiences of Castillo-Puche.

While much has been made of the psychological and existential aspects of the novels chosen, inadequate attention has been given so far in the criticism of Castillo-Puche to the notion of the religious vocation and the human conflicts that this involves. Yet it is through a closer examination of the religious ideal, the seminary and the priesthood that I think we can have a clearer picture of the author. Two other novels can be related to this theme. However, I decided not to include *Hicieron partes* among my choice of novels since it cannot be considered to be a study of the seminary but rather of the use and abuse of money. I also chose not to include *Jeremías, el anarquista* as it is concerned with the problems of infidelity and desertion after ordination, which is an area that was not experienced personally by the author.

The first novel to be studied, *Sin camino*, was particularly appealing in that it was written almost immediately after the author's departure from the senior seminary. In this way, it could potentially be considered the most autobiographical of all his works since many of his experiences were still fresh in his memory. The work contains many references to Comillas and Santander and the ongoing events of the Second World War and is also critical of the seminary regime of that time under the Jesuits. The critical nature of the novel led to the work being banned by the censors until it was eventually published in Argentina in 1956. It seems significant, also, that the title of this novel is the opposite of a book published in 1939 by Jose María Escrivá, the founder of the Opus Dei, entitled *Camino*.[7]

My second choice, *Como ovejas al matadero*, was published in 1971, almost twenty-five years after *Sin camino* was written and during the aftermath of the Second Vatican Council. This seemed to me a logical choice since, apart from the change of setting to Murcia, it shows how the author was still concerned with the conflicts and problems involved in seminary life. It is also a very critical work and, like *Sin camino*, concentrates on the conflict between natural instincts and the religious ideal. As well as contrasting the success and failure of the religious vocation, I was keen to highlight the author's concern about priestly celibacy which will be examined in the discussion of sexual repression.

The three novels of the *Trilogía de la liberación*, regarded as some of the best works written by Castillo-Puche,[8] are also connected to the notion of the religious vocation and worthy of study in their own right. The most attractive feature about the trilogy was the sense of self-exploration and self-analysis as the novels endeavour to probe the source and development of the religious ideal. In this examination of the early periods of the author's life during the 1920s and the 1930s, I will be looking especially at the external forces, both positive and negative, involved in the religious ideal and also the notion of personal commitment. Such an undertaking will necessarily include references to both historical and ecclesiastical perspectives as well as to certain psychological and philosophical interpretations, as is also the case with the earlier novels chosen.

Although all these novels are related to the same topic, the first and the last are separated by a period of almost forty years. Bearing this in mind, it seemed appropriate to examine each novel separately and in chronological order since the implied author of the mid-1940s would probably have a different perspective from the implied author of 1980. In this way, I hope to discover the changes and similarities between each novel and how the author's views have evolved and developed over the years.

NOTES

1. This work appeared in the form of a newspaper serial from 15 August to 1 October 1943 and has been reprinted in full by Emilio González-Grano de Oro. See *El español de José L. Castillo-Puche: estudio léxico* (Madrid: Gredos, 1983), 361-388.

2. References to the comments on realism by Gonzalo Sobejano and Marcelino Peñuelas are included in the later chapters on *Sin camino* and *El libro de las visiones y las apariciones* respectively.

3. Ramón Jiménez Madrid, *Novelistas murcianos actuales* (Murcia: Alfonso X el Sabio, 1982), 90.

4. Emilio González-Grano de Oro, "Visión y sabor del poso de la nada." *Cuadernos Hispanoamericanos* 388 (1982), 202.

5. "Escribir en Murcia.", lecture given by the author at the University of Murcia (1988).

6. "Escribir en Murcia."

7. A collection of meditations on the Christian way of life which first appeared in 1934 under the title of *Consideraciones espirituales* and which has been translated into several languages, including English. See *The Way* (Chicago: Scepter, 1965).

8. The third novel of the trilogy, *Conocerás el poso de la nada*, was awarded the Premio Nacional de literatura (novela y narrativa) in 1982.

CHAPTER 2
Sin camino

In a novel so evidently related to the author's own experience, one might
be tempted to ask to what extent *Sin camino* can still be regarded as a work of
fiction. While it is true that the novel does include reference to real situations,
like the Jesuit seminary in Comillas, and to historical events, like the great fire
of Santander, it would be wrong to compare every experience of Enrique, the
protagonist, with those of the author. In the late preface to the novel, written in
1983, the author answers the charge of being too autobiographical by referring
to the fire of Santander, an event which was not witnessed at first hand:[1]

> Tengo que decir que mi descripción del incendio de Santander es
> pura imaginación, por supuesto apoyada en una realidad
> solamente entrevista y de oídas. No presencié el incendio de
> Santander, pero pude narrarlo porque para eso soy un novelista.[2]

What is true is that the novel was written as a direct result of the author
abandoning the seminary, as he states in the same preface, and it becomes a
vehicle for criticism of the seminary system:

> Como era de esperar, escribo *Sin Camino*, una especie de alegato
> generacional frente al fallo de la educación eclesiástica y al
> fraude, la cobardía y el engaño de tantas conductas del seminario.[3]

In private conversation between Castillo-Puche and myself at a later date,
in 1985, he described two principal motives for writing the novel, namely
self-justification and liberation. The failure of the seminary education, the

hypocrisy of the superiors, and insincerity of the seminarians are all underlined as the causes for conflict and the eventual crisis of vocation:

> Todo eso está un poco recogido de una manera justificadora de la deserción de la vocación.[4]

As soon as Castillo-Puche left the seminary, the first thing he wanted to do was recount his own experiences and also the suffering that the seminary regime often imposed on him. He hoped that writing about these things and sharing them might provide some sort of liberation:

> No para un proceso masoquista, sino para liberarme totalmente de ese fantasma.[5]

To use the term 'fantasma' to describe the memories of his experiences in the seminary seems to suggest that the author was truly disturbed by what he saw in the religious life at that time. And we shall see how these feelings of resentment are reflected in the main character of the novel, Enrique, as he struggles to come to terms with the realities of seminary life and the uncertainty of his own vocation. Castillo-Puche has also admitted in the preface that the lack of charity and sacrifice which prevailed in the seminaries of the 1940s has given way to a new sense of commitment and sincerity thanks to the changes that have taken place since the Second Vatican Council:

> Afortunadamente, aquellos seminarios obsesivos, donde se enseñaban principalmente las artes del disimulo y la hipocresía, están pasando a la historia si no han pasado ya del todo. Hoy se vive la fe y la educación en los seminarios de una manera más honesta, más limpia, más verdadera.[6]

But the impact of the seminary system in the author's earlier days must have been powerful enough to make him consider *Sin camino* as a means of liberation. The sense of liberation for the author also implies that the later work *Trilogía de la liberación* is not unique, and that perhaps this motive can be applied to many of the author's works.

The novel describes the events in the life of Enrique, the protagonist, just prior to his departure from the seminary, a period of time in which he is involved in some critical experiences which will determine his later decisions about his vocation. During this short period also we witness all the anxieties and conflicts that are present in the mind of Enrique as he is confronted with the uncertainty of his vocation which is also challenged by the world outside and the memories of the life he tried to leave behind. The narrator goes beyond the external events to give us an inside view of the character's mind and the liberal use of the 'estilo indirecto libre' demonstrates an understanding between the narrator and character. However, the narrator is not always sympathetic to Enrique's plight as is sometimes seen in the changes from the 'estilo indirecto libre' to third-person narrative. Often the narrator is able to distance himself from Enrique and become rather critical of certain attitudes and behaviour.

The external setting, or the stage, of the novel consists of the seminary environment, in the first place, and then the world outside the seminary, that is, the local village, presumably referring to Comillas, and the capital of the province, Santander. The internal conflicts concerning the destiny of the protagonist, Enrique, can be divided into three major areas: the conflict between the individuality of Enrique and the general community of the seminary; the confrontation between genuine commitment to the vocation and attraction to the world; and the need for courage and resoluteness in the face of indecision. For a clearer understanding of the uncertainty of the destiny of Enrique, it is necessary to examine these conflicts separately.

A. THE SEMINARY ENVIRONMENT

Even in the early stages of the novel it is possible to sense the tension surrounding the presence of Enrique in the seminary. The narrator makes it clear from the start that Enrique is uncomfortable with his position and the signs of uncertainty, which is to be a major question throughout the novel, are already beginning to surface:

> Gravitaba dentro de la celda de Enrique una atmósfera de indecisión y hastío,de suma perplejidad y cansancio. (p.28)[7]

After spending five years of his life within the seminary without questioning any of the rules and traditions, the situation is now starting to change as Enrique begins to question the validity of his religious vocation and the sincerity of those around him. As the prospects of ordination to the priesthood draw nearer, the more restless and unhappy he becomes, yet it seems that Enrique is the only one suffering a crisis:

> Cada día sentía también mayor rencor por sus compañeros, como si no les perdonase que ellos siguieran adelante y fueran allí felices. (p.32)

The difference between Enrique and the rest is that while he is struggling to break with the past and to quieten the passions of his heart, the other seminarians seem to remain unperturbed without any complications as if exempt from any interior struggle:

> De ningún modo ellos podían sentir el amor como él. En su misma celda habrían parado ya muchos, pero ninguno habría experimentado la hermosa y dramática incertidumbre que a él le conmovía, ninguno seguramente estaba dispuesto a jugarse como él el destino a cara o cruz, ninguno vivía tan tenso y agónico. (p.35)

This conflict between the individual and the surrounding environment has been examined in detail by Oscar Barrero in his study of the post-war existential novel in Spain.[8] In this work Barrero not only studies the conflict between the individual and the environment but also other problems that are characteristic of existentialist philosophy in the works of several Spanish authors writing between 1946 and 1955. Among the works examined are two novels by Castillo-Puche, namely, *Sin camino* and *Con la muerte al hombro*. While commenting on the particular conflict between the individual and the external world as a general feature of existentialist thinking, Barrero finds it paradoxical that the Spanish existential novel should both speak favourably of mankind and yet often regard it with contempt. Barrero explains that the reason for this lies in the sterile environment produced by the external world from which the individual must alienate himself in order to aspire to a more authentic way of life:

> Por reacción negativa ante un gregarismo esterilizador, el personaje clama en defensa de su propio yo, siempre en lucha con el mundo circundante. En último termino, su aspiración es acceder a un estrato de plenitud vital más auténtica.[9]

In *Sin camino*, this view is illustrated when Enrique regards the other seminarians, with perhaps the exception of el Barón, as a community of individuals who display no passion or personality but rather remain in an atmosphere of obedience and subordination:

> Enrique estaba desorbitándose. La felicidad de la comunidad le parecía mansedumbre y la obediencia, insensibilidad. La comunidad para él eran almas sumisas sobre las que cualquier mano algo dura podía escribir en serie frases iguales. (p.41)

It was this kind of environment which clashed with the individuality of Enrique, and the unsettling effects eventually lead to a critical review of the religious vocation.

Another factor underlying the sense of uneasiness of Enrique in the seminary appears to be the failure of self-denial. His inability to deny self and his own will means he cannot surrender himself to the will of God, nor to the will of his superiors. The religious vocation requires complete mortification and the annihilation of self, as the Spiritual Director makes clear to Enrique. This condition of self-denial, which Enrique seems unable to accept, is fundamental to discipleship, as it states in the New Testament:

> Then to all he said, 'If anyone wants to be a follower of mine, let him renounce himself and take up his cross every day and follow me. For anyone who wants to save his life will lose it; but anyone who loses his life for my sake, that man will save it.'
> Luke 9.23-24

Oscar Barrero sees this failure to submit to the will of his superiors as further evidence of the inability of the individual to integrate into the general community life. In common with other existential novels, the protagonist tries, instead, to assert his own individuality:

> Común a buena parte de estos personajes es su sentimiento de superioridad sobre sus semejantes, derivado tanto de su reacción psicológica ante la imposibilidad de integrarse en la átona vida colectiva como de su propia necesidad de afirmación existencial.[10]

At the same time, the protagonist is aware that his individual condition cannot be shared or extended to the others in the external world, but rather remains something personal and singular. Consequently, there is no one else in the community surrounding Enrique who is able to share or understand his particular predicament:

> Pero, ¿es que algunos quieren, piensan, sienten y sueñan algo? Yo creo que no. Por no tener, no tienen ni pasiones, ni amor, ni dolor,

ni odio, ni tampoco ganas de tenerlos. (p.41)

This assertion of his own individuality and the sense of being on another wavelength makes not only the community alien to Enrique, but gradually forces him to believe that he is a different human being from the rest.

As Enrique gets a stronger sense of his own identity, it becomes even more difficult for him to practise self-renunciation and submit to the religious principles. He can no longer bow to the demands imposed by the Spiritual Director urging him to die to himself. As he has nothing in common with the other seminarians, the Spiritual Director will not be able to convince Enrique on the basis of the example shown by the others:

> Tienes que cambiar enteramente. ¿Entiendes? ¿No ves a los demás? ¿No ves a Juan, a Tomás, a tantos otros ...? Estás perdiendo un tiempo precioso. Tú mismo crees que quieres, pero, en el fondo, es que no quieres inmolarte. (p.54)

The Spiritual Director recognises that Enrique is being drawn towards the attractions of the material world and puts his problem down to the fact that he is not involved enough with spiritual matters as the other seminarians are:

> Mira a otros seminaristas, para los que sólo existen los libros de estudio y la Eucaristía. Los hay a los que sonreía el mundo y no se dejaron engañar. Y aquí los tienes dando ejemplo. (pp.56-57)

But Enrique is unlikely to be encouraged by the actions and attitude of others who exist in a world so foreign to him. As a different being unable to find solidarity, Enrique slowly drifts into a position of isolation, and isolation inevitably leads to loneliness. This isolationist attitude can be seen especially as ordination draws nearer and Enrique continues to conform externally to the seminary routine:

> Ahora era para Enrique más difícil aislarse. Sin embargo, aunque
> seguía la vida y la distribución del tiempo de sus compañeros, su
> alma permanecía ajena, como embotada. (p.244)

At the same time, his enthusiasm and religious fervour begin to wane as he often

becomes rather distracted:

> Mientras los demás ordenandos leían o meditaban, totalmente
> ajenos al cansancio y al aburrimiento, Enrique se entregaba a
> ensueños y monólogos, incapaz de concentrar su espíritu. (p.244)

This notion of feeling different from all the rest, then, must seriously

affect any chance of successful ordination to the priesthood. The lack of a

common bond in faith and friendship together with the failure of Enrique to

submit his own will and individuality to the general wishes of the establishment

lead to conflict and inevitable crisis. This internal struggle between Enrique and

the seminary environment is only revealed to the reader, however, as the narrator

employs the privilege of offering the reader alone an inside view of the workings

of the protagonist's mind. Although there may be the external signs of this

conflict in the attitude of Enrique, no other seminarian or superior is aware of

what he is thinking. Nobody, except the narrator and the reader, can know this.

Hence the Spiritual Director can only counsel Enrique on the basis of what the

latter reveals, namely, the more tangible conflict between his commitment to the

religious vocation and his fascination with the world outside. But this conflict,

too, is another major factor in determining the future of Enrique, as we shall now

see.

B. ATTRACTION TO THE WORLD

Although this conflict is more evident to other characters in the novel like

the Spiritual Director or other seminarians such as Gerardo or el Noli, Enrique remains adamant that his particular torment is not common to anyone else. He is convinced that the others cannot feel or experience the trauma of indecision in the same intense way as himself. While they excelled in control and conformity, Enrique yearned for life with all its passion and refused to be associated with the rest. Just as no other seminarian could understand this problem in the seminary, neither could anyone in the world outside understand him if they classified him in the same category as the other students. This feeling is seen during his special leave in Santander as he observes the women passing him in the street:

> No saben lo que soy; no lo descubren. Yo no soy tan basto y tan torpe como son allí la mayoría. (p.143)

It is as if Enrique is desperate to transmit his inner passions to an indifferent world and yet he is frustrated by the fact that he remains isolated and completely unknown to everyone else:

> Tanto sentir - recapacitaba -, tanta ternura como tengo oprimida dentro del pecho y nadie la conoce, nadie me ha regalado nunca ni una sonrisa. (p.143)

Being a seminarian had become a disadvantage and a barrier between himself and the world. As long as he remained in the category of 'seminarian' he would find it impossible to reveal himself as an individual with his own particular character and qualities.

The trip to Santander, then, would be doubly motivated. On the one hand, Enrique would be able to penetrate some of the secrets of the world outside and, on the other hand, this voyage of discovery would also enable him to show his true character:

> Debía, de una vez para siempre, tener una experiencia directa de lo que era el mundo. Para eso, por unas horas, era dueño de sus actos. (p.144)

However, before the journey into the provincial capital could be realised, the mind and heart of Enrique were persistently drifting off into the world outside the seminary. As Enrique feels uncomfortable in the negative environment of the seminary, he begins to adopt certain methods of distraction. One of these methods is the use of the imagination to escape into a distant world away from the monotony of study and prayer:

> Si Enrique había resistido tantos años de horas de estudio y oración era por esto, porque había logrado vivir dentro del Seminario enteramente derramado hacia afuera. Con la imaginación vivía muy lejos. El Seminario le asfixiaba. (p.88)

Another form of escape was to indulge in the reading of secular literature to compensate his lack of enthusiasm for theology, and most of this literature was considered dangerous to the religious vocation:

> Estaba seducido por el tono pasional y literario de ciertas obras que los demás seminaristas tenían y consideraban como condenatorias. Pero él iba leyendo meticulosamente toda esta literatura tensa y revolucionaria. (p.126)

The narrator here uses very emotive terms to describe the way in which this literature was gradually affecting Enrique, changing his beliefs and undermining his way of thinking:

> Pero lo cierto es que ciertos libros se le iban colando en el alma y cada uno de ellos era dentro de su espíritu como un espía de un fortín enemigo. Enrique iba vendiendo su alma lentamente. (pp.125-126)

This passion for literature is also demonstrated during the excursion to Santander when his first priority is to visit a bookshop and gaze in wonder at the variety of novels and poetry totally alien to the seminary library. His enthusiasm is such that he begins reading the works of Rilke and Miró, which he had bought, even as he walks along the street. This powerful attraction in Enrique towards literature is similar to the attitude of the author in his own seminary experience:

> Sobre todo, lleva en su interior el morbo literario. En Comillas, vuelve a la lectura obsesiva de los autores de su querencia: Miró, Unamuno, Ortega, Azorín ..., todos ellos más o menos prohibidos. Tenía que esconder los libros debajo del colchón y hasta en las maderas del suelo. Era una fiebre de lectura y clandestinidad que no se avenía con su sentido de la verdad y de la sinceridad.[11]

In the novel, it looks as if the Spiritual Director has noticed this deviation in Enrique and is afraid that his vocation may be affected by his passion for worldly attractions. In an earlier episode both the Spiritual Director and the Prefect share the concern that what they consider to be a valid vocation could be under threat from external influences:

> Lo que es indudable es que tiene algunos rasgos mundanos que no me gustan nada. Demuestra que su imaginación vive lejos del Seminario. (p.51)

This comment by the Spiritual Director and the fact that they both agree to look into the matter show that Enrique is not as isolated in this conflict as he thinks.

The attraction of the outside world gradually undermines the sincerity of his devotion and dedication. The painful sense of remorse is no longer present when he goes to confession, nor is there any inclination towards meditation and prayer during the celebration of Mass. All the time spent at seminary now seems like a meaningless existence as if both life and time had passed him by. Now and again his life is interrupted by the memories of what might have been had he decided to remain in the outside world. These moments afford him a certain degree of pleasure:

> Sin embargo, estos instantes de perplejidad, de descorazonamiento, de duda, de desarraigo, le atraían, porque vivía en ellos el goce de la obediencia expiadora y el anticipo de las rebeldías venideras. (p.132)

The problem of the attractiveness of the outside world is one of the central themes of the novel. The author has created an individual, Enrique, who is caught between two worlds, namely, the real world outside the seminary and the ideal world. But rather than being someone seeking to escape from the real world, the protagonist is portrayed as an individual with a passion for life. The fears that exist inside Enrique do not originate from the world outside but are produced by the seminary education with its obsession with renunciation and withdrawal. Indeed, Castillo-Puche claims that Enrique has a much wider vision of the Christian message than that offered by the seminary:

> El individuo tiene vitalidad suficiente para pensar que el Evangelio es algo más que lo que se predica.[12]

Speaking forty years on from the time the novel was written, Castillo-Puche outlined in private conversation the primary features he intended to put across in the novel:

> Yo creo que lo primero que se ve en *Sin camino* es que hay desconfianza interior o una duda, una especie de soltura, un resquicio de liberalidad de este espíritu.[13]

The great love of the protagonist for the life which lies on the other side of the seminary wall creates anguish, doubt and indecision. The ideal of the priesthood and its implications of sacrifice and self-denial is challenged by the desire to experience, to indulge in the world of the senses. This world of the senses is discovered even when Enrique takes the short walk to the local village:

Al menos era ya suficiente ver que los pájaros andaban sueltos por
los jardines, que las ramas de los árboles se iban vistiendo de
hojas nuevas, que había seres humanos que se pasaban la tarde en
la playa, zambulléndose en el agua o jugando; que existía otra
vida. (p.105)

It is this desire to experience and enjoy life in all its variety which clashes with

the ideal of self-sacrifice required by the Spiritual Director. The author now

emphasises how natural this attraction to life is for Enrique:

Se da a la vida porque le atrae tanto. La lleva dentro. Sabe que allí
hay algo hermoso y que hay belleza. Y como es artista, lo
siente.[14]

Equally, for the author, Enrique could not conform to the idea that life was

nothing more than resignation and submission:

Por el sistema impositivo y totalmente aniquilador, del nacimiento
al cadáver, el hombre tiene que ser totalmente entregado a seguir
los dictados como un fantasma viviente, ambulante. No termina
de entrar en la sumisión plena del cadáver.[15]

In solidarity with the protagonist, Castillo-Puche resists the notion of life as

negation of everything as if the main purpose of our existence was to be

submerged in mortification and desperation. Instead, he identifies with Enrique

and his inevitable conflict:

Tiene una aceptación de la vida, de que la vida es como es y que
hay que aceptarla. Lo que pasa es que trata de compaginar su
vocación con eso y allí hay una lucha.[16]

While in Santander, Enrique is fascinated by every aspect of the outside

world: the shops, the bars, the streets and parks. Everything that he sees is accessible to him. He is, for the moment, not controlled by any rules and no one can forbid him doing whatever he pleases. This is the most important feature for Enrique about being part of the world, namely, the sense of freedom:

> Si esto durara, si esto pudiera seguir, si yo pudiera mirar las cosas abiertamente, ser libre, tener independencia, gozar la vida. Y, sin embargo, la realidad es que puedo. ¿Quién me lo prohibe? (p.147)

The notion of freedom is emphasised by Gonzalo Sobejano, among his list of potential obstacles to the vocation, as the crucial attraction of the world over and above all the other factors which prevent Enrique from dedicating his life to the religious vocation:

> Lo impide el descubrimiento de no pocas mezquindades en el ambiente del seminario, lo impide la inteligencia decepcionada en la selva de la teología, lo impide el instinto erótico que vuelve por sus derechos, lo impiden súbitas experiencias del mundo como fuente de placer y, sobre todo, de hermosa e integral libertad.[17]

Enrique begins to realise that his vocation to the priesthood is an ideal which now proves difficult to accomplish, despite his intial optimism and romanticism:

> Creí que era fuerte para encerrarme, para intimar conmigo mismo hasta el punto de agradecer que mi corazón estuviera hecho para un amor eterno, sin nostalgias estériles. Creí que me podría crear una vida propia a base de mis propios sueños y esto veo que es mi aniquilación. (p.140)

Other contributory factors in his decision to enter the seminary were the Civil War and its aftermath of desolation with his own family left devastated by the events. The seminary provided a welcome escape from these depressing circumstances and offered a better existence. But Castillo-Puche points out later that the liberation which Enrique seeks is not just from the external situation, but it is also from his internal conflicts and uncertainty, and he discovers that the seminary does not solve his problems:

> El individuo se comporta como un ser que va buscando su propia libertad interior, y en la libertad interior encuentra que la vocación es la anulación.[18]

Living according to ideals and dreams, then, is not the way to discover his own individuality or identity. Enrique is aware that this romantic ideal of the vocation is in conflict with the physical and visible reality around him:

> El cree que va a hacer una ofrenda, una oblación de su persona y va, y tiene un sentido de entrega romántica. Pero en la experiencia sucumbe, porque podía más en él la vida de los sentidos que la vida del espíritu.[19]

This victory of the senses over the spirit is illustrated when Enrique contemplates certain features of the landscape surrounding the seminary and how they affected him differently when he first entered the seminary from the way he now interprets them. While, at first, nature represented the beauty of the spiritual realm and reflected the greatness of the Creator, now it expressed a direct invitation to sample the wonders of the physical world through the senses:

> Esta fronda vegetal desbordada, este color triste de las piedras de las casonas, esta niebla, los troncos húmedos, el verde mullido y blanco, los pinos, las rocas desnudas, el mar, todo, todo me pide como una satisfacción que no me da ni me puede dar el espíritu. (p.139)

Enrique feels more in union with the natural world than with the spiritual sphere. This conflict between nature and the soul has been at the root of all world religions and philosophies and Christianity is no exception, as St Paul clearly illustrates:

> The impulses of nature and the impulses of the spirit are at war
> with one another; either is clean contrary to the other, and that is
> why you cannot do all that your will approves.
>
> Galatians 5.17

This tension is also manifest in Enrique and is one of the major causes of his perpetual uncertainty. Castillo-Puche admits that he wanted to make this struggle one of the principal themes of the novel: to emphasise how much one is restricted to the world of nature and must conform to natural laws despite any desire for some higher spiritual plane:

> El hombre está imperado, obligado, ceñido y totalmente constreñido a la naturaleza.[20]

While St Paul is urging Christians to be prepared for warfare, Castillo-Puche seems to be saying that the battle is already lost and that man must inevitably surrender to the natural world.

In the novel, the experience of life in the world outside is united to the world of the senses and, for Enrique, it is only by entering into and experiencing this world that he will discover his true self. Hence he feels he must break with the spiritual order and cross over to this other world if he is to attain fulfilment. Enrique believes that the opportunity for this arrives in Santander when the encounter with the prostitute Marisol offers him the possible experience of sexual intercourse:

> Esa frontera en la que tú me esperabas, era para mí insalvable. No podía ser. No podía ser de otro modo. Estuve ciego. Ahora, tarde, irremisiblemente tarde, sé quién soy, de dónde vengo y a dónde iba. (p.184)

But before the sexual act can be realised, both Enrique and Marisol find themselves in the middle of the great fire which is destroying the city.

This episode demonstrates a certain degree of distance between the implied author and the character Enrique. Not only is the character placed in a situation in Santander that was foreign to the author but there is also an air of criticism of the excessive sense of self-importance in Enrique who sees himself at the centre of this catastrophe. This self-importance is connected to the notion of guilt, a problem which will re-appear in *Como ovejas al matadero* and the trilogy. In a similar fashion to the thunderstorm sequence in *El amargo sabor de la retama*, when one of the characters, Matilde, regarded the storm as the wrath of God, so Enrique is ridiculously assuming that this disaster is aimed directly at him.[21] The woman responsible for the temptation into the realm of sensual pleasure now becomes a source of embarrassment to Enrique:

> La mujer de su placer comenzaba a ser la de su dolor, y le hacía sufrir extraordinariamente que le llevara cogido del brazo. Aquello, ¿no era motivar más indignación y más castigo por parte del Cielo, que había presenciado claramente su caída y reaccionaba según la tradición bíblica? (p.174)

As the fire engulfs the city and everyone is panic-stricken, the only matter of any importance for him was his sin and its apparent consequences. While Enrique is convinced he is responsible for what is happening, Marisol is bewildered by the extravagance of his claims:

> Era para inquietarse. Aquel hombre no sólo decía cosas absurdas, sino que ponía toda su pasión en querer hacer del espectáculo devastador del fuego un secreto de su persona. (p.182)

This episode also represents a clear example of the inability of Enrique to cope with a sexual relationship. It is not the only instance where his attempts at establishing contact with women end in frustration and disaster. His previous relationship with Isabel before he entered the seminary seems to have been promising initially yet it ended in failure because of the lack of courage and commitment in Enrique:

> - Realmente soy un tipo raro o estoy loco. ¿Por qué no le cogí la
> mano entonces y le dije la verdad? ... Y ahora me paso los días
> pensando en ella ... (p.32)

His failure to declare his true feelings for Isabel is also reflected in his shyness towards another girl, Inés, who lived near the seminary and often attended the church services. Indeed, there is a continual sense not only of the uncomfortable effects caused by Inés, but also of the threatening closeness of all the young women in the village. Whether Enrique is unable to commit himself to the opposite sex or whether any attempt to do so ends in frustration, the result is that Enrique considers the opposite sex to be unattainable. This view is complemented by the Spiritual Director's warning of the dangers of involvement with women:

> Estás sobre el abismo, Enrique. La mujer es el lodo infame que
> todo lo mancha. ¡Siempre la mujer, causa de maldición! (p.55)

Women, then, are clearly out of bounds for Enrique and are certainly not compatible with the vocation to the priesthood.

Besides the Spiritual Director, Enrique is also advised by his mother not to be seduced by the attraction to worldly pleasures. As a consistent factor throughout many of the works of Castillo-Puche, the mother is presented as a powerful influence on the religious vocation. Often, as in this novel, it is the fulfilment of the mother's dreams which halts any decision by the protagonist to abandon his vocation and, whenever there are doubts, it is usually the memories of his mother's encouragement which alone can sustain her son's presence in the seminary. Examples of the pressure exerted by the mother can be found in a letter written to Enrique:

> Tú ya sabes que yo lo único que quiero es que seas un sacerdote
> santo y que mi único consejo ha sido siempre decirte que las cosas
> de la tierra no valen nada y todas son desengaños. (p.40)

If Enrique could become a priest it would be the climax of his mother's dreams even if she was not still there to witness it:

> ¡Qué feliz seré yo aunque esté en el cielo viendo que tú salvas
> muchas almas ...! (p.40)

Clearly inspired by these words of encouragement from his mother, Enrique decides to put aside all obstacles and distractions and reinforce his efforts to become a priest:

> Es mi madre la que tiene razón. Puedo ser sacerdote. Puedo si
> quiero. Lo de la chiquilla del chalecito, una simple distracción. Lo
> de Isabel, ganas de complicarme la vida. Nada más. Lo importante
> es recordar unas cosas y olvidar otras. (p.42)

In the face of all these images of the past and the present complications involving Inés and his yearning for life, Enrique makes a renewed commitment through prayer and study. Although the world outside may be associated with feelings of liberation, Enrique seems determined to stand firm in his vocation, and his resoluteness is revealed by the narrator in a clear illustration of the 'estilo indirecto libre':

> A la fuerza, nunca dejaría el Seminario. Él era tan capaz como el
> primero de aquel sacrificio. (p.201)

Furthermore, recognising his resolve is vulnerable, Enrique turns to God in an attempt to surrender his own will into God's hands, hoping to be carried through by a greater, more powerful force:

Es cosa de mi voluntad, que la tengo débil, que la tengo enferma, que no tengo voluntad. Pero Tú, que has hecho tantos milagros, deberías quitarme la poca voluntad que tengo y podrías hacer ya siempre lo que quisieras. Yo sería feliz dejándome llevar por Ti, por ese camino tuyo, que eres Tú mismo y en el cual está ciertamente mi salvación. (p.45)

On top of this prayerful commitment comes the practice of the lashes. This act of self-inflicted pain was actually recommended by his superiors as a means of disciplining the flesh when temptations were threatening. In this case, any thought of women or the outside world must be driven out:

- Toma, Enrique, y no huyas. Para que aprendas. Toma, Inés, para que aprendas a cerrar los ojos. Toma, uno, dos, tres ... Pero no siempre en el mismo sitio. Toma ahora por Isabel. Para que aprendas a enterrar y pudrir los recuerdos. (p.46)

As the narrator here introduces the protagonist talking to himself in the second person, it seems as if Enrique is detaching himself from that wretched, awful body which is so vulnerable. When the narrator of the later *Trilogía de la liberación* changes from the first person to the second person narrative, it often occurs at moments of intense guilt and self-accusation, similar to what happens here in *Sin camino*. Enrique is employing this practice so that the body will submit to the will and both will unite into one in a determined effort to become a priest. It is as if the body is a separate part of him which had to be controlled:

Tú, toma, toma, toma, tienes vocación. Tienes que tenerla. Quiere Dios que la tengas. Lo quiere tu madre. Debes tenerla. (p.47)

The ferocity of this self-imposed punishment is an indication of just how much Enrique does, in fact, want to be a priest. Being in the seminary was not just an escape from the past and a chaotic situation, nor could his presence there be reduced to a simple search for authenticity. On the contrary, the narrator reveals that the ideal of the priesthood is something that has been desired ever since childhood and has remained with Enrique right up to the first signs of manhood:

> Sueño de su niñez que se evaporaba como las gotas de agua en un cristal cuando las besa el sol. Ordenarse había sido también anhelo de su adolescencia, su adolescencia que era ahora como el roce intacto de una flor sobre los párpados, puro ensueño hacia un ideal. Y en su juventud, cuando se imponía el comprobar la vocación, había surgido la mujer. La mujer, la imaginación, acaso la literatura, los sentidos ... (p.250)

These three periods mentioned here in the protagonist's life seem identical with the three novels of the *Trilogía de la liberación* which is similarly concerned with the problem of the religious vocation. But what is important is that the priesthood is something which Enrique always desired and that the decision to enter the seminary was not due merely to external factors. Yet although there are still times when he yearns to be free from the seminary environment and hopes that some external event will change his situation, Enrique will remind himself that his religious vocation was freely accepted:

> ¿Pero él no está allí porque quiere? Porque quiere está allí; nada más. También está porque esto hace feliz a su madre y no ha querido matarla de un disgusto. Bueno, se acabó. Yo estoy aquí porque quiero, porque lo he querido. (p.73)

The recognition of his own freedom to decide for himself means that Enrique must accept responsibility for this situation and reject the tendency to put the blame on other people or external events. This theme of personal responsibility is discussed by the psychologist John Powell of the Loyola University of Chicago.[22] Most of Powell's work is concerned with human growth and self-awareness and tendencies within people to behave in a way that is detrimental to growth as a person. Whenever an individual is uncomfortable with his situation, he is sometimes inclined to attribute the cause of this discomfort to someone else or some other event. This kind of reaction is described by Powell as a form of ego defence called 'projection'. In other words, the individual develops a defence system in order to compensate for some defect or handicap within himself. Through 'projection' the individual tends to see his own defects in others:

> All of us tend to disown things in ourselves and to "project" them into others. We try to rid ourselves of our own limitations by attributing them to someone else.[23]

Powell gives a simple illustration of this trend by referring to the episode of Adam and Eve in the Garden of Eden when they eat the forbidden fruit. After their offence had been discovered, Adam automatically blamed Eve for tempting him, and Eve likewise blamed her own action on the serpent.

It is very common for human beings, Powell claims, to attribute their own failures not only to other individuals but also to external circumstances:

> It is also projection when we blame other things for our own failures, like the circumstances, the tools I had to work with, the position of the stars.[24]

The consequence of such ego defence is to camouflage and disguise the real person within and, by distorting the truth, the individual becomes unable to share himself with anyone else. As a result, the individual fails to grow and develop as a human being. As Enrique feels uncertain about his vocation he is tempted to look back on past events like the Civil War, his relationship with Isabel, or the emotional pressure from his mother as possible underlying factors of his present predicament. Although he may display resentment towards people and towards the seminary environment, Enrique is aware that he alone is to blame for the present dilemma:

> Lo que ocurre es que soy un cobarde. Siempre lo he sido. Cobarde
> al terminar la guerra y venirme aquí. Cobarde por continuar aquí
> y no marcharme. Cobarde y más cobarde cada minuto que pasa.
> (p.36)

By admitting his own failure, Enrique is taking important steps towards his own self-development as opposed to remaining stagnant in a constant feeling of resentment. For Powell, the resentful attitude is unfounded, for though other people may do wrong to us, we still have our own will and freedom to act for ourselves, and can never blame anyone for the way we are:

> No one's feelings are caused by others. Our feelings are caused by
> our own emotional response, our own choices and reactions.[25]

According to Powell, one of the most positive advantages of growing into a fully human individual is that the fully developed person is not affected by the moods and emotions of others and does not let others dictate how he should act:

> That the "fully human" person is "his own person", that he does
> not bend to every wind which blows, that he is not at the mercy
> of all the pettiness, the meanness, the impatience and anger of
> others. Atmospheres do not transform him as much as he
> transforms them.[26]

While many of us are at the mercy of other people, being affected by their manner, and consequently blaming them for our course of action, the fully human person is aware that his own actions depend entirely on himself, and not on other people or circumstances:

> The fully human person, as Shakespeare put it in Julius Caesar,
> knows that: 'The fault, dear Brutus, is not with our stars, but with
> ourselves ...'. We can rise above the dust of daily battle that

chokes and blinds so many of us in the process of growth as a person.[27]

For Powell, to be fully alive and fully human is never to surrender to the senses or the emotions when external factors try to affect us because unconditional surrender would mean the inevitable abdication of our own will and intellect.

Thus we have two different ways of understanding the complexity of Enrique's predicament in the seminary: the existentialist and the psychological. It has already been seen, in existentialist terms, that the reason for Enrique's resentment lies in the conflict between the individual and the seminary environment in which Enrique reacts against the sterile atmosphere by defending his own individuality. This notion of defence is also evident in Powell's psychology but, in this case, the way in which the individual tries to defend himself is negative and detrimental. Whereas the existentialist basis for ego defence lies in the individual's need to aspire to a more fulfilling way of life than what is presented around him, the psychological definition leans more towards the notion of compensation and camouflage of some personal handicaps. In the psychological sense, the individual is deluded into thinking that the employment of ego defence is beneficial and rewarding whereas the opposite is true.

Another important aspect of the two interpretations is the question of will: in other words, the existentialist emphasis lies in the affirmation of the individual will and the psychological view affirms that the individual loses the power of his own will if he allows himself to be affected and influenced by those around him and every changing mood and circumstance.

A clear example of both attitudes, that of self-affirmation and that of projection, can be seen when Enrique is confronted with the official document for application for ordination to the priesthood. On the one hand, we see him attempting to establish his own identity over and above the identity about to be imposed upon him through the impending ordination ceremony:

Enrique ... Mi nombre no es sólo un nombre, mi nombre soy yo,
que tengo un destino propio, un destino único, un destino mío.
(p.247)

Then, in the next instance, Enrique suggests that the Civil War may have
contributed to his present situation:

Si no hubiera ocurrido todo lo de la guerra, quizá tampoco tuviera
yo tanto que pensar. (p.247)

This kind of psychological defence is clearly detrimental and the narrator appears
quite critical of Enrique's sense of resentment and attempts at self-justification.
The narrator's critical attitude can be seen especially in the shift from 'estilo
indirecto libre' to third-person narrative:

Aunque quería a algunos, a todos les fundía en aquel momento en
una fila compacta de rencor. Tenía que despreciarlos a todos para
justificar su impotencia o fracaso. (p.251)

Both the existentialist and psychological interpretations are
complementary in that they are both concerned with self-affirmation in the face
of a sterile environment and the moods and influences of other people and events.
Seen in this way, both views affirm the freedom of the individual, and help us
understand perhaps the reasons behind certain characteristics in Enrique's
behaviour, especially with regard to his inability to make a firm decision, an
aspect we will now examine.

C. INDECISION

It is clear, then, that the religious vocation is something chosen by
Enrique and ordination to the priesthood has been the ambition of his entire life

till now. There is no doubt, either, that Enrique now feels attracted to the world
and that he wants to experience the natural side of life. The problem is that he
cannot have both and, therefore, he must choose between the vocation or the
world. But his inability to decide responsibly about his future leads him to
withdraw into an isolated life of uncertainty and passivity. Unable to act for
himself, Enrique lets himself be carried along by the external routine. The
anxiety surrounding the uncertainty of his position makes him a completely
passive individual, hoping that events will dictate the course of his future, as in
the case of the possibility of Spain taking part in the Second World War:

> La guerra, la guerra podía ser un remedio, piensa. La guerra podía
> ser también la perdición. Por lo pronto, la guerra sería la libertad.
> (p.73)

As the Civil War is seen by Enrique as being a contributory factor to his decision
to enter the seminary, so now the news of Spain's potential participation in the
World War could mean his life being transformed and given a completely new
direction:

> Una movilización representaba la destrucción de todos sus ideales
> pero no le atemorizaba, más bien interiormente le emocionaba y
> atraía. Una guerra en aquel momento podía trastrocarse en la
> mayor de las aventuras. ¿No necesitaría él de otro choque externo
> que le lanzase definitivamente por la senda elegida? (pp.72-73)

As ordination draws nearer, Enrique still hopes that something external will either
reinforce his commitment to the vocation or change the course of events. Either
way, he cannot make a decision for himself, so something else would have to
make it for him, as, he recalls, has often occurred in the past:

> Sin embargo, él esperaba aún que algo externo viniera a
> removerle, a obligarle. Esperaba que algo sucedería que, en el
> último momento, sacase a su enferma voluntad de aquel sopor.

> Siempre había sucedido así. Siempre él se había dejado arrastrar
> por los hechos e impresionar por algún acontecimiento que le
> electrizase. (p.244)

We can see how closely this passive attitude of 'dejarse llevar' conforms to Powell's earlier description of the abdication of the will.

The more the indecision continues, the more anguish is experienced by Enrique in this immense struggle between the ideal and the awareness of human limitations. Though it is painful to admit, it seems Enrique is becoming more and more convinced that he ought to abandon the vocation and take up some other profession. Without doubting the sincerity of his intentions, he gives the impression that if any decision was to be made, it would be the decision to leave. The fact that during every summer vacation Enrique hoped that something would happen to prevent him returning to the seminary emphasises this yearning to leave. However, Enrique recognises his lack of courage by always returning to the Community and resents this tendency within him to avoid the truth:

> Lo que tenía que haber hecho era decirles terminantemente que a
> él no tenían que recogerlo de ningún modo, que él dejaba
> espontáneamente el Seminario y que se proponía ser libre desde
> ahora. Pero, como siempre, se escondía en sí mismo, huía de
> afrontar las situaciones. (p.195)

This passive attitude, however, is not confined to the seminary, for even in the episode with the prostitute in the city there is a sense of Enrique going along with the situation. Before Enrique crosses the frontier into the world of sensuality and the subsequent feeling of self-knowledge and awareness, there are moments when he is unable to recognise himself. While drinking with the prostitute in the club he denies any involvement of his real self:

> Yo no estoy aquí, soy un ser incorpóreo. A posteriori nadie se
> espanta de nada. (p.165)

This problem regarding the sense of non-being will appear again in the later novels to be studied. Shortly afterwards, just before entering the house with her, Enrique sees his own image reflected in the mirror:

> Reconoció su persona como algo esencialmente propio, aunque
> ajeno al espacio que ocupaba. (p.171)

It seems that as he is being driven into unknown circumstances the protagonist attempts to alienate himself from any participation in the forbidden events. Not only does the surrounding atmosphere become alien but, in his anguish, Enrique tries to flee from the uncomfortable predicament by denying his own presence and thus denying any personal responsibility:

> Que comprenda Dios que yo no hago más que dejarme llevar. Que
> yo no siento nada. Que no quiero nada. Pero soy débil, soy
> cobarde. (p.170)

The passiveness displayed here by Enrique is common to that shown by other characters in the Spanish existential novels, according to Oscar Barrero.[28] It is as if the individual is unwilling or unable to act in the face of unknown circumstances:

> Subyace en esta suerte de abulia existencial un fatalismo ... que
> induce a los personajes a la no actuación ante lo que consideran
> como imposición de las circunstancias externas sobre la propia
> voluntad.[29]

His own will redundant, Enrique decided to go along with the events, yet these events prove crucial to Enrique in the determination of his future destiny. It is interesting to note how this attitude compares with the existentialist ideal of refusing to submit the individual's will to the general will. The notion of strong individuality and self-affirmation seems suddenly to give way in the face of unfamiliar surroundings.

However, while Enrique maintains his inactive stance in the seminary, he is fully aware that this attitude is both negative and obstructive to progress, and he also recognises the consequences of such an attitude. In the first place, by not declaring his true feelings and simply going along with the situation, Enrique is distorting the truth about himself and this results in falsehood and deception. In the second place, by not being true to self, he is hindering any chance of growth in self-affirmation or as an individual and hence is unable to discover himself.

From the earliest part of the novel it is evident that Enrique resents having to feign devotion and deceive those around him:

> Era el suyo indudablemente un naufragio sin testigos, desesperado
> y exasperante. Estaba harto de mentir y fingir. De rezar
> inútilmente y de pecar en la peor de las soledades. (p.28)

Apart from deceiving himself and the rest of the community, one of the major victims of his deception is Enrique's mother. As in the author's other novels about the religious vocation, the mother must be taken into account with regard to any decision by the protagonist about his vocation. It could even be said here that she too bears great responsibility for the predicament in which her son now finds himself. There is clearly great emotional pressure from the mother on Enrique to continue and endure in a way of life which is now becoming so ridiculously false to him. Concha Alborg, when comparing Enrique to other principal characters in the early works of the author, emphasises the importance of the mother's pressure in *Sin camino* in the decision about the vocation:

> La madre del protagonista, hasta cierto punto, ejerce una
> influencia más fuerte sobre él. Es a ella a quien le entusiasma la
> idea de tener un hijo sacerdote; la carta que le escribe es
> indicativede una religiosidad acerbada que le hace sentirse
> culpable a Enrique cuando considera la posibilidad de abandonar

el sacerdocio.[30]

If Enrique is to feel guilty about deciding his future because of his mother, then the mother becomes a negative element since she is not concerned with her son's happiness but rather with her own dreams being fulfilled. So deciding to abandon the vocation is going to be difficult since Enrique wants to avoid causing any distress to his mother, and thus the deception continues:

> No pudo terminar la carta. Su madre le recrudecía e incrementaba el dolor de una herida insufrible. La tenía tan engañada como se tenía a sí mismo. (p.40)

Even when Enrique sometimes imagines himself as an ordained priest, sound in wisdom and an exemplary figure, it is his mother's happiness which is taken into account. Enrique knows that he possesses the qualities to become a good priest but it seems that his success as a priest would depend entirely on his mother's reactions. But dreams of this kind only served to heighten his anxiety and prolong the deception:

> Así difería el compromiso y el duelo entablado entre su voluntad y su vocación. Y cada día era menos capaz de decisión y de sinceridad. (p.203)

Thoughts of an ideal future are overwhelmed by the reality of indecision and doubt about his vocation, yet he still conceals his real feelings when writing to his mother. Consequently, she continues to believe in her son's commitment and devotion:

> Cuanto más caído estaba, más se sentía en el deber de adormecer a su madre con aquellos arrebatos que no existían sino en su imaginación y en su rapto de piedad filial. (p.245)

However, as ordination draws closer, the mother's emotional pressure gradually loses its hold on Enrique. Reading some of her letters becomes more and more intolerable as Enrique shows the first signs of rebellion and independence. Eventually her letters are left unopened and Enrique becomes immune to his mother's pressure. Now he realises that the real test of courage lies in his ability to break free from his mother's influence:

Sin embargo, era por ella, quizás, por lo que necesitaba más valor para abandonar el Seminario que para quedarse en él.(pp.244-245)

Having allowed himself to be influenced for so long by his mother, Enrique now understands that he has not been in control of his own life and this fact not only led to the current state of indecision and deception but also prevented Enrique from getting to know and understand himself. He realises that his identity was being imposed by external elements:

Pero, una vez más, pensó también en que él no era dueño de su destino, que él no se pertenecía por entero. Estaba también su madre, ilusionada por su sacerdocio. (p.196)

Indecision and passivity, then, have been negative attitudes which have blocked the path to self-knowledge and self-discovery. Instead, we are left with an individual who is unsure of himself and whose only alternative is to consciously deceive his mother and the seminary community as to the validity of his commitment. Eventually, though, Enrique becomes tired of this perpetual charade and realises that the only way to put an end to this life of falsehood is to seek a complete change of direction:

Estaba dispuesto a hacer algo. Algo que tenía que hacer. No siempre iba a continuar lo mismo, dejándose llevar. Él tenía una vida propia, anhelos, sentimientos, fervores, dudas, y todo tenía que existir dentro de sí mismo con una vida oculta y casi

anónima.Era necesario que empezara de una vez para siempre a
conocerse. (pp.28-29)

The dilemma which faces Enrique as the novel progresses is that of
cowardice. The question he must confront is whether it is cowardly to abandon
his ideal and surrender to his natural impulses or whether the cowardice lies in
not admitting the truth that his vocation is no longer sincere. As Enrique feels that
to defy his mother's emotional pressure would take the greatest amount of
courage so it would seem more cowardly to submit and continue to ordination:

¿No podría yo salvarme fuera? Hay que ser más valiente ahora
mismo para irse, que para continuar. Seguir es lo fácil, tenderse
en el suelo, decir que sí, y subir las gradas, tanquam oves ad
occisionem!!! (p.250)

As earlier we saw three periods of Enrique's life, namely, his childhood,
adolescence and early manhood, described as the likely basis for the author's later
Liberation Trilogy, so now this later phrase taken from the forty-fourth Psalm in
the Old Testament would provide the inspiration for another novel about the
religious vocation, *Como ovejas al matadero*. The Latin phrase used by Enrique
coincides with the Latin wording of the 'Letras Dimisorias', the official
document for application for ordination, which Enrique had just completed but
from this cynical usage of the phrase we detect the sense of submission which
ordination would imply.

In the struggle between different and incompatible impulses Enrique still
will not let go of the ideal and, even when his decision to leave has all but been
made, he still hopes that commitment might still be possible:

Hasta el final cabía esperar que su naturaleza y su imaginación
cedieran a la Gracia y a la disciplina. Pero ya su voluntad no tenia
nada que hacer. Se hallaba gastada casi por entero. Con la poca
que le quedaba debía entrar en el mundo y empezar una vida

nueva. (p.250)

It becomes clear that the sincerity and intentions are no longer in evidence and Enrique has demonstrated by his behaviour that his heart lies in the outside world. So also, for Enrique, the disasters which normally accompanied his worldly escapades like the fire of Santander and the tragic death of Ricardo, the military acquaintance of Inés, were another indication of the failure of Enrique's vocation. He feels that all this misery could have been avoided if he had only listened to the voice of brother Gabriel when he first entered the seminary:

> Y de nuevo oyó claramente la voz del Hermano aquella noche de su llegada: "¿Qué haces tú aquí?" Él tenía razón. El había visto con los ojos de la eternidad. Debía haberse marchado entonces. (p.236)

The feeling of uncertainty which is present all through the novel is still in evidence even when he finally decides to leave the seminary. Now, however, the uncertainty is more concerned with the challenge of an unknown destiny, a destiny which will be entirely of his own making. When Castillo-Puche commented on the novel much later, he stated that the problem of uncertainty is the central theme of the novel. What the author attempts to explore is not merely the problems of doubt or speculation surrounding the religious vocation but the wider question of human choice and human destiny:

> Esta novela no está hecha desde el punto de vista del análisis mental, filosófico, ni siquiera moral, sino desde el punto de vista de incertidumbre humana: de ¿qué hago con mi destino, con mi vida? Una vez sólo puedo elegir y elijo esto y ¿por qué? Este sentido es totalmente existencial.[31]

This statement by the author would suggest that there is no hidden truth concerning Enrique and, furthermore, that the novel is not a religious novel that was meant to appeal to a certain section of the public. The main object of the

novel is not concerned with anything spiritual or metaphysical, but rather with the
fundamental problems of human existence:

> La novela mía está hecha con los sentidos, y con la carne y con la
> vida.[32]

Although the setting of the novel is the Jesuit seminary of Comillas just after the
Civil War and all the observances and practices of a typical Catholic
establishment are brought into play, the main emphasis of the novel is centred on
Enrique, not principally as a seminarian, but as a human being in a particular
situation. In this way, the author claims that the novel is therefore not a religious
work, but the product of an existential writer:

> Yo soy existencialista porque mi naturaleza me hace vivir de lo
> que soy, de mi existencia. No es que olvide la esencia de las
> cosas. En la novela aparece que en la existencia está la esencia.[33]

Gonzalo Sobejano, writing on the modern Spanish novel, would agree
with the author's assertion that he cannot be classified as a Catholic or religious
novelist. The key to this lies in the fact that none of the problems in the novels are
resolved by reference to Catholic doctrine or spirituality:

> Las decisiones de los protagonistas conflictivos - que en el fondo
> son un solo y mismo personaje: el autor - no terminan en la meta
> de la salvación por la fe o la gracia. El desenlace ... tiene lugar
> hacia dentro del mundo, fuera del supremo negocio ignaciano de
> salvar o no el alma.[34]

In the same way, Enrique does not solve the crisis by remaining in the seminary
but will only discover his own will as he steps out into the world:

> Todo lo pasado no había sido más que el vago presentimiento de
> un hombre que comenzaba a vivir con vida propia y que salía
> dispuesto a crearse una voluntad. (p.260)

Once the decision is made and there is a new-found sense of freedom, Enrique can only regret that he never acted sooner and so saved himself and others a lot of worry and pain:

> Había sufrido mucho. Había sido un loco. Había querido armonizar en él lo inarmonizable. Él no servía para aquello. (p.260)

It is this sense of appealing to the general audience of humanity with the universal problems and anxieties of the human situation which surely dismisses the idea of Castillo-Puche as a Catholic novelist. The ability to emphasise values that are common to most human beings is one of the main ingredients of a successful novel. This point is discussed by Wayne Booth when writing on general language and form in fiction.[35] Booth claims that some authors possess that special gift of bringing together, through their writing, people of different backgrounds and convictions. A successful work will incorporate values which are universal, overriding all the barriers of beliefs and cultures, as do the plays, for example, of Shakespeare:

> Platonist and Aristotelian, Catholic and Protestant, liberal and conservative, can agree that these lives are comic and those tragic, that this behaviour is vicious and that admirable, that somehow, in fact, these plays express existentially, as the current fashion puts it, what life means.[36]

In a similar way, Castillo-Puche is not intending to put across an argument either against or in favour of the Christian faith, but rather wants the reader to sympathise and feel solidarity with the anxieties experienced by Enrique. As Booth indicates, it is when a work tries to convince the reader of a specific set of beliefs that it would be classified as doctrinal or religious:

It is only when a work seems explicitly doctrinaire, or when reasonable men can be in serious disagreement about its values, that the question of belief arises for discussion.[37]

The problems of the human condition which qualify the author as existentialist are also extended, however, in this novel, to the Christian ideal. Speaking in 1985, Castillo-Puche claims that Enrique is portrayed as someone who wants to remove Christianity from the purely spiritual or theological realm and associate Christ with the problems of human experience:

Quiere humanizar a Cristo. Quiere acercar a Cristo al Ser, a la contingencia y al problema del hombre en sus dudas y en sus cosas.[38]

This attitude is seen at the end of the novel when Enrique is about to abandon the seminary and go directly into the outside world. Leaving behind the routine of prayer and study does not, for Enrique, imply the abandonment of belief. On the contrary, Enrique is about to discover the real presence of God in the human condition, in the simple ordinary events of everyday life:

Él se iba detrás del Dios de los caminos, de los que quieren a Dios sin analizarlo, de los que lo quieren y lo sienten en su carne sin haberlo estudiado en los libros de teología, de los que sin tener hábitos ascéticos lo siguen por los campos y las ciudades heroicamente sin saberlo apenas. Se iba detrás de un Dios mucho más difícil y exigente. (p261)

As Enrique sets out 'con paso firme' into the world, we must conclude that, in the struggle between nature and the soul, it is the world of the senses which appears to have triumphed. Although Sobejano has suggested that the solutions here can only be found in the material world, I think it is wrong to assume that Enrique has therefore abandoned all religious hope and belief. It is not the faith of Enrique that is questioned by the decision to leave the seminary. On the contrary, as Oscar Barrero indicates, his departure from the seminary signifies the beginning of a new search for God, different from the image presented in the seminary:

> Enrique, persistiendo en su propósito de autenticidad, se dirigirá al encuentro de un Dios quizá diferente del aprendido, un Dios humano y comprensivo.[39]

Although the feeling of uncertainty continues out in the world there is, at least, a kind of liberation and recuperation of an individual whose lack of decision was leading him into a miserable existence. Yet, through all the novel, there is a persistent sense of conflict which leaves the reader uncertain as to which direction Enrique should take. The fact that he does yearn to be a priest and that his heroic ideal is not far from being realised makes it more difficult to support the decision to abandon the ideal. But the attraction to literature, to women, and to nature prove equally desirable and, in the end, one desire had surrender to the other. It appears rather unfortunate, or perhaps cruel, that the Catholic Church should present the vocation with so many conditions attached, especially concerning the matter of celibacy. The narrator gives the impression that Enrique is not looking to blame anyone for his failed vocation but, instead, we see Enrique accepting full responsibility for his decision. The frequent inside views, the use of the 'estilo indirecto libre', and the sympathetic treatment of Enrique suggest a certain degree of solidarity between the narrator and the character. As Wayne Booth indicates, the use of the inside view itself can sometimes be enough in transforming the role of the character:

> We should remind ourselves that any sustained inside view, of whatever depth, temporarily turns the character whose mind is shown into a narrator.[40]

We have seen that Sobejano does not distinguish between author and any conflictive character, and the author has implied in the preface that his own experiences are reflected in Enrique. Nevertheless, there is equally enough evidence of criticism of Enrique's attitude and actions to suggest that the author is not wholly identified with the character. At the same time, however, within such a short time after his real-life abandonment of vocation, it would be wrong to assume that Castillo-Puche had created a completely fictitious character in Enrique. While admitting that many of the events in this novel are fiction, it is clear also that the anguish and uncertainty of Enrique in the novel were plainly shared by the author at the time of writing.

NOTES

1. 'El 15 de febrero de 1941 una inesperada catástrofe sobrecogió a España entera. Un horroroso huracán azotó Santander, acompañado de un incendio que destruyó la tercera parte de la ciudad.' *Enciclopedia universal ilustrada, europea-americana* (Madrid: Espasa-Calpe, 1958), suplemento anual 1940-1941, 765.

2. Preface to the latest edition of *Sin camino* (Barcelona: Destino, 1983), 8.

3. Preface to *Sin camino*, 6-7.

4. Private conversations with the author in Madrid (September 1985).

5. Private conversations (1985).

6. Preface to *Sin camino*, 9.

7. All subsequent quotations will be taken from the 1983 edition.

8. See Oscar Barrero Pérez, *La novela existencial española de posguerra* (Madrid: Gredos, 1987), 81-92: "El conflicto de la individualidad con el medio exterior."

9. Barrero Pérez, 81.

10. Barrero Pérez, 85.

11. Author's Curriculum Vitae, 2.

12. Private conversations (1985).

13. Conversations (1985).

14. Conversations (1985).

15. Conversations (1985).

16. Conversations (1985).

17. Gonzalo Sobejano, *Novela española de nuestro tiempo*, 2nd. ed. (Madrid: Prensa Española, 1975), 260-261.

18. Private conversations (1985).

19. Conversations (1985).

20. Conversations (1985).

21. Compare the sense of disaster and punishment found in the storm sequence in *El amargo sabor de la retama* (Barcelona: Destino, 1979), 94-128.

22. See John Powell, *Why am I afraid to tell you who I am?* (Hong Kong: Fontana, 1975).

23. Powell, 110.

24. Powell, 110.

25. Powell, 161.

26. Powell, 39.

27. Powell, 42.

28. See Barrero Pérez, 108-110.

29. Barrero Pérez, 110.

30. Concha Alborg, "Tres personajes de Castillo-Puche en busca de un camino." *Anales de Filología Hispánica* 2, (1986), 117-125.

31. Private conversations (1985).

32. Conversations (1985).

33. Conversations (1985).

34. Sobejano, 268.

35. See Wayne C. Booth, *The Rhetoric of Fiction*. 2nd. Ed. (London: Penguin, 1991), 137-144: "General Rules, IV: Emotion, Beliefs, and the Reader's Objectivity".

36. Booth, 141.

37. Booth, 142.

38. Private conversations (1985).

39. Barrero Pérez, 196.

40. Booth, 164.

CHAPTER 3
Como ovejas al matadero

From the isolation and uncertainty of the seminarian Enrique who finally decided to abandon his religious vocation in the first novel, *Sin camino*, we move to the tense and apprehensive situation of four ordinands on the very day of ordination to the priesthood. The scene is the chapel of the Episcopal Palace in Murcia and the time is July 1936, just prior to the outbreak of Civil War. Although the title of the novel together with the timing of the impending conflict might suggest that the main concern of the novel was with the precarious situation confronting the Spanish clergy in 1936, we soon discover that the novel has very little to do with the political implications of the period. What is more important seems to be human nature and the effects, both physical and emotional, that the demands of religious life of that time imposed upon individuals. These effects are never more evident than at the crucial moment of ordination when the four 'misacantanos' are confronted with the memories of certain experiences of the past which have determined their present predicament. Many of these experiences have taken place within the seminary period but the narrator often refers to incidents in the years preceding their entry into the seminary so that the reader can have a fairly clear picture of the four distinct backgrounds.

Although written some twenty-five years after his first novel, *Sin camino*, *Como ovejas al matadero* reveals a continuity in the author's concern for the problems of the human limitations within the particular environment of the religious institution. As in *Sin camino*, in *Como ovejas al matadero* Castillo-Puche is primarily interested in human problems as he maintains his existential position which remains unconcerned with the investigation of faith or religious dogma. At the same time, however, we witness in *Sin camino* a clear desire to transfer Christianity from the exclusive world of the religious institution to the wider secular world when Enrique steps out into an uncertain future. In a similar way, the seminary institution in *Como ovejas al matadero* is criticised by the narrator for its policy of isolation from the problems of human beings in the world. The attitude of the Church in the novel is that no vocation is fruitful without sacrifice and that there can be no real sacrifice unless there is total renunciation of everything worldly:

> La vocación había sido siempre un campo roturado de carteles con 'vedado' por aquí, 'vedado' por allá, como si la vocación fuera una incursión orgullosa en la entrega y en la renuncia total a la vez, y que se hacía obligado condenar de antemano precisamente el mundo que se intentaba salvar. (p.13)[1]

The consequence of this hostile attitude towards the world is a conflict between the human and the spiritual, between nature and soul, between solidarity and solitude, and this is precisely what is examined in the conscience of each seminarian as he approaches the consummation of the sacrifice:

> Los seminaristas se pasaban los años entre la soledad y el deseo, entre el miedo y la nostalgia, en pugna constante entre los dones y las gracias del Espíritu y lo que se llaman pasiones terrenales, que a veces también se convertían en fondo disimulado de sus existencias. (p.13)

The narrator introduces here the basis for the entire novel, that is, the conflict between the spirit and human nature that exists in the religious vocation as it is described in the novel. The important terms to describe this conflict are salvation and condemnation, as we have just seen, since the seminarians are under the impression that all that is worldly is condemned and that salvation lies outwith the physical realm. These two opposing terms are described by Pablo

Corbalán, in his article about the novel, as the source of every struggle and anxiety present in the conscience of the seminarian:

> Estas palabras plantean el problema fundamental ... Y de ellas nace todo el drama angustioso, pesadamente angustioso, áspero, casi ululante en la lucha entre la sencillez vocacional y el salto casi en el vacío - por ignorado - que se va a dar de un momento a otro.[2]

If the human and physical side of us is to be condemned, as we saw also in the words of the Spiritual Director in *Sin camino*, then the seminarian is faced with a whole new set of questions as to the significance of his existence, as Corbalán indicated:

> ¿Cómo esa condena? ¿Cómo esa salvación? Y, entre una y otra pregunta, ¿quién soy yo, cómo soy, cómo salgo de la condena y entro en la salvación?[3]

These are the questions facing the four ordinands in the last twenty-four hours leading to the most important decision of their lives. But the four candidates are quite different from one another and while two of them, Ramiro and Fulgencio, represent sincere and heroic vocations, the other two, Cosme and Alfredo, are examples of individuals in conflict with their humanity, especially their sexual nature. Indeed, the problems of sexual repression and homosexuality depicted by Alfredo and Cosme respectively form a major part of the novel. But before dealing with this feature, it is also important to examine the conflict between nature and spirit in terms of social justice, or Christianity in the world, on the one hand, and the ideal of sacrifice, on the other.

A. SOCIAL JUSTICE

In a similar way to *Sin camino*, the narrator of *Como ovejas al matadero* is able to offer inside views of all four characters. But whereas *Sin camino* was principally concerned with showing us the events and how they affected the protagonist, the difference in *Como ovejas al matadero* is that the action is limited to a very short period of time and we are told about the events already experienced by each of the principal characters. The past experiences are revealed by the omniscient narrator so that we come to know the characters not through their action within the time-scale of the novel but only from what they have already done, as described by the narrator. In this way, the narrator takes us back to the family backgrounds of each character and reveals the origins and causes either of heroic virtue, in the case of Ramiro and Fulgencio, or of the physical and emotional problems of Cosme and Alfredo.

The concern for social justice manifested by Ramiro, for example, can be linked to a religious vocation which developed in the face of an indifferent or hostile environment. The sincerity of Ramiro's vocation was strengthened by the fact that he was neither encouraged nor assisted by anyone outwith or even within his own family. For the narrator, a vocation that was based on a personal decision and not on the persuasions of others would be a stronger and more genuine vocation:

> Su destino no había sido impuesto ni amañado por nadie sino forjado por él mismo en un arranque de disolución familiar. (p.21)

The strength of his vocation lay too with the notion of sacrifice since he had renounced a comfortable middle-class lifestyle and a prosperous future in order to embrace a life of poverty. In this way, he was able to exchange his association with the rich for solidarity with the needy:

> Para Ramiro, el sacerdocio no había sido, como en tantos casos, una liberación de la pobreza, sino más bien lo contrario, un abrazo con el riesgo y la soledad de los desheredados, precozmente aburrido de la rutinaria y engañosa felicidad en que vivía su

familia. (p.143)

Also important is the fact that his decision to become a priest was directly opposed to the republican and atheistic views upheld by his father, a successful psychiatrist. In a sense, Ramiro sees his sacrifice as perhaps the only way of convincing his father of his religious belief:

> Ser sacerdote era lo único que él podía ser ante un padre vanidoso, y si no impío, por lo menos no creyente. La vocación había sido inconscientemente la lucha contra el padre, frente al padre, y que éste era el único milagro o por lo menos el único testimonio que su padre podría entender, porque en los otros, manifiestamente, no creía. (p.21)

It was not only the attitude of Ramiro in the face of opposition from the world outside which determined the strength of his commitment, but also, the narrator authoritatively tells us, it was his ability to resist all the negative elements that existed within the seminary itself:

> Que su vocación era genuina partiendo del sentimiento de la caridad, había quedado probado por su capacidad para resistir de un modo objetivo, casi frío, todo lo horrendo y vulgar que había encontrado en la vida del seminario, la zafiedad intelectual, la espantable ascética y el fácil disparadero hacia una mística de consolaciones. (p.21)

Although the narrator presents Ramiro's vocation as genuine, he suggests that the seminary is populated by many individuals whose vocation has been implanted by others. There is a profound contrast between the careful preparations and counselling undertaken by Ramiro before entering the seminary in order to discern the validity of his calling and the facile vocations already predetermined by others:

> No era fácil encajar una vocación de este tipo dentro del rebato

de las vocaciones predeterminadas desde pequeños por el cura, la
madre, el tío sacerdote, ayudados por las circunstancias
económicas de familias indigentes que ven en el seminario y en
el sacerdocio el camino hacia una redención más mezquina y
limitada incomparablemente que la que Cristo selló con su
sangre. (p.146)

The reference here to the influence of the mother and the religious uncle is linked

to the *Trilogía de la liberación* in which the young protagonist, Pepico, is also

affected by the resolutions of his family to send him to the seminary. There

appears to be a similarity between the pressure of the mother on Pepico in the

trilogy and the emotional influence exercised by the mother of Alfredo in this

novel which suggests that Alfredo's vocation, like Pepico's in the trilogy, would

fall into that category of 'vocaciones predeterminadas'. We shall observe later

in our study of the trilogy how the character of the mother in the three novels

closely resembles the author's own mother in reality, and how she did have a

great deal of influence on the religious vocation. It may be the case, therefore,

that, although the virtues and attitudes of Ramiro are presented favourably by the

narrator, it is the background of Alfredo and not Ramiro that is more identifiable

with the author.

Apart from the negative features displayed by his peers, Ramiro also

objected to the kind of education offered by the seminary:

Teología de machamartillo que en vez de enfrentar al alumno con
el misterio y con la ciencia disponible, lo dejaban como un corcho
flotando en el mar de las dudas. (p.147)

Nevertheless, Ramiro had never allowed his ideals to be defeated by the

behaviour of his family nor by the attitude of other seminarians, and he would not

be deterred either by the stuffiness of the religious education. It appears that

whenever there were obstacles, Ramiro possessed the ability and determination

to transform negative situations through Christian action:

> Y el seminario, que pudo ser embalsamiento en la retórica o
> esterilidad en el autoclave para Ramiro, se hizo aventura donde
> ásperos espinos, arenas fangosas y espejismos engañosos no
> sirvieron más que para crearle la necesidad de hacer vergel, oasis
> y huerta frondosa a costa de derramar misericordias. (p.147)

It is interesting to note the difference in attitude between Enrique of *Sin camino* who, in the face of a negative environment, reacted by alienating himself from the situation, and Ramiro, who uses these occasions as challenges for growth.

There are three main positive factors concerning Ramiro's vocation, namely, the sacrifice involved in renouncing a wealthy lifestyle for the sake of an ideal, the courage to decide his own future for himself, and his attitude towards Christianity which brings God into the world and human experience. This last factor is principally connected to the idea of social justice and on this point there is a similarity between the ideals of Ramiro and Enrique of *Sin camino*. Both want to see God actively involved in human circumstances just as Christ was, but where they differ is how to bring this about. For Enrique, since he felt religious life was separated from human problems, the only solution was to abandon the seminary and go into the world. But Ramiro, on the other hand, is able to combine his ideal of social justice with ordination to the priesthood and, what is more, if the Church is lacking in this respect, then, as we have seen, Ramiro had the courage to change the situation. One of his methods was to blend traditional teaching with modern sociology and psychology and incorporate them under the Church's social doctrine. In this way, Ramiro could bring the priesthood that bit closer to the problems of modern man:

> Para Ramiro el Evangelio era una empresa nueva, y dentro del
> sacerdocio, cuanto más sacrificado mejor, estaba la esperanza del
> hombre actual. (p.38)

Just as Christ was associated with the plight of the poor, the sick and the sinner, so Ramiro saw Christianity essentially involved wherever there was poverty or injustice. This is demonstrated by his desire to be chaplain to the working-class communities:

> Quería entregarse al proletariado en cualquiera de sus formas y le interesaban las fábricas y las Casas del Pueblo más que las cofradías y las congregaciones piadosas. (p.76)

Ramiro saw the priesthood as the abandonment of personal security and complete solidarity with ordinary people:

> Había que saber lo que es el reparto de un sueldo, incluso el no reparto de ningún sueldo en las épocas de brazos caídos o cierre transitorio. (p.76)

There is a suggestion that Ramiro was attracted to the notion of 'worker' priests which was a phenomenon which sprang up in Spain especially during the late 1960s and 1970s due to the influence of the Second Vatican Council.[4] This trend among the clergy, as John Hooper indicates, must be viewed as a complete reversal of the Church in its attitude towards the Franco regime:

> The gap between what the regime promised and what it delivered in the way of social justice grew wider every year and was quite soon demonstrably at variance with Christian ideals.[5]

Hooper explains that the Church's renewed links with the working class began to surface in the 1950s with the creation of new societies like 'Hermandades Obreras de Acción Católica' and continued to strengthen through the 1960s and 1970s as more priests integrated with the poor communities in the search for complete solidarity:

> This was the heyday of the *curas rojos* (red priests), who took advantage of the privileges and immunities granted to the Church

by Franco to allow strike meetings in the vestry and sit-ins in the nave.[6]

All these innovative measures seemed to have the approval of the Vatican and this is demonstrated in the teachings of the Second Vatican Council which has a section dedicated to the ministry of the priesthood.[7] The Council emphasises that all priests are united in the one purpose though each may bring this about in varied and different roles:

> All priests are sent forth as co-workers on the same undertaking, whether they are engaged in a parochial or super-parochial ministry, whether they devote their efforts to scientific research or teaching, whether by manual labour they share in the lot of the workers themselves - if there seems to be need for this and competent authority approves - or whether they fulfil any other apostolic tasks or labours related to the apostolate. All indeed are united in the single goal of building up Christ's body, a work requiring manifold rules and new adjustments, especially nowadays.[8]

Since the novel *Como ovejas al matadero* was published in 1971 it is likely that Castillo-Puche was influenced by the teachings of the Council which were first published in 1966, and which generated a period of transition in the Catholic Church. It is unlikely, however, though not impossible, that Ramiro would be expressing the same sentiments of solidarity and social justice in the summer of 1936, the period depicted in the novel. It is as if the author were wishing that this change of direction in the Church had come about earlier and so helped to reconcile the divisions in Spanish society which led to the outbreak of Civil War. At the same time, however, it should be said that many of the ideas put forward in *Sin camino*, written between 1944 and 1947, express a longing for change in the Church's attitude towards society and human needs, and this novel long predates the Second Vatican Council. This fact indicates that the author felt just as strongly in his earlier years as he did when change eventually came about in the Church's social doctrine. It seems clear that prior to the Civil War, the Catholic Church in Spain had alienated itself from the plight of the poor and working-class. This process of alienation began in the nineteenth century and continued right up to the outbreak of the Civil War.[9] It was during this critical period, as Stanley Payne indicates, that the poorer classes gradually became disillusioned with the Church:

> Much of the peasantry lived in a great spiritual void and was filled with social and economic resentment against the clergy, who were identified with the upper classes.[10]

Gerald Brenan, writing just after the Civil War, also points out that, despite this growing separation, the Church seemed either incapable of, or uninterested in, narrowing the gap:

> Just as in the sixteenth century it showed neither the will nor the patience necessary for converting the Moors, but used its influence with the State to have them driven out altogether, so today it has refused (until too late) to take the appropriate measures for arresting the steady de-Christianization of the working classes.[11]

With the Church failing to establish solidarity with ordinary working people we find yet further evidence of the distance between nature and the soul, between social needs and spiritual welfare. The result is a people in conflict, devoid of any sense of social harmony and justice, as Fulgencio reflects in the novel:

> Un pueblo vacío de dirección y azuzado a la agresión por ambas partes contemplaba, entre resignado y receloso, el desbarajuste total y, si unos hablaban de los valores del espíritu, los otros invocaban las exigencias del proletariado. (p.89)

Fulgencio, like Ramiro, is also presented by the narrator as one who wants to be involved with the poorer classes. It often seems to be the author's own views which are expressed through both Ramiro and Fulgencio as when, for example, Fulgencio was dismayed at the intransigence of the opposing factions during 1936. On the one hand, there was the traditional Catholic stance which was unconcerned with charity or social justice:

> Los que ponían por delante el nombre de Dios no urgían por el milagro de convertirse a conductas de justicia sino que el único milagro que pedían era la destrucción del enemigo con todas sus peticiones, algunas de ellas muy justas. (p.89)

On the other hand, meantime, those who claimed to be standing for workers' rights were bent on violence and settling old scores:

> Mientras los que no se quitaban de la boca la palabra 'pueblo' y la 'causa del pueblo', más que normales niveles de existencia lo que reclamaban eran armas y armas para imponer por la fuerza, a costa de lo que fuera, la revancha también total. (pp.89-90)

Like Ramiro once again, Fulgencio saw the priesthood as an heroic sacrifice which scorned any association with 'providencialismo' or any political affiliation.

Both Ramiro and Fulgencio are presented sympathetically by the narrator as examples of genuine sacrifice and commitment. Both characters are critical of the Church and a seminary system which churns out great numbers of ordained priests, many of whom have no authentic vocation and likewise no understanding of social problems. The more seminarians released into the world without proper training and awareness, the greater will be their alienation from the people and the more injustice will be ignored. The result, Ramiro thinks, will be a passive and conformist Church that is unable to change a society where the privileged prosper at the cost of the poor:

> No tenemos derecho a pronunciar la palabra caridad cuando alrededor nuestro, como si fuéramos sus guardianes, todo es vandalismo legal, explotación inicua y monopolio del bienestar

exclusivo por los egoísmos privilegiados, como si estuviéramos
haciendo una farsa de lo que es el auténtico drama de la
humanidad. (p.176)

The personal views of Castillo-Puche on the Church's attitude towards
social injustice are clearly expressed in his comments on Sender's *Réquiem por
un campesino español*. Sender, a writer in exile from Spain, was accompanied by
Castillo-Puche on his return to Spain in 1974. Over the years, the two writers
became closely acquainted and Castillo-Puche was clearly impressed enough to
write a book on Sender which includes a special tribute to *Réquiem*.[12] The
Réquiem is described as the classic tragedy of Spanish rural life in which the
supposed saviour of the community, the priest, commits the grave iniquity of
betraying a good man into the hands of his enemies. As in the novels by
Castillo-Puche, the Civil War forms an integral part of the events but
Castillo-Puche believes that *Réquiem* is not principally a novel about war:

> Hay, pues, en la obra una denuncia de la injusticia social, de la
> opresión ejercida sin piedad por los ricos, y de la rutina y el
> conformismo tradicional de la iglesia que la hace antievangélica
> e inoperante.[13]

For Castillo-Puche, the most important features in the works of Sender are the
notion of social conflict, the human condition and the problems of Spanish
society, riddled as it is with so much injustice:

> Realismo del hombre español y sátira de sus quimeras es lo que
> se adensa en las páginas de Sender; explicación racional y
> profunda del fracaso de nuestros sueños de convivencia y de paz;
> análisis de aquellas influencias nefastas que, en determinados
> momentos históricos, nos han impedido ser lo que queremos ser.[14]

Both Sender and Castillo-Puche appear to agree in their criticisms of the
Church and its failure to stand up for justice and peace, and Castillo-Puche tries

to link this failure to a seminary system which allows so many individuals to pass into the ministry without any understanding either of Christianity or of social problems. It takes an exceptional kind of character like Ramiro or Fulgencio who, despite the seminary education, can still maintain within themselves the potential for reform. However, in reality, the Church and Spanish society had to wait some time before reform came about with the Second Vatican Council in 1965.[15] It was during the period of renewal afterwards that the Catholic Church in Spain recognised its own failure to bring peace and reconciliation in the past, especially during the conflict and division of the Civil War. In his study of the Church under Franco, José Chao Rego refers to the following declaration issued by the Spanish bishops in September 1971:

> Si decimos que no hemos pecado, hacemos a Dios mentiroso y su palabra no está en nosotros (I JN, 1,10). Así, pues, reconocemos humildemente y pedimos perdón, porque nosotros no supimos a su tiempo ser verdaderos 'ministros de reconciliación' en el seno de nuestro pueblo, dividido por una guerra entre hermanos.[16]

There is already the suggestion in the earlier novel *Sin camino*, set in the 1940s, that the seminary was awaiting some kind of reform from Rome which never seemed to arrive, and this desire for renewal is also very much apparent in this novel. The Church of the 1930s was obviously lacking in the spirit of reconciliation and justice by its decision to ignore the plight of the weak and to side, instead, with the powerful. However, this has not always been the case. In more recent times in countries like El Salvador, for example, the Church has rejected its association with the ruling classes and opted, instead, to side with the poor and oppressed. In a similar way, Castillo-Puche believes Spain needs not a political Church but a Church that cares for the people and that can encourage social justice and peace, as expressed in the ideal of Ramiro:

> No hay más testamento que cumplir que el de Jesús ni más tesoro

que los pobres y los necesitados de justicia. (pp.175-176)

B. SACRIFICE

Connected to the notion of social justice is the call for self-sacrifice, something which is indispensable to the priesthood. The title of the novel is taken both from the Forty-fourth Psalm and the prophet Isaiah, the latter being regarded as directly referring to the sacrificial death of Christ:

> Harshly dealt with, he bore it humbly,
> he never opened his mouth,
> like a lamb that is led to the slaughter-house,
> like a sheep that is dumb before its shearers
> never opening its mouth.
>
> Isaiah 53.7

The sense of dumbness and resignation to describe the attitude of Christ is also reflected in the four ordinands at the crucial moment of the imposition of hands, which symbolises the bestowal of divine grace:

> Fulgencio, Ramiro, Alfredo y Cosme permanecen mudos, espantados de su real ministerio y asustados por la tremenda responsabilidad. (p.163)

No distinction is made between the priesthood and Christ since the newly-ordained priests are to continue the same mission that Christ himself had. Castillo-Puche, speaking about the novel in 1985, refers to this notion of the priest as another Christ:

> Ese sentido es el que yo he querido llevar, porque como siempre que se repite que el sacerdote es 'alter Christus', entonces siempre es otro cordero y un cordero que se va a sacrificar.[17]

The dating of the novel in 1936 also indicates that, with the wave of anti-clericalism and violence against the Church, the likelihood of giving one's life was a reality that each of the four ordinands had to face up to. The narrator implies that the atrocities about to be committed against the Church with the deaths of so many priests can be compared to the persecution of Christ:

> Pero si es evidente que no ha de faltar Cristo a su Iglesia, tampoco faltarán nuevos sacerdotes, aunque sean pocos, que como otros Cristos den el testimonio de esta hora, el testimonio más comprometido porque no sólo se trata de la gloria de su Iglesia sino también de su debilidad, todo lo que hay de gracia en el mensaje de Jesús, pero también todo lo que hay de escándalo y contradicción. (p.163)

It is difficult to see how the sense of martyrdom can be attributed to the victims of persecution of the 1930s since the Catholic Church had always been associated with the wealthier classes, as Hooper indicates:

> Whenever, during the late nineteenth and early twentieth centuries, the right lost its grip on the levers of power there were frenzied outbursts of violence directed against Catholicism and its representatives. Churches were burned or desecrated. On occasions, priests were killed and nuns raped.[18]

The notion of Christian martyrdom seems more appropriately identified with the defence of social justice than with those who defended traditional values. In other words, the Spanish Church of the 1930s seems to have been hated not for its Christian activity but for its isolation from the poor.

Although the narrator of the novel rightly criticises the Church's lack of concern for social issues, there seems to be a sudden change in tone as he comes to the Church's defence in the face of persecution and hostility. There is a sense that if the priests are persecuted or killed this would be something martyr-like or heroic:

> En pureza de interpretación ellos están siendo constituidos servidores del pueblo, no sólo, además, del pueblo fiel y cristiano, y tanto es así que a veces por salvar al pueblo serán arrastrados por este mismo pueblo. (p.162)

Nevertheless, it seems to be recognised by the author, speaking some fourteen years after the work was published, that much of this sacrifice must be questioned as to the value and motives involved. Since it is clear that many seminarians find their way through the seminary without any real commitment to Christianity, it could be considered somewhat illogical that these individuals should later be regarded as martyrs for Christ:

> Hay como una alarma profética en el libro sobre dos entregas: la entrega cotidiana normal que parece inconsciente para algunos y la entrega total que después va a dar testimonio del sacerdocio, y morirán como ovejas, y algunos morirán sin tener por dentro la conciencia limpia ni tendrán el testimonio.[19]

We have seen that Ramiro and Fulgencio are exemplary figures since they both worked hard at their religious vocation and would be willing to sacrifice themselves for Christ and for the Church. But we know that the novel is not just about elevating the religious vocation and Castillo-Puche later gave his views on the novel's theme of sacrifice:

> Todo el proceso interior de la novela es la inmolación consciente o inconsciente.[20]

The author maintains that many individuals in the seminary, especially before the advent of the Second Vatican Council, were ignorant of the true meaning of priesthood and sacrifice. As was also demonstrated in *Sin camino* much of the commitment was only superficial and the seminarians often displayed deviant tendencies. Castillo-Puche is trying to examine the phenomenon of the vocation and how to distinguish between the true vocation and the false or perhaps imposed vocation:

> ¿Cómo se entregan, se immolan? y ¿ cómo, muchas veces, no saben el sentido altísimo transcendental que tiene la inmolación? Y entonces unos van con ilusión. Otros van con fe, y otros van de una manera vulgar, anodina.[21]

If a vocation is not genuine, then others may be responsible for promoting and encouraging an individual to continue to ordination:

> Entonces el sentido mío fue: ¿Qué fenómeno de opresión, de represión, de coacción, de invitación, de sugerencia, de solicitud hay en la vocación? ¿Dónde termina el mundo de la persuasión y empieza el mundo de la coacción, de la violencia?[22]

Those others would include, for example, the Spiritual Director and also the mother of Enrique in *Sin camino*, while in *Como ovejas al matadero* the mother of Alfredo plays a similar role of emotional involvement in the vocation. However, the point seems to be that if an individual is going to sacrifice his life for an ideal, then he must be equipped for that sacrifice and all it entails. One of the greatest obstacles to self-sacrifice which the novel gives so much importance to is the sexual condition, which shall now be discussed.

C. SEXUAL REPRESSION

In stark contrast with the heroic virtues of Ramiro and Fulgencio and their genuine commitment to the religious vocation, the narrator reveals the disturbing side of religious life in the characters of Alfredo and Cosme. In an interview with Miguel Fernández-Braso in 1971, Castillo-Puche explained why his intention was not just to show the positive ideals of the priesthood but to expose the realities of Spanish Catholicism:

Desnudar el alma del catolicismo español. Virtudes externas y vicios internos. Se puede saber morir por la fe y no saber vivir según la caridad: se puede dar la apariencia de una castidad combativa y ser un monstruo: se puede ser ejemplo de fidelidad a la llamada jerarquía y ser un monumento circulante de egoísmo o un emblema de injusticia social.[23]

The author describes the novel as a realistic approach to seminary life which is ready to exalt the qualities of the priesthood without forgetting the dangers and pitfalls. In the same article, the author claims that the novel attempts to give a complete picture of the religious situation and that must include the pain as much as the glory:

Y no huir, ni escaparse, tampoco, de flaquezas y debilidades, que tantas veces son parte del testimonio.[24]

The attempt to highlight the negative side of the vocation is not done for the sake of 'tremendismo' but rather to draw the reader's attention to the magnitude of the problem. The religious life is plagued with human problems and it is only by taking our humanity into account that we can assess the situation with honesty:

Hay que ser sinceros, terriblemente sinceros en los conflictos religiosos, porque la vitalidad dominante hay que contrastarla con otra muy bella ciertamente, pero condenada al tormento.[25]

Castillo-Puche refers here to the other important dimension of human beings, that is, sexuality: human love and procreation. This is an integral part of the definition of our humanity and must be regarded as a beautiful aspect of human nature. Quite often, however, the Church has presented sexuality as an enemy or has simply tried to ignore its presence altogether. But if sexuality is seen as something which interferes with our total well-being, then seminarians who have this impression will inevitably run into problems, as is seen in the novel, in the case of Alfredo.

The title of the trilogy, which begins with *Como ovejas al matadero*, reflects the importance given to the theme of sexuality. *El cíngulo*, which translates the word 'cincture' or 'girdle', is an essential part of the priestly attire and is a symbol of the priest's commitment to chastity. When, early on in the novel, Alfredo is seen accidentally dropping the girdle, this accident becomes a sign of the troubles already experienced and the terrible outcome that was still to befall him. It had been impressed upon the seminarians that the 'cingulum castitatis' was the greatest and most precious sign of their priesthood. Just as Enrique was warned of the dangers of women and the flesh by the Spiritual Director in *Sin camino*, so the seminarians of this novel are told of the terrible consequences of failing to remain faithful to their oath:

> De no cumplir con la pureza sacerdotal, era preferible cien veces que cogieran la cuerda del cíngulo, un cíngulo que si lo conservaban sin mácula les serviría para atar al Cordero Celestial, pero que si lo manchaban sería preferible que lo volvieran rojo de latigazos sobre la propia carne, ya que desertar en la castidad era peor que hacer un nudo corredizo con el propio cíngulo y ahorcarse como Judas. (p.25)

This ludicrous attitude towards sex by imposing a sense of terror around natural impulses shows that the primary responsibility for any sexual problems must be with the teaching of the Church at that time and the superiors of the seminary. This warning had created such an impression on Alfredo that even at the moment of communion thoughts of the betrayal of Judas were very much on his mind:

> Todavía faltaba beber el cáliz, beber del cáliz de la eterna salud, pero también el cáliz de la posible perdición eterna, según tantas veces le habían advertido. Judas también estuvo en el cenáculo. (p.231)

As Alfredo became more aware of his sexuality, so he became increasingly obsessed with his own sinfulness and unworthiness since the natural urges in his body would force him to betray Christ. The body is made to become an obstacle to sanctity and the 'cingulum castitatis' is not strong enough to repress the sexual feelings that make him so unworthy:

> Por lo tanto, para él el prodigio no ha terminado de consumarse, acaso por ser un pecador él, están retenidas sobre él las manos del obispo. Por eso él todavía no es poseedor de la dádiva de las dádivas. Pero no es esto sólo, es que por todas y de todas partes le llega un susurro amenazante que dice: 'el cíngulo', 'ese cíngulo', 'cuidado con el cíngulo'. (p.226)

According to the author, the use of the term 'cíngulo' as a general heading is symbolic. In the same interview with Fernández-Braso, Castillo-Puche explains that the cincture is of double significance in the novel since it not only symbolises the priestly ideal as the Church would see it but it also represents man's captivity to human nature:

> Se trata de establecer aquellos símbolos profundos que precisamente por diarios no apreciamos. 'El cíngulo' es una alegoría, una metáfora que quiere ser de orden superior, porque el sacerdote, como hombre, está atado, ligado, colgado de realidades inevitables.[26]

The author maintains that these realities cannot be ignored and hopes that openly recognising these problems in the novel may bring about a greater understanding of the dilemma and provide a change in attitudes:

> Intentar sortearlas por arte de magia podría ser disímulo ohipocresía. Afrontarlas puede ser una experiencia saludable.[27]

Since sexuality was regarded as something hostile to God's kingdom, so too would women as the object of sexual desire be condemned. As the Church had taught the seminarians that women represented nothing but sensuality, passion, and sin, there was no way the vocation could be compatible with relationships with the opposite sex:

> Era una pena que el ideal del sacerdocio no fuera conciliable con la mujer, la enemiga, la trampa, la que vendía pasión a cambio deternura, la que repartía vicio en vez de compañía, la que incendiaba la soledad con el pecado, la que proporcionaba carne también dañada en lugar de prodigar espíritu. (p.231)

Yet Alfredo fought very hard to impose the demands of holiness upon the natural instincts, and to give precedence to the spiritual realm over the natural world. His failure to achieve this led him to despise his body as something corrupt and unworthy, and this attitude of repugnance is the key to the whole issue of sexual repression.

As the narrator reveals the important factors which have determined the lives of the four ordinands, the episodes of the sexual experiences of both Alfredo and Cosme are recorded in such detail that the emphasis on sexuality far outweighs that of the virtues attributed to Ramiro and Fulgencio. While Cosme is afflicted with the memory of his homosexual advances towards the adolescent Camilín, Alfredo is tormented by the memory of two distinct experiences with the opposite sex - with Tomasa 'hija de los labradores' and the maid in the 'fonda "la Confianza"'. There is quite a difference in this novel in the presentation of women compared with the images of Isabel and Inés in *Sin camino*. While the opposite sex was still presented as a threat to the vocation, Isabel and Inés are presented by the narrator in a somewhat gentle manner and are by no means scorned or hated. But in this novel the sensual experiences with women are presented very negatively as Alfredo displays sentiments of remorse and hostility towards them. This is perhaps not so much a demonstration of the narrator's animosity as an illustration of the attitude of Catholic education and the effects of this upon a character like Alfredo. In other words, the repugnance felt by Alfredo is due to the fact that he had never experienced any wholesome education regarding sex and therefore could only show an unhealthy attitude towards the subject.

This attitude is reflected in the experiences with Tomasa which took place during the vacation while Alfredo was already attending the seminary. Tomasa is presented in a similar way to the prostitute in *Sin camino* as the one responsible for introducing Alfredo to the world of sensual pleasure. But crossing the frontier between chastity and carnal knowledge only served to produce an immense feeling of guilt and remorse and a subsequent reaction of hostility:

> Tenía que haberla abofeteado por aquella ciencia de corrupción
> que le había hecho compartir, una culpa nueva, una culpa que era
> como la cumbre en la montaña de las culpas solitarias. (p.69)

Alfredo, like Enrique, had reached the point of no return and the depth of emotional response to the incident is similar enough in both novels to suggest a sense of solidarity between the narrators of both works and the respective characters. In both cases, the narrator highlights the transformation between the innocence of chastity and the guilt of sexual activity. For Alfredo, the awakening experience and the associated remorse were to remain forever present:

> Pero es que el olor de Tomasa, su rechinar de fiera en celo, le
> perseguían de continuo. Y Alfredo aceptó aquel olor como el cuño
> vil del pecado. (p.69)

Since Tomasa was the cause of this horrendous guilt, so both women and his own sexual condition were seen as despicable for creating such an ugly feeling. Yet these feelings did not originate from Tomasa or from his own sexuality but rather from his own misguided and unhealthy attitude towards the functions of the body. How could Alfredo's understanding of the matter be any different since this negative view of women had been taught from the Church's earliest times?:

> Ahora se percataba Alfredo de lo dicho por los Santos Padres, en
> todos los sentidos, que la mujer es cepo de obscenidad, estopa de
> delirios carnales, vaso de corrupción, engendro de Satanás. (p.67)

In this way, what was natural for every human being was converted into an

obstacle and a threat, and what was unnatural, the celibate state, was imposed as

an essential condition for sanctity.

Both the sexual repression of Alfredo and the perversion of Cosme are

related to the notion of human sexuality as something disgusting. The critic

Rafael Vázquez Zamora examines this notion of repugnance in an article about

the novel, written in 1971, where he indicates that this sense of disgust was at the

root both of Alfredo's masturbation and the homosexuality of Cosme:

> Su homosexualidad, aunque fomentada por haber encontrado a
> algún inocente efebo en el seminario, tenía ya hondas raíces en la
> repugnancia que le habían causado los exhibicionismos de sus
> propios hermanos, así como Alfredo, que había pasado por
> deprimentes experiencias 'normales', estaba asqueado de esos
> breves contactos con la sexualidad 'externa' y se refugiaba en una
> tremenda masturbación que le iba desesperando y deshaciéndole
> la vocación.[28]

The difference, however, between Cosme and Alfredo is that the guilt and disgust

which gradually destroy the mind of Alfredo are reduced and controlled by

Cosme who is able to accept that the failings of his human condition can receive

Divine forgiveness:

> Era barro y barro miserable y no era digno de estar allí, pero
> aceptaría el reto de bondad de la divina misericordia y entraría en
> el sacerdocio con alas más que con pies, como un 'hombre nuevo'
> que quiere acercarse al *alter Christus*. (p.85)

But while Cosme was aware of his sexual inclinations and could justify himself through his belief in God's mercy, Alfredo was weighed down by the inevitability of surrendering to the sexual urges and the consequent feeling of remorse. As Alfredo saw sexuality as opposed to his vocation so there is a sense of desperation that sex would have to remain an inaccessible world to him. It was quite early on in the seminary when the notions of despair and disgust about sexuality began to surface, and particularly at the moment of witnessing the naked farm-workers at the baths during the summer vacation:

> Nunca como entonces llegó a sentir tanta rabia como curiosidad por el sexo, y a la curiosidad se mezclaron luego el desprecio y la pena, porque también los hombres desnudos frente a sí hablaban del paraíso imposible. (p.52)

It soon becomes clear that Alfredo does not have the ability to cope with sexual pressure despite his sincere yearning to impose his religious ideals upon his natural instincts. The result of such sexual repression is a continuous cycle of guilt and the attempt at repentance which inevitably ends in failure:

> Y era un no dormir y la necesidad de la confesión con la terquedad de la caída, del arrepentimiento y del perdón, todo en cadena, una cadena peor que la de los condenados al infierno. (p.53)

This pattern of relentless falling and subsequent guilt can prove no benefit to anyone and the inability to understand this problem leads to more severe difficulties as Alfredo discovered. At the earlier stages of the problem, however, although Alfredo seems unaware of it, the narrator points out that celibacy is a demand too great for the likes of Alfredo:

> Entre los pasos del Vía Crucis, uno se sentía fuerte y Alfredo prometía lo que estaba por encima de sus fuerzas y hasta llegaba a enamorarse de la lucha desigual. (p.53)

Another consequence of this repression is that the object to be ignored quickly becomes the most significant, and Alfredo is caught in the realm of sexual obsession. In other words, the more he tries to control the urge, the more obsessed he becomes with its power and soon his whole life is overcome by this obsession:

> No sólo en sueños ni en el retrete, sino en la calle y hasta en la iglesia, había tenido que pactar, o disimular al menos, este imperio grosero, despótico, inhumano. (p.187)

The natural urges are transformed into such a dominating force that Alfredo is unable to concentrate on other matters:

> Era su gran obsesión, la gran ignorancia, el gran miedo, la grandísima dictadura. En la raíz misma de su naturaleza latía la patología del sexo, una angustia, una curiosidad, una enorme debilidad. (p.186)

Alfredo's obsession with sex soon turns to hatred for his sexual organ as he regards this as the source of all guilt and misery preventing him from achieving holiness and this absurd attitude is demonstrated when Alfredo sees himself in the mirror:

> Fuente del deleite que aproxima a la muerte, como un suicidio inicial, o al menos membrocidio, venganza y tiranía, culto exprimido y bastón de dominio, hipnosis y fertilidad inútiles. (p.187)

This harmful attitude towards sex is discussed by Castillo-Puche while commenting on the plight of Alfredo in the novel as representative of what was a serious problem in the seminary and one which very few superiors were able to detect. In conversations with the author in 1985, he stated that the most alarming aspect of Alfredo's case is that his condition was not treated until too late:

> Principalmente es un caso de obsesión sexual: que hay un individuo que ha pasado disimulado, tapado, oscuro y con el timo incluso a los superiores y a los padres espirituales de que está dispuesto y es apto para el sacerdocio.[29]

The author uses the novel as a vehicle for criticism of the traditional seminary education which turned a blind eye to sexuality. Since there was no opportunity for dialogue and discussion on the subject many seminarians could only endure or disguise any problems they had with sex:

> La obsesión sexual que no es percibida. No hay trato. No hay verdadera relación. No hay diálogo entre superior y discípulo, entre maestro de espíritu y almas.[30]

The dangers of sexual repression and keeping such problems to oneself are seen in the deterioration of the mental health of Alfredo when he believes that, during the ordination ceremony, the rector also is aware of Alfredo's sinfulness and disguise:

> Y lo más seguro era que había llegado a penetrar su pensamiento y sabía que él no tenía fronteras y que iba y venía creyendo no ser descubierto, pero lo había cogido seguramente por el olfato. (p.193)

Alfredo had become so paranoid about his problem that even a chance look by a member of staff was able to uncover the entire history of sinful masturbation which Alfredo felt so guilty and dirty about:

> El rector aspiraba y olía y estaba oliendo policiacamente todo aquello, todos los olores dejados en tantos sitios, todo su rastrerío de esperma. (p.193)

The truth, however, is exactly the opposite and it seems that Alfredo's problems are very distant from the concerns of his superiors.

It is the mental deterioration of Alfredo which becomes the central issue in the novel and which binds the narrative together. At the beginning of the novel we are told that there was a noticeable change in Alfredo's behaviour ever since the spiritual retreat which he made prior to the ordination ceremony. His ever-increasing reticence and alienation were to become the signs of an internal psychological conflict centred around his sexuality.

The madness of Alfredo can be seen especially in the way the external surroundings become altered and transformed in Alfredo's mind as the ordination ceremony proceeds. Both the people present at the ceremony and the fittings and structure of the cathedral fall victim to his hallucinations:

> Por si fuera poco, Alfredo está convencido de que la enorme lámpara que hay en el centro mismo del presbiterio guarda una especie de venganza contra él. De la alucinante araña de cristal de roca salen unos brazos que despiden fuego. y estos brazos tratan de apresarlo, como los de una araña gigante. (pp.152-153)

In the growing struggle between reality and illusion there are indications in the earlier stages of the ceremony of Alfredo trying desperately to hold on to his sanity:

> Alfredo, al darse a sí mismo conocimiento de lo que estaba pensando, fuera del tiempo, notó que su imaginación llevaba un derrotero extraviado, que ya no provenía de su voluntad, y por eso, dándose un coscorrón contra el suelo, mascullaba de modo imperativo:
>
> - ¡No, no y no! ¡He dicho que no! (p.120)

But as his mental condition worsens at the crucial moments of the ceremony, even the image of the bishop changes dramatically:

De repente Alfredo se sintió sacudido por una intensa
obnubilación y el rostro del obispo se hizo por momentos ancho,
redondo, enorme, amenazante incluso. (p.209)

The most graphic imagery of all, however, is normally associated with the
uncontrollable power of his sexual organ:

Alfredo se está descomponiendo. De momento comienza a sentir
el crecimiento de aquel culebrón de cabeza gorda y rosada, boca
de ofidio sin dientes que escupirá simiente si enloquece, que
esparcirá inútil y malsana semilla de hombre a los cuatro vientos
sin poder evitarlo. (p.108)

This gradual deterioration of the mental condition of Alfredo is a very
dramatic illustration of the effects of sexual repression and constitutes a powerful
attack on celibacy by the author. It is certain that this attack on the Church's
policy on celibacy not only coincides with the new age of reform initiated by the
Second Vatican Council but also with the crisis in vocations which, by the early
1970s, was widespread in the Church. This crisis, as John Hooper points out, was
caused in large part by a clerical revolution against celibacy:

During the sixties more priests are reckoned to have renounced
their vows in Spain than in any country except Brazil and
Holland. .....The main reason for this wave of secularizations was
the Church's policy on celibacy.[31]

Comments on the novel by Sobejano in 1975 suggest this linkage between the
protests of the clergy and the timing of *Como ovejas al matadero*:

La crudeza con que se ofrece aquí el problema de la castración
sacerdotal sirve a una actitud dimanada del actual reformismo,
como también subrayan esta tónica postconciliar las ideas que
Ramiro fomenta mientras sueña con la urgente apertura social de
la Iglesia.[32]

At the same time, Sobejano believes that Castillo-Puche is sufficiently qualified to expose the problem because of his own experiences and he is therefore able to transmit in detail the trauma and reality of man's enslavement to his body:

> No es el mensaje reformador lo que justifica la novela; es el sostenido temple patético de ésta (pese a cierta prolijidad en la evocación de la ceremonia), su impresionante aprehensión de la servidumbre al cuerpo, y su poderoso reflejo del delirio de una conciencia atormentada por la represión sexual, lo que imprime vigor transcendente a aquel mensaje.[33]

The reality of man's enslavement to nature is also considered by Pablo Corbalán as a fundamental obstacle to priestly celibacy in the novel. Corbalán makes the point that the concept of choice must be taken into account since most people in society do not choose careers conducive to a confrontation with their human condition. As celibacy is an essential requirement for the priesthood, then the priesthood creates this confrontation with nature. If celibacy can only be achieved by divine grace, then the confrontation is really between this desired spiritual state and the natural control of the physical condition, a confrontation which pertains only to that minority who aspire to the religious life. For the great majority of people who marry, this conflict, at least in the realm of sexuality, does not exist:

> Este enfrentamiento es el de la gracia religiosa, el de la llama mística de la consagración. Problema difícil de abarcar fuera de la situación en lo que estos hombres se encuentran, pero no por ello menos real, menos dramática e incluso trágica.[34]

But the point being made in the novel is that, for certain individuals like Alfredo, this aspiration is not practical and that sexuality is in no way diminished by divine grace. If celibacy is only possible through divine grace then clearly

Alfredo, like many others, was not in possession of this gift. In Alfredo's case, it appears that every attempt to subdue nature results in an ever greater response from the physical impulses as they impose their authority with a vengeance:

> Ni la vocación religiosa ni la gracia anulan al hombre - nos viene a decir Castillo-Puche -; es decir, es frente a la vocación y la gracia cuando la condición humana se exacerba con todo lo que ésta significa de impureza ante la voluntad de pureza, ante la corriente que aparece como purificadora, y tan difícil es de seguir.[35]

The novel, nevertheless, does not suggest that the vow of chastity is totally inhuman and should be scrapped. The celibate ideal still holds good for certain temperaments who are able to channel their sexual energy in other ways. Fulgencio is an example of one who is not frustrated by the sexual urge but whose main concern about chastity was the notion of loneliness and its dangers:

> Para Fulgencio existían contrastes de tentación en lo que se refiere a la castidad, no ya tanto como rebelión de la carne, sino como necesidad de librarse de los peligros de la soledad para el corazón, pero aun así, no había problema esencial, con un limpio deportivismo del espíritu iba dejando a un lado todas las torvas insinuaciones que más bien consideraba cosa enfermiza, propia de temperamentos débiles o pocos francos consigo mismos. (p.178)

From this inside view of Fulgencio comes the suggestion of a division between the weak and the strong and that sexual problems will probably affect certain types of individuals more than others. But the narrator does not imply that these weaker temperaments are without faith but rather, as Ramiro concludes after Alfredo's crisis, often faith by itself is not enough:

> Pero ¿qué tenía el pobre Alfredo? Nada más que la fe, nada más que un sueño loco de llegar, un ansia enferma de coronar la empresa a despecho, no a despecho sino en contra de la propia naturaleza. Y es que se cometen muchos disparates en nombre de

la santidad. (p.291)

The novel still presents chastity as a worthy virtue but chastity itself is not considered solely a divine gift since effort has to be made on the part of the individual. Just as Cosme recognises the need for God's grace if he is to be truly repentant, so Fulgencio expresses the narrator's view that it is also by grace that the vow of chastity will be preserved:

> En todo caso, conservar estas virtudes era un don de Dios que había que ponerse en condiciones de merecerlo. (p.178)

The question that is asked at the end of the novel is whether there is something psychologically wrong with Alfredo anyway or whether the breakdown is entirely due to the seminary experience and his struggle against nature:

> ¿Le habría pasado aquello no obligado al duelo de su castidad, en otra situación distinta que no fuera la de la ordenación sacerdotal? (p.289)

Ramiro lays the blame for Alfredo's mental condition purely on the basis of the seminary education which has been responsible for blocking rather than channelling nature, and therefore if Alfredo had chosen some other career he may have been sexually healthy. So the question still remains as to why Alfredo chose to endure such torture rather than seek an alternative lifestyle. This question is also asked by the critic José Domingo in his article on the novel shortly after its publication:

> La reacción humana ante el fracaso es preguntarse si le habría pasado lo mismo de no haber intentado seguir, un mucho por inercia, por miedo a luchar contra los convencionalismos, esa corriente a la que se había dejado arrastrar falto de valor para salirse de ella.[36]

The answer could be that Alfredo was afflicted with the same sense of uncertainty that is found in the other seminarian characters of Enrique in *Sin camino* and Pepico in *Conocerás el poso de la nada*, both of whom are guilty of the attitude of 'dejarse llevar' instead of coming to terms with the situation. There is a close identification of the three characters, especially in the yearning for liberation and experiencing life in the world. Even Alfredo himself is seen questioning the wisdom of entering the seminary in the first place (p.47) suggesting that he is also aware that another career may have prevented a lot of suffering and repression. Yet, despite this awareness, Alfredo continues to endure his own self-deterioration.

The symbolism of water representing liberation in the three novels of the *Trilogía de la liberación* is also found in this novel as Alfredo contemplates a possible escape from his predicament:

> Acaso era el momento de huir y escaparse. Sí, salir corriendo hasta la esquina de los bomberos y luego hasta el puente y acaso tirarse al río gritando: 'Agua, agua'. El río de la ciudad había sido su escape y su sueño de fuga desde las ventanas cuando se pasó una temporada en la enfermería. (p.47)

There are also instances when, like Enrique, Alfredo is drawn towards the outside world, and associated with this are also the notions of vitality and freedom as Alfredo observes life in the street:

> Una celda que daba a un patio cerrado por donde pasaban los muchachos y las muchachas que estudiaban para vivir en la calle, en el mundo, en el cochino mundo, acaso hermoso mundo si las cosas no fueran como tenían que ser, implacablemente ... (p.48)

Another comparison can be made with the influence of the mother as a determining factor in Alfredo's inability to leave the seminary. Just as with

Enrique and, to a greater degree, Pepico, the emotional pressure from the mother is instrumental in the pursuit of ordination. In Alfredo's case we can observe the powerful effects of his mother's dying wish:

> Ella sí que tenía vocación o por lo menos de ella era el mérito de la propia, ... 'Santo, sólo te quiero santo, santo o nada, santo, santo', habían sido sus últimas palabras cuando el carro tuvo que subir la cuesta. (p.56)

Although the mother is scarcely mentioned in the novel compared to the powerful role she exercises in the *Trilogía de la liberación*, the emotional pressure is just as evident and her influence on Alfredo must be taken into account in the final assessment of his problems. The vocation must inevitably be of personal choice, but his mother was really leaving Alfredo with little freedom:

> Pero tú serás sacerdote, tú mejor que nadie tienes que absolverme, tú que estás bendecido por Dios desde que naciste, tú ... (p.54)

It is interesting to note just how much the character's mother is intrinsically related to the religious vocation in the novels mentioned. It appears that the characters of Alfredo, Enrique and Pepico are not only influenced by the mother but find their lives answerable only to her as if she were the greatest beneficiary of her son's career. As the different characters seem intent on a lifestyle which primarily pleases the mother, so the mother becomes the motor and source of continuity.

This desire in the different characters to please the mother seems to be a reflection of the author's own experiences which will be examined in the next chapter. In a similar way, the torture of sexual repression suffered by Alfredo appears to be related to the author's personal struggle with the ideal of chastity. Evidence of this association between Castillo-Puche and the character Alfredo can be seen at the critical moment of sexual obsession which comes across in the novel in disturbing and apparently blasphemous detail. In his cell in the mental asylum after the crisis at the ordination ceremony Alfredo is shown obsessed with his sexual organ and the unusual scene is witnessed by both Ramiro and Fulgencio:

> El falo entronizado, no en símbolo sino en carne, por unas manos recién consagradas provocaba más que malestar físico repugnancia espiritual. (p.289)

But it is the blasphemous use of the words of the Consecration of the Mass which proves the greatest shock of all for his newly-ordained companions:

> Concretamente los dos estaban pensando en lo mismo: en la fusión desdichada del culto enloquecido al miembro viril con las palabras sacrosantas de la consagración: 'Hoc est enim corpus meum'. Solamente la locura en su versión más blasfema e impura. (p.287)

Castillo-Puche had stated in private conversation that the phrase was introduced as a symbolic way of portraying the exclusion of Alfredo from the heavenly banquet. In other words, Alfredo cannot attain sanctity because of his sexuality and therefore the forces of his own human body prevent him, so he is convinced, from becoming a member of the Body of Christ:

> Y entonces es el gran monólogo, el gran coloquio consigo mismo y con su miembro con las palabras de la Consagración, en lo cual no hay una blasfemia, sino que hay un verdadero conocimiento de donde empieza mi cuerpo, y de donde empieza el cuerpo de Cristo, porque yo no pertenezco al convivio de la Sangre de Cristo porque no he podido entrar.[37]

The use here of the first person by the author could be understood as a way of identifying Alfredo with the author's own experience of the problems of sexuality in relation to priestly celibacy. However, this understanding of the author and his character Alfredo should be viewed from a psychological standpoint, since theologically the argument is far from sound. There is nothing in the Scriptures or in the Church's teaching to suggest that one's sexuality can exclude one from the community of the faithful, so the view expressed by the author must relate to a psychological sense of guilt and failure, feelings which were not eased by the attitude of his superiors.

After the mental shock of witnessing the condition of their companion, there are attempts both by Ramiro and Fulgencio to offer explanations for this disastrous outcome and it seems to be Ramiro who wants to provide the positive dimension to the plight of Alfredo. Ramiro believes that it was the attempt to suppress the natural urges and the consequent suffering caused by this which gives Alfredo an air of nobility. In other words, it was precisely the hidden anxiety and the persistence in the struggle which demonstrated the saintliness of Alfredo:

> Y ahora, querido Fulgencio, es cuando nos podemos dar cuenta de lo que ha sido seguramente el martirio, el sufrimiento, la lucha estéril de Alfredo. Nadie cae de ese modo sin dejarse una parte importante de la carne, de los sentidos, de la razón también, en la prueba. Seguramente (no te escandalices) Alfredo es un santo, quiso ser un santo, al menos (¿me entiendes?) ... (p.291)

Ramiro reiterates this view in a previous statement which attacks a religious system which excludes human nature from the realm of holiness and thus prevented Alfredo having a healthy understanding of his humanity:

> Hay métodos que no es ya que violenten (de la violencia puede salir fuerza y luz), sino que pervierten en cierto modo (que Dios me perdone, pero creo que es así) la naturaleza, por lo menos en ciertos seres. La santidad no tiene que ser anti-natural, tiene que haber una santidad hecha con la naturaleza sublimada. (p.291)

And Alfredo's inability to control his sexuality does not imply insignificance in the sight of God. Being sexual like every other person does not diminish the right to faith and holiness. Therefore nature cannot be dismissed or suppressed in this way as something contrary to faith as Ramiro makes clear:

> Y es que la naturaleza no se puede detener como quien pone un paredón al río, hay que encauzarla, pero no de este modo frustrador. (p.291)

Ramiro here appears as a spokesman for the narrator as he expresses a clear protest against the treatment of human beings in such a misguided manner. The opinion of Ramiro is also a reflection of the author's viewpoint which was emphasised during private conversation while commenting on the impact of Alfredo's breakdown:

> Y entonces es una explosión reveladora de que la naturaleza no se puede violentar hasta límites insospechables. Entre la naturaleza y el espíritu, tiene que haber una concordia y entonces la vocación puede ser fructífera, pero no en una especie de revancha y de agresividad mutua.[38]

The madness of Alfredo, then, becomes a symbol of sexual repression and its destructive effects upon an individual. While Ramiro and Fulgencio become concerned about the possibilities of diabolical intervention in Alfredo's illness, they soon realise that the real culprits are nature itself and the mistaken attempts to repress it. Castillo-Puche indicates that the madness of Alfredo has nothing to do with anything spiritual:

> Pero no es la gracia, ni es el demonio, sino es la perturbación total de un ser. Y en eso hay una alegoría, hay paralelismos porque muchos (sacerdotes) ... no son sacerdotes ni son hombres ... no son sensatos ni razonables, no tienen la mansedumbre de Cristo ni tienen nada.[39]

From this the author seems to suggest that many ordained priests in his own experience should not have been ordained since these inner conflicts remained unresolved. He also confirmed in conversation that some individuals who became priests ended up broken people as a result of problems undetected and untreated:

> Es más corriente que lo que parece y algunos terminan anulados, aniquilados, y terminan con una doble personalidad totalmente hipócrita o simplemente sufriendo una congoja interior inexplicable.[40]

Whether or not the author is saying that these misfortunes are entirely due to sexual repression is not clear, but it seems that the message for the reader is that priests should not be regarded as robots who perform their ministerial duties but that they are just as human and just as much part of nature as any other person. It is the priests' humanity which concerns Castillo-Puche:

> El sacerdote no se puede ver de una manera fácil: va, viene, predica y reparte. Hay un conflicto interior y ese conflicto es de hombre.[41]

In the same way, the picture of a newly-ordained priest obsessed with his sexual organ in the mental institution has not been created in order to shock the reader with some kind of blasphemy or profanity, but rather it represents the most powerful and dramatic means of transmitting a problem which, though common, is so often hidden and disguised:

> Esto a alguno le pareció una profanación o un sacrilegio. Cuando la gente examina esto despacio, empieza a meditar, porque las cosas no están hechas para escandalizar ni para perturbar a nadie, sino para una auto-reflexión más seria, más profunda.[42]

Before we allow ourselves to be convinced that the priesthood only represents misery and repression we should remember that neither the sacrifice nor the virtues are wiped out. Castillo-Puche remains convinced of the existence

of the valid religious vocation expressed in the characters of Ramiro and
Fulgencio who both pursued their ideals with honesty and determination. Nor
must it be thought that chastity or celibacy are impossible virtues since Fulgencio
and Ramiro did possess the ability to cope with their sexuality and this is
demonstrated by Ramiro as he ponders the fate of Alfredo:

> Nos podía haber pasado a cualquiera, a ti y a mí, si no tuviéramos
> otras cosas, otra disposición, yo qué sé ... (p.291)

And the author makes clear that the novel is not an attack on celibacy:

> Yo no ataco el celibato. Yo creo que el celibato es un don especial
> y una gracia especial que es carismática.[43]

He goes on to say that, despite being something given to individuals from above,
to remain celibate will necessarily involve a certain amount of struggle and
restraint:

> El que se considera con virtud para eso debe luchar y, aunque no
> consiga ser casto toda su vida, en la lucha está su mérito, está su
> martirio y su esfuerzo.[44]

There is an indication here of Ramiro's reference to the struggle of Alfredo as
something heroic and saintly despite the tragic outcome of this struggle. Yet no
matter how highly regarded the virtues and vows of the priesthood may appear
they are inevitably diminished in the novel by the tragedy and failures of that
same ideal.

The predominant atmosphere of the novel is one of failure, and if there are
triumphs they only come after many defeats. This is illustrated at the glorious
singing of the *Te Deum* while Alfredo was suffering a crisis in the sacristy:

> Se canta la gloria del día soñado, gloria que pesa como un

madero, porque en el sacerdocio no hay salmo ni puede haberlo de ascensión y triunfo sin antes haber apurado hasta las heces los cálices más amargos: derrotas personales, incomprensión de los superiores, máquinas de estampillar la mayoría de las veces, soledad frente a unos padres espirituales aburridos y cansados ya de recomendar lo imposible para quedarse en la consolación de las medianías. (p.245)

The title suggests that this novel would not present the priesthood in a good light and Alfredo's breakdown seems the inevitable outcome of a character growing more and more disturbed as the novel unfolds. In the end, we are left with a person destroyed by his own ideals and stubbornness. The author points out that this negative dimension is essential to the purpose of the novel:

Es un estudio del sacerdote, víctima: víctima de su propia ignorancia, de su propio egoísmo, víctima de su propia fe, de su ilusión también.[45]

His aim is to abolish the mistaken notion of the priesthood as something noble and glorious and to show, instead, the inseparable elements of weakness and failure, as the author admitted to Fernández-Braso:

Mi novela no presenta el sacerdocio como triunfo, sino como impotencia; no como victoria, sino como fracaso. Y este concepto, esta idea, esta experiencia es parte del mismo sacerdocio.[46]

It seems that there exists some identification so far between the author and the characters of Enrique in *Sin camino* and Alfredo in this novel. Both are presented as individuals tormented by guilt and failure and, in both cases, the abandoning of the vocation by Enrique and the mental crisis of Alfredo are justified by the respective narrators. In the first case, Enrique is justified by following the path of God in the world and, in the latter, Alfredo is considered saintly for persisting in the struggle. But if there is identification between these characters and the author, then it suggests that the author continued to be troubled with his own failure to become a priest. Such a powerful attack on sexual repression implies too that the author may harbour resentment towards the religious establishment and, like *Sin camino*, *Como ovejas al matadero* is yet another vehicle for expressing resentment for his own failure or for liberation of any guilt or bitterness. Yet, as we have discovered, the virtues of the priesthood are still evident and the ideal is still a worthy one. So it may be concluded that Ramiro and Fulgencio represent what could have been, and Alfredo becomes a symbolic figure of failure and the limits of the human condition.

NOTES

1. *Como ovejas al matadero* (Barcelona: Destino, 1971). All subsequent bracketed references are to this edition.

2. Pablo Corbalán, "Castillo-Puche, entre la liberación y la fe." *Informaciones* 1 de julio de 1971.

3. "Castillo-Puche, entre la liberación y la fe."

4. See John Hooper, *The New Spaniards* (London: Penguin, 1995), 126-145: "Religion and the Church".

5. Hooper, 136.

6. Hooper, 137.

7. See "Decree on the Ministry and Life of Priests." (Presbyterorum Ordinis) in Walter M. Abbott ed., *The Documents of Vatican II* (London: Geoffrey Chapman, 1966), 532-576.

8. *The Documents of Vatican II*, 549-550.

9. See Gerald Brenan, *The Spanish Labyrinth.* 2nd. ed. (Cambridge: CUP, 1962), 37-56: "The Liberals and the Church".

10. Stanley Payne, *The Spanish Revolution* (London: Weidenfeld & Nicolson, 1970), 25.

11. Brenan, 52.

12. See *Ramón J. Sender: el distanciamiento del exilio* (Barcelona: Destinolibro, 1985), 75-83.

13. *Ramón J. Sender: el distanciamiento del exilio*, 79.

14. *Ramón J. Sender: el distanciamiento del exilio*, 83.

15. The Council formally opened on 11 October 1962, and was concluded on 8 December 1965.

16. José Chao Rego, *La iglesia en el franquismo* (Madrid: Ediciones Felmar, 1976), 75.

17. Private conversations (1985).

18. Hooper, 136.

19. Private conversations (1985).

20. Conversations (1985).

21. Conversations (1985).

22. Conversations (1985).

23. Miguel Fernández-Braso, "Castillo-Puche a cuerpo limpio." *Pueblo*, 7 de julio de 1971.

24. Fernández-Braso.

25. Fernández-Braso.

26. Fernández-Braso.

27. Fernández-Braso.

28. Rafael Vázquez Zamora, "José Luis Castillo-Puche: El cíngulo. Como ovejas al matadero." *Destino* 28 de agosto de 1971, 45

29. Conversations (1985).

30. Conversations (1985).

31. Hooper, 135.

32. Sobejano, 267-268.

33. Sobejano, 268.

34. "Castillo-Puche entre la liberación y la fe."

35. "Castillo-Puche entre la liberación y la fe."

36. José Domingo, "Del seminario a la isla. Castillo-Puche. García Ramos." *Insula*, 302 (1982), 6.

37. Conversations (1985).

38. Conversations (1985).

39. Conversations (1985).

40. Conversations (1985).

41. Conversations (1985).

42. Conversations (1985).

43. Conversations (1985).

44. Conversations (1985).

45. Conversations (1985).

46. Fernández-Braso.

CHAPTER 4
Trilogía de la liberación: Introduction

In the two novels already studied, both narrators were closely involved with the characters of the story. Despite the use of third person narrative, the narrators were able to reveal to the reader just what was going on in the minds of Enrique in *Sin camino* and all four characters of *Como ovejas al matadero*, especially Alfredo. Now, in a completely different narrative style and a change to first person narrative, the three novels of the *Trilogía de la liberación* present a narrator directly involved in the action as he recalls his childhood in *El libro de las visiones y las apariciones*, his adolescent years in *El amargo sabor de la retama*, and early manhood in *Conocerás el poso de la nada*. The trilogy introduces a radical change from a classic story-telling narrative style to a much more evocative, unstructured, 'stream-of-consciousness' kind of writing, which we shall look at later in this chapter.

The narrator speaks directly to the reader from the green valleys of the Basque country where he relives the memories of his early life in the village of Hécula. The age of the narrator is not revealed and all the reader knows is that some time has passed between the narrator writing down his memoirs in the present and the twelve or thirteen year period in which the events of the novels take place. So we must assume that the narrator is a mature adult and that a transition has taken place in his life enabling him to recall these events in Hécula at a safe distance away from them in some green haven in the north. In the trilogy, the choice of first person narration means that there can only be identification between the narrator and the protagonist since the narrator is the only character who can be seen from the inside. Sometimes the views in the novels are expressed directly by the adult narrator and sometimes the world is seen through the eyes of the young child, Pepico, as the narrator was called. But the most important factor here in the use of first person narrative is that the narrator establishes a personal relationship with the reader as the reader cannot help but accompany the narrator on his journey through the past.

As the narrator takes us through the often painful experiences of his early life it is quite easy for the reader to get involved with the emotions and reactions of the same narrator displayed during the most sensitive and intense episodes of his youth. Just as the narrators in *Sin camino* and *Como ovejas al matadero* involve the reader in the condemnation of the seminary education which helped to produce such crises in the lives of Enrique and Alfredo, so the narrator of the trilogy involves us on his side in exposing and condemning the elements of oppression responsible for so much ruin and affliction, not only in the life of Pepico but in the lives of many victims of Spanish society at that time. This inclusion of the wider Spanish public is illustrated in the author's dedication at the beginning of *El libro de las visiones y las apariciones*:

> Dedico esta novela a Hécula, mi pueblo, pero en ella a todos los pueblos que han sufrido - o gozado, quién sabe - bajo el terror del fanatismo religioso, el oscurantismo y el miedo al infierno.[1]

Hécula, the village where the story begins and which remains as a symbol of oppression throughout the trilogy, is clearly based on the historical village of Yecla where the author spent his own childhood. The reader should be aware from the start, then, that the aim of the first part of the trilogy at least is to uncover the terrors and nightmares imposed upon a young child by a misguided religious environment. In the novel this particular environment is found in Hécula, but Hécula, though based on reality, is symbolic of any Spanish village which generates this kind of fanaticism, and indeed, it need not apply to Spain but could be a universal symbol, as the author himself pointed out in a lecture given in 1988:

> La realidad de Hécula en mis obras es una realidad parabólica, paradigmática, casi emblemática; es decir, se trata de una realidad como pretexto de determinadas indagaciones, es una realidad lo suficientemente profunda y simbólica para que pueda servir igualmente para otras realidades, otros pueblos, otras tierras, otras vidas, y casi diría que vale para cualquier tierra y cualquier pueblo donde se produzcan con la misma intensidad la opresión, el fanatismo religioso y el oscurantismo cultural.[2]

The author makes his original intentions clear to the reader, and the reader will be shown the experience of living in such an environment through the eyes and thoughts of a young boy. But a literary experience can never be the same as the experience in reality since what took place in the author's own experience has not been directly transferred to the pages of the novels of the trilogy. While it is clear that certain elements and characters may originate from the author's life, it is also likely that many of these elements have been transformed and altered in the creation of the novels. We shall now examine those characters and elements in the novels which are taken from reality to see how much of a transformation, if any, these have undergone as their image unfolds in the novels.

A. LIFE AND LITERATURE

Even the fact that the narrator of the trilogy finds himself in the Basque country writing his memoirs could be related to the author's own experience. It is well established, for instance, that Castillo-Puche was acquainted with the famous Basque writer, Pío Baroja, who was a great source of encouragement and inspiration for the author. It is also worth noting the friendship between Castillo-Puche and Ernest Hemingway who had enormous admiration for Baroja and the Basque people in general, as was demonstrated in the visits by both authors to Pamplona.[3] So the author's own involvement with the Basque culture could suggest that the Basque location in the novels is not merely coincidental. It should be said, however, that there is no resemblance between the author and the narrator with regard to living and working in the area. The narrator is presented as someone who has settled in the Basque country and who is employed at a local factory whereas there is no indication in Castillo-Puche's life that he had undergone a similar experience.

What is more important here is the influence of Baroja upon the author since Baroja, unlike Ortega, was particularly keen on the inclusion of life and reality in the novel.[4] While Ortega is said to support the use of creative imagination in the novel, Baroja upheld the concept of the novel as essentially linked to experience and observation. In the prologue to Baroja's novel *La nave de los locos* he affirms the author's own privileged use of invention and imagination in the novel, but these must have their foundation in reality:

> El escritor puede imaginar, naturalmente, tipos e intrigas que no
> ha visto; pero necesita siempre el trampolín de la realidad para dar
> saltos maravillosos en el aire.[5]

The notion of the springboard of reality is clearly reflected in the writing of Castillo-Puche and Baroja's views were recently echoed by the author in a lecture given in several American universities in 1985:

> Yo no soy un autor realista, o un novelista de realidades externas,
> digamos un narrador de historias más o menos verdaderas o más
> o menos verosímiles. La realidad, aunque sea realidad tremendista
> de mi pueblo, no es para mí más que un trampolín en que
> apoyarme para una indagación de tipo interior, transcendente y
> profunda.[6]

Another influence of Baroja on Castillo-Puche is seen in the construction of the novel. Baroja believed in open-ended, free-flowing narratives in order to reflect properly the patternless cycle of events which characterise our experience of reality. In other words, Baroja, and other writers of his generation, were opposed to well-organised plots in the novel since an account of the world in this way did not conform to reality. The writing of Castillo-Puche also appears to follow this trend of mere successiveness in an attempt to reflect the indeterminate nature of life in the world, and this technique is employed to the greatest degree in the trilogy. Related also to this type of construction could also be the existential philosophy of Baroja, shared by others of his generation and also by Castillo-Puche, which concentrates on the aimlessness of existence. In his study of the generation of 1898, Donald Shaw affirms that the type of narrative construction will also reflect certain characteristics of the author:

> Since every serious literary novel is in some degree 'a novel-shaped account of the world', it follows that the reaction against tidy plots and clear definition of character, visible in all the novelists of the generation of 1898 (but most clearly enunciated theoretically by Baroja), is fully in line with their general vision of life as mere contingency without purpose or pattern.[7]

The difference between reality and the novel is that the novel can never be neutral, and anything that is taken from real life, whether it is people, places, or events, are all transformed by the author according to his view of the world. In his book *Language of Fiction* David Lodge rejects the view that a novel can successfully reflect the 'open-endedness' of reality since the author will exercise his ability to select and emphasise certain features which a neutral reality can never do. While admitting that reality and experience do form an integral part of the novel, Lodge maintains that these will be included according to the motives of the author and the effects which the author wants the novel to give. Yet the use of circumstantial details in the novel can also be seen as an attempt to incorporate the novel into reality:

> The circumstantial particularity of the novel is thus a kind of
> anti-convention. It attempts to disguise the fact that a novel is
> discontinuous with real life. It suggests that the life of a novel is
> a bit of real life which we happen not to have heard about before,
> but which somewhere is or was going on.[8]

But the point being made is that what the novel creates is only a fictional likeness of reality no matter how much the characters and places resemble the real world. At the end of every movie in the cinema we are told that all characters and events are fictitious, unless the film is deliberately biographical, and that no resemblance to real life is intended. Although Castillo-Puche would claim that this is the case in all his novels, as he stated at the beginning of *Jeremías el anarquista*[9], it is still true that certain characters in the trilogy, like the mother, and certain places, like Hécula, are directly related to life. As the trilogy does contain many references to the real world, it is important to analyse how certain characters, places, and events in the novels are based on reality and how the author continues or transforms their images according to the aim of the work.

In the trilogy certain characters and features of life are presented favourably while others come across as negative. The negative elements include, besides Hécula, the Civil War, uncle Cirilo, and uncle Cayetano to a lesser degree, and the effects of these upon Pepico are a dominant feature of the trilogy. Following the trend of his predecessors Baroja, in his novel *Camino de perfección*, and Azorín, in *Las confesiones de un pequeño filósofo* and *La voluntad*, Castillo-Puche converts his native village of Yecla in Murcia into a symbol of morbidity and oppression. It is not the first occasion, of course, that the author uses his native village as similar references can be found in *Con la muerte al hombro*, *El vengador*, *El perro loco* and *Jeremías el anarquista*, just as the Basques are also seen in earlier works like *América de cabo a rabo* and *Oro blanco*. The author, in private conversations, made his reasons quite clear for choosing Yecla as the symbol of all that is backward and oppressive in Spanish rural life:

> Se ha convertido en esquema representativo de la España oscura,
> de la España difícil, de la España negra, terrorífica, y es el pueblo
> que yo he tenido como espejo, como fondo, como escenario.[10]

Although these problems were widespread at the time, the author can only speak

from his own experience and thus will principally refer to his own background:

> Porque he nacido allí. No lo he elegido caprichosamente. No es un
> pueblo aislado, pero es un pueblo juntado y da carácter, y es la
> caracterización de muchos pueblos que son iguales en ignorancia,
> en furores, en los ímpetus locos sociales de anarquía y de
> revolución.[11]

There is little doubt, then, that Hécula is based on Yecla, and that,

furthermore, the inhabitants, streets and events mentioned in the trilogy perhaps

relate to actual people and places in the village. One such place is the 'ermita',

the chapel named after Saint Cajetan, which stood in the centre of the village, and

which became for Pepico in *El libro de las visiones y las apariciones* a building

of mystery where the lighting and images often became a source of illusion and

fear. In present-day Yecla, the chapel no longer exists and in its place stands a

market-place in the square that is still named after the saint, as Miguel Ortuño

explains in his book *Las calles de Yecla*:

> El nombre se debe a la ermita de San Cayetano. Fue edificada por
> el vecindario a raíz de la más horrorosa tormenta conocida,
> ocurrida el 7 de agosto de 1805. Sería destruída y arrasada en
> 1936. Sobre esta bella ermita ha escrito mucho el genial novelista
> José Luis Castillo-Puche, vecino de la misma por su nacimiento
> y niñez.[12]

In the novels also the destruction of the chapel is included to coincide with the

outbreak of hostilities and the narrator tells of the devastating effects this event

has upon Cayetano, who was responsible for establishing devotion to the saint.

Saint Cajetan is referred to in the trilogy as the patron saint of Providence and this also conforms to his image in reality as Miguel Ortuño explains:

> El italiano San Cayetano de Tiene (1480-1547) funda la Orden de los Teatinos. Muere en Nápoles. Canonizado por Clemente X en 1673. Es el santo de la providencia, su imagen suele estar en las despensas de las casas. Su fiesta se conmemoraba tradicionalmente el 7 de agosto, y en la actualidad el 8 del mismo mes.[13]

The author explained in private conversation that the character Cayetano in the trilogy corresponds to an uncle of his in reality:

> Cayetano no se llamaba Cayetano. Era un sacerdote que había vivido mucho tiempo en Madrid, siendo capellán de una de las familias de más alta alcurnia de España.[14]

And it was this same uncle, known as Pascual, who raised the necessary funds for the building of the chapel dedicated to Saint Cajetan:

> El levantó esa iglesia y consiguió que personajes de mi familia que eran muy ricos y pudientes entregaran parte de sus bienes para esa iglesia y él entonces se refugió allí cuando terminó su vida en Jumilla. Le llamaban todos un nombre cariñoso, don Pascualico, y era muy conocido.

Both his uncle and devotion to the saint became very popular throughout Yecla and consequently the destruction of the chapel during the Civil War was a great blow not only to his uncle but to the entire village. The author describes how his uncle painfully witnessed the removal of the chapel's foundations:

> Murió viendo desde la casa del otro hermano cómo levantaron los cimientos de la iglesia que él había levantado para hacer un mercado. Que toda la ilusión lo puso en levantar esa iglesia. Todo el mundo se enamoró del culto que él puso allí a San Cayetano, de

novenas, llevaba grandes predicadores, había grandes fiestas.

In the second part of the trilogy, *El amargo sabor de la retama*, Pepico describes how his uncle Cayetano had a solid relationship with the ordinary people and how highly regarded he was. This is seen as particularly crucial at the outbreak of war when many religious lived in fear for their safety. The town of Jumilla is known as Pinilla in the trilogy and it was from there that the socialists came to Cayetano to reassure him of their protection:

> Que todos recordaban que en los años que mi tío había estado allí de cura se había portado como un cura del pueblo y para el pueblo, y hablaba con la gente humilde y alguna vez hasta había hecho gratis bodas o bautizos, y ahora quien quisiera hacerle daño tendría que enfrentarse con ellos.[15]

The high respect demonstrated here by the socialists in the trilogy for Cayetano also corresponds to actual events:

> Cuando empezó la guerra los socialistas de Jumilla fueron a Murcia a buscar a mi tío que estaba escondido y entonces le llevaron con ellos para que estuviera como sacerdote metido en un convento que había en Jumilla para que él los pudiera casar o lo que quisieran.

The author's uncle was equally popular with the inhabitants of Jumilla as he was with the people of Yecla and, during the war, the socialists wanted to repay some of his kindness:

> Que no le faltaba nada, porque había bautizado y confirmado medio pueblo de Jumilla y de Yecla y entonces le querían mucho.

The author reveals that this good relationship between his uncle and those of the political left was very rare indeed at a time when a lot of socialists were excluded or expelled from the body of the Church:

Antes de la guerra había criterios de anatema para todo el que estuviera, por ejemplo, apuntado al socialismo o que estuviera en un ala que, por ser obrero, no estaba en la Iglesia. Estos criterios no imperaban ante mi tío porque él creía en algo más que eso: él creía en el hombre, que vive, que va a morir mañana, que se confiesa, que pasa muchos apuros, que tiene virtudes que nunca asoman. Entonces era un hombre apostólico, no de la propaganda externa del apostolado sino interior.

Even after the war was over, the author explains that his uncle was offered a high position in the Curia by the bishops of Astorga and Madrid but his uncle's dedication to the poor prevailed over any attraction to esteem and position:

No acepta ningún cargo, entonces estos cargos tenían una renta grande. No acepta y se queda totalmente para atender a la familia y para ser una especie de padre de todos los parientes pobres.

The most important feature of his uncle's priesthood was his ability to counsel and offer reconciliation to individuals, particularly the young:

Era un gran confesor ... su confesonario era el más famoso que había en Murcia, sobre todo, para la gente joven; era muy fácil tener una cola de treinta o cuarenta cuando él estaba en la catedral o en San Bartolomeo y nadie preguntaba qué pasaba allí, todo el mundo sabía que era él, era un don grande.

Very little of this, however, is mentioned in the novels despite the author's evident admiration for this man. It is true that certain positive features are attributed to Cayetano but nothing compared to the saintly qualities which the real uncle appeared to have. The omission of these qualities is perhaps a sign of the author's desire to make the novels as objective and neutral as possible and to avoid any hint of partiality:

Yo, en la novela, no he querido hacer una obra carismática, ni apologética, ni de conversión porque entonces me hubiera fijado mucho en ésta.

On the contrary, there is a parallel here with *Como ovejas al matadero* where the faults and failures are even more in evidence than the virtues and heroism of the priesthood. In a similar way in the trilogy the author concentrates more on the negative aspects not so much of Cayetano, but of Cirilo:

> Yo he querido destacar las virtudes negativas, impositivas y anuladoras del tío Cirilo que ni siquiera deja ser a su hermano Cayetano todo lo santo que tenía que ser, porque en un momento determinado, cree que algunas cosas son condescendencia con el mundo.

While Cayetano in the novel remains a man of humility and charity, Cirilo comes across as a total fanatic imposing strict rules and observance on Cayetano, Pepico and the rest of the family. When asked if Cirilo, like Cayetano, was based upon a real-life character, Castillo-Puche denied that Cirilo strictly resembles any one relative while admitting, at the same time, that certain features of Cirilo do originate from the author's own experience:

> Los novelistas, cuando hacen una cosa, juntan en un personaje co-arquetipo, un personaje que parece un emblema, un prototipo de las cosas, juntan varios personajes. No hay personajes tan netos como el tío Cirilo, pero sí había algún pariente al que se podía aproximar; en un plan de antítesis y de compensación yo pongo este personaje que además tiene muchos rasgos de realidad, de un personaje vivido.

While the author claims that the role of Cirilo is more symbolic in the novel, the existence of the mother's two missionary nephews is directly related to reality:

> Ha habido casos en mi familia: sobrinos de mi madre han sido jesuitas, un jesuita misionero en la India, otro misionero que

> estuvo en Bélgica y que ha estado por Europa, y que ha hecho muchas cosas sociales ... De los hijos de un hermano de mi madre, todos fueron religiosos. Entonces había como una emulación de que eso era un don de Dios a la familia.

Here lies the source of the author's own experience in the seminary since his mother was greatly influenced by the ideals of her religious brothers and wanted her own family to follow the example of their uncle and cousins. Consequently, it is likely that the central theme of the religious vocation in the trilogy and the connection with the mother and the uncles originates from the author's own experience. It is clear that the mother was influential on the vocation by wanting her own sons to emulate the family of her brother, and it appears she did, in fact, exert some pressure on her son to become a priest:

> La vocación religiosa parte de que la madre tiene un hermano sacerdote, y que tiene otro hermano que tiene todos estos hijos religiosos.

This demonstrates that influence and pressure have as much a part to play in the religious vocation as do personal ambition and heroic ideals.

In the trilogy, the author is not interested in presenting his relatives in a favourable light, but instead, all personal affection has been placed aside in order to present both positive and negative aspects of these religious relatives before young Pepico:

> Yo he tenido que poner ante el péndulo de la atención de un muchacho que va hacia el sacerdocio, como en un espejo ideal hay que poner lo que es atractivo y lo que es repulsivo. He tragado el sentimiento y el afecto y las ideas propias de los personajes, porque para mí valían más los esquemas, es decir, ¿por qué Cirilo con una fe casi patológica imponía a Cayetano criterios que no eran estrictamente apostólicos o sacerdotales?

In the novels the relatives have been altered in accordance with the aims of the author who wants the married uncle to act as if he were the priest and the one ordained to be reduced to a weaker and more humble level. The dictates and reproofs of Cirilo have more weight than the simplicity and charity of Cayetano:

> He hecho una especie de combinación en el cual el furor sacerdotal está de parte del que no es sacerdote, pero tiene autoridad grande, porque él tiene dos hijos misioneros. Es como si él participara del sacerdocio con el rigor más estricto y el otro fuera un hombre abandonado al mundo y a sus cosas.

One of the ways in which Cirilo demonstrates his authority is seen especially in the first part of the trilogy when young Pepico is forced into a series of religious devotions which he can neither endure nor understand. Among these devotions were the 'Via Crucis' which was carried out in the 'ermita' and more especially the vigil for the dying, known locally as 'los auroros'. The tradition of 'los auroros' plays a very important part in the religious traditions of Yecla, as Miguel Ortuño explains:

> Constituyen los auroros una secular tradición local, con sus cantos y plegarias en honor de la Virgen. La imagen de la Virgen de la Aurora, titular de la Cofradía del Santo Rosario, se trajo a Yecla el 28 de enero de 1752. Desde entonces van de casa en casa, semanalmente; dejan el cuadro de la Virgen y todas las noches le dedican oraciones y cantos.[16]

If Cirilo is to be regarded as a negative element in the novels, then persuading his nephew to attend these devotions must also be seen as negative since, no matter how good the intentions of Cirilo, the 'auroros' remained for the narrator a sombre encounter with suffering and death.

In a similar way to the alteration and virtual reversal of roles that takes place between Cirilo and Cayetano insofar as it is the lay person who is the more fanatical and obsessive, the brothers Pascual and Manolo are also involved in contradictory roles. While the mother in the novels, for example, would be under the impression that to fight on the side of religion was the noble thing to do, it is Manolo, who is on the republican side, who is described as the kinder and more helpful one. His brother Pascual, supposedly fighting on the side of God, is presented as hard and obstinate. When asked if the opposition between the two brothers could be identified with real events in the author's life, Castillo-Puche would only admit to a limited similarity:

> Son vocaciones extremas de lo cual hay algo en la realidad pero no todo. Lo que sí hay en mi familia es que he tenido parientes, que unos han estado en la zona roja y otros en la zona nacional y que han sido muy contrapuestos.

While the reality of his brothers' political affiliations remains unclear, the reference to the sister Rosa and the scandal caused by her elopement in the novel has its roots in real life. The author describes how his sister fell in love with a man who led her into the extremely dangerous world of Spanish politics at that time:

> La vocación que tuvo fue política. Al empezar la guerra, se le truncó totalmente la vida porque se encontró con un hombre que la arrastró y la sedujo hacia una lucha que era probablemente lo que es el falangismo: las armas, la violencia etc.

At the early age of twenty-two, she was heavily involved in politics, speaking publicly and promoting new ideas:

> El amor de ella era tan grande que se entregó a ese hombre aun cuando ella había sido una especie de líder a los veintidós años. Hablaba en público del comienzo de la democracia cristiana en España, que era la redistribución de la riqueza y la concordia de los españoles. Ella presentó a varios diputados en Yecla. En Murcia mi hermana intervino presentando a Gil Robles.

The image of Rosa is presented favourably in the trilogy as someone admired by the narrator, but his brothers are often viewed as people caught up in a world of women and vice. While the narrator shows resentment towards his brothers' lack of virtue, Rosa is shown an attitude of compassion and understanding despite the scandal:

> He querido conservar una resistencia grande a los vicios y también he querido poner un gran sentido de perdón y de comprensión y de indulgencia cara a la hermana.

So Rosa is one of the few characters in the trilogy who is a source of comfort and inspiration, but the supreme positive character of the trilogy is, without doubt, the mother.

The notion of the mother as a symbol of tenderness and happiness is significant throughout the trilogy and especially in *El amargo sabor de la retama*. Castillo-Puche considers himself fortunate to have had such a caring mother in his own life and the symbolism in the trilogy is directly connected to experience:

> Sale de la vida. No surge de que yo lo haya inventado. La madre existe. Es decir, yo he tenido una madre que era una madre excepcional, he sido un hombre muy afortunado con una madre que tenía mucho carácter, mucha bondad.[17]

The author explains that it was not just maternal qualities she possessed but to everyone she knew she became a constant source of warmth and understanding:

> Una mujer excepcional, y no a nivel del cariño de un hijo sino a nivel del pueblo. Una mujer hasta muy revolucionaria, pero muy saludable, muy llena del evangelio.[18]

Though she had not dedicated herself to the religious life, the author gives the impression that she was a better person than all her religious relatives. Here again we witness the best qualities coming from the humblest source though this time the figure of the mother in the novels seems almost identical with reality.

In all of this, we have seen to what extent the author has included locations, characters and images from his own experience and how some remain identical, like Hécula and the mother, and how others undergo a transformation in accordance with the author's creativity. All we can say at this stage is that what has been altered seems to have been done in order to reverse roles or to suggest the unexpected. Before proceeding to examine the various characters and events and their symbolic values in the three novels, it is necessary to look at the technique used in the narrative which remains constant all through the trilogy.

B. NARRATIVE

In the trilogy, as in the previous two novels examined, the reader must depend on the narrator's commentary and inside views of the characters in order to understand the story. But unlike Enrique of *Sin camino* and the four ordinands in *Como ovejas al matadero*, the main character in the trilogy, Pepico, is the younger version of the narrator himself. The main difference between the trilogy and the other novels studied is that while in *Sin camino* and *Como ovejas al matadero* the events are interrupted by flashbacks and inside views of past experiences of the characters, in the trilogy the past experiences themselves form the basis of the novels with interruptions coming from the narrator speaking in the present. However, although the narrator and Pepico are one and the same, the narrator does not merely tell the reader how the events happened, instead he allows the reader to follow the events as they happen in the life of Pepico. The reader is transported into the past world of Hécula and the free-flowing narrative allows one event to follow another without any necessary linkage or set pattern. In this way, scene predominates over summary, yet the reader must still rely on information given by the narrator about himself and other characters. Often the vision of the world is seen through the eyes of Pepico, as a child, an adolescent or a young man, but sometimes the views and emotions come directly from the adult narrator. In this way the adult narrator in the present is often distinguished from Pepico in the past while both remain equally involved in the distressful experiences of injustice and oppression which are frequent throughout the trilogy. This separation between adult narrator and young Pepico can normally be observed in the distinction between the 'yo' of the memory and the 'yo' of the events.

While the narrative style of the trilogy is quite different from any previous work of the author, it is not the first work to be written in the first person since this happened in *Con la muerte al hombro* and *El vengador*. Now, with the trilogy, the author introduces a new dimension in the use of first person narrative alternating with second person narrative to produce the effect of dialogue between the narrator, searching for both liberation and self-discovery, and his *alter ego* in both the past and present. This notion of dialogue is mentioned by Gemma Roberts in a study of the final part of the trilogy, *Conocerás el poso de la nada*:

> El yo presente que recuerda (el narrador) tiene que reconocerse en
> el yo pasado (el protagonista), el yo que ahora evoca los hechos
> se desdobla en un 'tú' para dialogar consigo mismo.[19]

This would suggest that the narrator is finding difficulty in relating himself as he is in the present to the image of himself found in Pepico. It is this difficulty of being unable to recognise himself which makes the narrator create his *alter ego* through which he can find dialogue and solidarity. The author has also suggested in private conversation that solidarity is one of the key motives in the introduction of the second person which tends to appear at moments of intense emotion and drama:

> El individuo busca una solidaridad en las cosas trágicas de la vida
> en un 'tú' que es el reflejo del yo, manifestación o complemento
> del yo.

Apart from solidarity, the author claims that the dialogue with the 'tú' signals a departure from the mere memory of the events in order to make these events closer and more intimate:

> Es el tú del pasado, y es el tú del acercamiento, de la proximidad, de la intimidad.

So, on the one hand, the 'tú' is introduced to bring both past and present together:

> Entonces el 'tú' siempre es un modo de romper la barrera del tiempo muchas veces y del espacio también, que, siendo mayor, se siente pequeño porque alude a edades y a tiempos que pasaron sin nominar y que él trata de reincorporar, resucitar o rememorar de una manera afectiva.

And, on the other hand, it is seen as an attempt to go beyond the external surface of the events:

> Es un modo de romper la costra de los hechos puramente memorables por una biografía, por la cobertura de lo histórico, es decir, el tú es una apelación a la intimidad, a un recuerdo más cálido, como romper la cáscara del huevo.

It is evident, however, that the second person is employed over a far wider scale than that suggested by the author. Very often the 'tú' is introduced when situations seem negative and pessimistic. It is introduced, for example, at times of guilt and recrimination when the narrator blames himself for failing to prevent a situation, as when he was sexually abused by the Spiritual Director don Crisanto in *Conocerás el poso de la nada*:

> Y cómo no habías salido corriendo de la cama, y cómo no habías reaccionado, luego tú tenías también culpa, confiésalo, tú habías cedido incluso a la espera del placer, entre el asco y el miedo.[20]

There are also many instances in the same novel when he accuses himself of failure:

> Y para qué seguir, que ni has sido consuelo ni apoyo a tanto desvalimiento, porque acaso tú eras el más desvalido, si puedes recordar, que ni eras tú ni eras el que eres, aunque ahora no tengas más remedio que aceptar o adoptar una identidad. (p.51)

The narrator also addresses Hécula sometimes in the second person in the form of accusation or condemnation and this extends the application of the second person to things outwith his own person. However, as can be seen in *El libro de las visiones y las apariciones*, the narrator often gives the impression that both Hécula and himself are inseparable:

> Tú eres esqueleto de tus propios sueños en medio del páramo con ilusiones de huerto, y aunque te tenga en la entraña, como tú me tienes a mí, abusas del poder de mi recuerdo y por eso siempre nos encontraremos en una pugna enconada y dolorosa. (p.21)

The view expressed by Gemma Roberts on the narrator's need to recognise himself in the protagonist Pepico conforms to the existentialist conflict between the individual and his own individuality, a theme that is also examined by Oscar Barrero.[21] We already saw Oscar Barrero discussing how the individual finds difficulty in relating to the surrounding environment and this was evident in *Sin camino*. Barrero claims that it is not only other people who remain alien to the individual in the existential novel but, indeed, his own individuality seems inaccessible to him:

> Se abre así un nuevo frente de conflicto para el personaje que, encastillado (voluntaria o forzosamente) en su soledad, se siente incapaz de acceder al tú, pero también de conocerse a sí mismo.[22]

Although the causes of this conflict are not altogether clear, Barrero thinks that in certain Spanish existential novels there is evidence of internal disintegration of the personality of the characters which could contribute towards the conflict. In the trilogy also there is more than a suggestion that the narrator is not at one with himself, as is seen when Pepico is leaving Hécula for the countryside towards the end of *El libro de las visiones y las apariciones*:

> Y entonces me entraba un miedo grande a la soledad, a verme partido en dos, algo mío quedaba en el pueblo aunque yo estuviera en el campo, y acababa por no saber dónde estaba yo, ni quién era, y esta misma sensación la tuve siendo ya mayor, que me parecía estar en dos sitios distintos, y esto me pasó desde entonces. (p.180)

Here too is an indication of why Hécula should be included in the dialogue between first and second person since the narrator saw his true self still imprisoned in Hécula:

> Y aquel viaje fue fatal, porque sentí por primera vez en mi vida aquello que había de ser un desdoblamiento de mi ser ... porque me parecía estar en otro lado y era como si el que iba en el carro fuera solamente la funda de mí mismo, una cáscara vacía, y mi verdadero yo se quedara allá en la habitación de arriba, sujeta a los recuerdos, a las pesadillas y a las apariciones. (pp.180-181)

This split personality could be related to the notion of conflict between the individual and his own individuality, as Oscar Barrero suggests. It is clear that the narrator of the trilogy experiences liberation as he writes down the memories of all the horrific and tragic events of his past, but if the trilogy is also an attempt at self-exploration and self-knowledge then this will lead to frustration as the narrator discovers in *Conocerás el poso de la nada*:

> Lo que eres y siempre has sido es un prófugo de ti mismo, un fantasma de otro al que persigues y sigues inútilmente, un ser dividido y roto. (p.51)

It is possible that the dialogue between narrator and this *alter ego*, between first and second person, has its roots in this split personality which the narrator painfully acknowledges.

114

NOTES

1. *El libro de las visiones y las apariciones* (Barcelona: Destino, 1977), 7. All subsequent bracketed references are to this edition.

2. "Escribir en Murcia."

3. See *Hemingway entre la vida y la muerte* (Barcelona: Destino, 1968), 416-440.

4. See Donald L. Shaw, *The Generation of 1898 in Spain* (London: Benn, 1975), 109-116: "Baroja's Theory of the Novel".

5. Pío Baroja, *Obras completas* 2nd ed. (Madrid: Biblioteca Nueva, 1973), IV, 320.

6. Lecture given by the author at several American universities in 1985. Parts of this lecture have since been published under the title "En torno a mis novelas" in Belchí Arévalo, Cecilia, and María Martínez del Portal, ed. *Estudios sobre José Luis Castillo-Puche* (Murcia: Alfonso X el Sabio, 1988), 15-24.

7. Donald Shaw, 111.

8. David Lodge, *Language of Fiction* (London: Routledge & Kegan Paul, 1966), 42.

9. The author felt it necessary to make this claim in response to an accusation that a character in the novel bore too much resemblance to a person in real life. See *Jeremías el anarquista* (Barcelona: Destino, 1975), 7-8.

10. Conversations (1985).

11. Conversations (1985).

12. Miguel Ortuño Palao, *Las calles de Yecla* (Yecla: La Levantina, 1982), 159.

13. Ortuño Palao, 159.

14. Private conversations with the author at his home in Madrid during

January 1987. Subsequent quotations from the author in this chapter are from these conversations, except when reference is made to the earlier conversations in 1985.

15.   *El amargo sabor de la retama* (Barcelona: Destino, 1979), 90. All subsequent bracketed references are to this edition.

16.   Ortuño Palao, 71.

17.   Conversations (1985).

18.   Conversations (1985).

19.   Gemma Roberts, "Memoria e identidad en *Conocerás el poso de la nada* de José Luis Castillo-Puche.", *Revista Canadiense de Estudios Hispánicos*, 12, no. 1 (Otoño, 1987), 93-108 (95).

20.   *Conocerás el poso de la nada* (Barcelona: Destino, 1982), 55. All subsequent bracketed references are to this edition.

21.   See Barrero Pérez, 92-103: "El conflicto con la propia individualidad".

22.   Barrero Pérez, 92.

1. At the Collegiate Church of San vicente de la Barquera (Asturias), Castillo-Puche (second from right on second row) with fellow seminarians, of whom several became bishops, from the Pontifical University of Comillas in 1942.

2. Castillo-Puche discussing one of his works with Pío Baroja in 1953.

3. Castillo-Puche in 1977, the year he published *El libro de las visiones y las apariciones.*

4. Castillo-Puche at one of his meetings with King Juan Carlos I of Spain.

CHAPTER 5
El libro de las visiones y las apariciones

We have seen how many characters and other elements in the trilogy are taken from the author's own experience and how these are altered in order to create the desired impact upon the reader. As the title of the trilogy suggests, the aim is to liberate an adult narrator still tormented by the harmful experiences of his past. One possible means of liberation seems to lie in the process of recounting those negative experiences associated with certain characters, places or events. Therefore, the three novels of the trilogy become a sort of exorcism by which all the demons of the past are cast out. In his article on the first novel, Corbalán indicates that this exorcism is not just for the author, but indeed for the entire Spanish society which appeared to be under the same spell:

> Nos encontramos en el fondo de la gárgola barroca de donde nacen los murciélagos y las humillaciones, el hedor de las cárceles interiores, la hipocresía disciplinada, la imaginación enferma, la intransigencia espiritual y física, y donde se vive una especie de ultratumba indecisa entre el acá y el más allá. Es decir, nos encontramos en la grieta por la que se entrevé el espíritu de un país siniestrista sobre el que Castillo Puche ha oficiado la ceremonia de exorcizarse de todos sus demonios.[1]

The claim that the novel embraces a wider national dimension than just the particular background of the author is shared also by Marcelino Peñuelas who feels that the novel is concerned with exposing certain negative elements of the entire national culture:

Aspectos que a través de los siglos han obstaculizado, con
resonancias que sin exagerar pueden llamarse patológicas, el
desarrollo normal del país. En este sentido el libro de Castillo
Puche, aparte su valor literario y humano, cobra dimensiones de
un impresionante documento socio-cultural.[2]

Both critics agree that the novel attempts to deal with the problems
common to Spanish rural life and therefore the novel is very much involved with
reality as we have already indicated. But despite all the references to real
situations in the life of the author, there is enough evidence to suggest that the
novel is fictional as much as it is autobiographical, as Peñuelas affirms:

La dimensión autobiográfica del relato es evidente. El autor no
intenta en ningún momento eludir o disimular su papel de
narrador-protagonista en la voz del niño Pepico. Pero aún en la
más estricta y verídica autobiografía el elemento ficcional no deja
de aparecer, aunque sea marginalmente y sin que el propio autor
pueda evitarlo.[3]

The fictional element can be seen in certain episodes of both horror and humour
which are scattered throughout the novel, as well as being evident in the
characters themselves.

Most of the characters and elements included are either presented
favourably or unfavourably and likewise become symbols of oppression or
symbols of liberation. It is clear, for example, that Hécula is meant to be negative
and this is emphasised by describing the town and everything in it as morbidly
and destructively as the narrator possibly can:

Porque Hécula influía poderosamente sobre mí con su trasunto de
exacerbada religiosidad y brujería, patología mística colectiva e
instintiva, monstruosidad también colectiva. (p.52)

Similar treatment is given to the subject of death and the exaggerated obsession of the inhabitants of Hécula with regard to the subject:

> Destrucción macabra que a veces parecía desencadenar el rapto
> místico o revolucionario de mis paisanos, gente que en medio de
> la orgía frenética de la vida metía siempre la tasa niveladora de la
> muerte, pavor y goce, rebeldía y postración, todo junto. (p.145)

Every element which the author wishes to highlight either positively or negatively is adorned with superior qualities on the one hand or grotesque features on the other. The goodness and kindness of the mother, for instance, are not just shown in contrast to the failings of Cirilo and Cayetano, but whenever she is mentioned the narrator suddenly becomes enraptured by her saintliness and is filled with praise and homage:

> Que yo no sé si ha habido o hay santas, pero si ha habido alguna
> alguna vez, ella fue una o la primera, o la última ciertamente, por
> el poderoso, por el potente, por el sublime cúmulo de fortaleza
> silencios que supo sostener sobre el humanísimo montoncillo de
> su carne. (p.29)

In this way, we can see how each character and element is turned into a symbol of goodness or badness, and although there are examples of relief and liberation in certain elements, the overall atmosphere of the novel is one of pessimism, morbidity and oppression. I now wish to identify these symbols of oppression and examine the particular effects each has upon the protagonist and narrator.

A. SYMBOLS OF OPPRESSION

We have seen already two of the principal symbols of oppression, namely, Hécula and death, but associated with both elements are certain negative characters with somewhat minor roles. Among these we find doña Cesárea, Andresico and don Roque who are all presented unfavourably by the narrator.

All three minor characters are linked to the notion of death: doña Cesárea is involved in spiritualism, Andresico is the strange and cynical undertaker, while don Roque is suspected of trying to murder Pepico's cat, Susto. Even more strongly linked with death is the practice of the 'auroros' which, with its emphasis on prayers for the dying, had such an impact on the child. Probably the chief symbol of oppression is his uncle Cirilo, who is responsible for the initiation of Pepico into the customary procession of the 'auroros' and whose fanaticism and religious observances seem to do more harm than good. To a lesser degree there is also the oppression of Cayetano, who, together with Cirilo, forms an alliance against the integrity of the mother and the wonders of childhood. All of these factors are responsible for creating not only a confused child, but also an adult narrator still haunted and tormented by their memory. The symbol of oppression that is intrinsically connected to the narrator is, without doubt, the village of Hécula which, as we have seen, seems to form part of his very self.

1. Hécula

Although the child Pepico is aware of the oppressive nature of Hécula the criticism and attacks seem to come mainly from the adult narrator. The reason for this is distance from the geographical centre of events, that is to say, the narrator can view his native village from a safe distance and condemn all its faults and failings. Young Pepico has not experienced any other environment outside Hécula, at least not until the end of the novel when he and his mother move to the countryside and later to Alicante. The adult narrator, on the other hand, appears to have spent some time in his new surroundings in the north and is thus in the privileged position of being able to compare the two different environments of the Basque country and Hécula. Likewise, we find that many of the attacks on Hécula are normally made in the light of a better situation. In other words, what is negative in Hécula is accentuated by contrasting it with the positive features of the north:

> Quizá nunca más volvería, que los muertos enterraran a los muertos, que se abrieran las tumbas de una vez, que cayera del cielo una gran nevada de fuego, que la tierra vomitara monstruos y el pueblo enloqueciera más de lo que estaba, gentes cainescas o cainianas, Hécula remota y perdida, a la que ahora recuerdo con pena desde esta catarata de verdes voluptuosos y plácidos. (pp.39-40)

In some instances the comparisons are made between the landscape surrounding Hécula and the very different environment of the Basque country. In Hécula there are visions of an angry sun beating down on the dry, red earth while in the north the sun is often hidden by clouds, and the rain showers maintain a landscape of moisture and greenery:

> Aquí no llueve tierra roja como allí, ni las encinas, ni los olivos ni las viñas ni la jara aparecen por la mañana con ese rocío de cristal, sino más bien humedecidos y gratos. (p.40)

Now that the narrator has experienced a more gentle environment, he can recall the extreme heat and dust which characterise Hécula and which also contribute to the notion of Hécula as a symbol of oppression. Unlike the cloudy sky in the north, the sky of Hécula was responsible for the destruction and desolation of the landscape:

> En este torbellino verde que me circunda aquí, tienes hasta un cielo menos implacable, cielo terrible aquél, por la mañana blanco como una mortaja, por la tarde rojo como una enagua de muchacha recién violada sobre el trigo, cielo que solamente se sentía cielo descargando piedra o rayos, la maldición sobre los pámpanos, los olivos y los trigales hasta reventar las ramblas, mientras que aquí los ríos tienen fango y peces, y las tapias descuelgan hiedras y madreselvas y la llovida niebla hace

122

voluptuoso el canto del mirlo y de los ruiseñores, un abismo por
no decir una gran diferencia. (p.23)

In Hécula, both nature and the landscape are presented as victims of an
extreme climate whereas in the north all wildlife and cultivation appear to be
flourishing. And the climate seems also to affect the people since the narrator
associates the relentless sky of Hécula with the aggressiveness of its inhabitants,
but in the new surroundings the narrator himself admits to a change of
temperament:

Aquí, en este plácido valle, sin navaja cabritera en el bolsillo, con
la memoria del pan y del queso, noto y tú adviertes, tú y yo
notamos, que he perdido dureza y ferocidad. (pp.21-22)

Included also in the list of differences are the women of the north who are
seen as tender and ladylike in comparison with the wild and fiery nature of the
women of Hécula:

Aquí, son otra cosa, yo creo que más finas, más calladas o más
astutas, no sé, y no se ponen coloradas tan fácilmente, pero
tampoco te hacen la gran faena, aquí las mujeres no tienen en los
ojos el mismo ardor y ese sudorcillo como de fruta pasada. (p.49)

Indeed, the narrator holds the view that the women in Hécula may have been
responsible for many of the problems in the village:

Aquí las mujeres son como terneras, allá como cabras locas, yo
creo que allí la gente se ahorca pródigamente no sólo por el viento
y los vinos, sino por las hembras, todas chaladas, que lo mismo
les da por Cristo que por Mahoma y que gozan poniendo cuernos,
la madre que las parió. (p.48)

It appears then that the women were also influenced by the harshness of the
region and that their nature, along with that of the rest of the inhabitants and the

wildlife, was an accurate reflection of an aggressive and oppressive climate.

Another contrast between north and south is also observed in the practice of religion. The Basque people seem to be just as Catholic as the rest of Spain but there appears to be not the same degree of fanaticism as there is in Hécula, perhaps because their faith is linked with other important areas of daily life such as work, politics, and recreation. The Basques also treat the clergy as their equals and do not cower before them as they have to do in Hécula under the authority of Cayetano. In general, religion in the north seems to be taken in moderation while in Hécula religious observances and devotions are verging on the obsessive:

> Que allí siempre están de Horas Santas, de Adoraciones Nocturnas, de Jubileos, de Misiones, de Ejercicios espirituales, de procesiones, de peregrinaciones, de años santos, del mes de las flores, del mes de las ánimas, de cuaresmas, con el Cristo para arriba y para abajo, con la Virgen para abajo y para arriba, y yo creo que aquello era ya una exageración. (pp.106-107)

The adult narrator reflects on the enthusiasm in Hécula for parading along the street with statues and banners in a proud display of their faith. However, the impression that all this left upon the narrator was hardly favourable since he remembers all these practices as something morbid and superficial:

> Yo recordaré siempre las espinas de los Cristos, las espadas de dolor o los puñales de las Vírgenes, o simplemente los hachones o las velas de los entierros y la macabra melopea de los cantores o cofrades, y el paso como de bueyes de los reverendos cansinos que miraban a través de lentes o cristales de aumento, y Hécula vivía solamente para estas ocasiones de despliegue de cruces y estandartes, de cintas colgantes y de penachos de plumas, de bocas humeantes de arcabuz, de mechas encendidas. (p.77)

Though all of this is remembered by the adult narrator and compared to the different attitudes in his new surroundings, there are also occasions when the horrors of Hécula were felt by the child Pepico. This is seen especially when

Pepico experiences life in the country and the first sensation of freedom from the fear imposed by Hécula:

> Y allí sentiste por primera vez la vida sin vértigos, sin sudores pálidos y sin terrores, lejos del precinto atosigante de Hécula. (p.190)

The feelings of Pepico are suddenly transferred and amplified by the adult narrator:

> Oh Hécula, de las calles rectas, de las casas vigilantes, de los 'auroros' vespertinos, de las jaculatorias y las penitencias, Hécula de los vientos y del polvo, pegado a las ventanas y al alma ... (p.190)

Despite the apparent liberation experienced by Pepico at the end of the novel and the new life that is found by the adult narrator, the fear that was engendered by Hécula had maintained its grip on the narrator:

> Y todo desde entonces en tu vida ha sido desconcierto, perplejidad, miedo, miedo incluso ahora mismo a contarte las cosas que sucedieron en tu casa y en las casas vecinas por aquellos tiempos, y aunque lo revistas de broma algo tendrá que haber en el fondo, pues todo lo de Hécula es un poco macabro. (p.50)

While rejoicing in a region where drought is replaced by rain, red is replaced by green, where harshness gives way to gentleness and fanaticism gives way to moderation, the narrator knows that he is still not completely free from Hécula:

> No puedo menos de quedarme recostado en la interminable frescura del verdor circundante y soñar que todo aquello queda muy lejos, y sin embargo, ¿por qué incoerciblemente evoco la truculencia de aquellos años? (p.40)

Since the narrator sometimes addresses Hécula in the second person, the reader has the unmistakeable impression that Hécula remains a part of the narrator himself. And as Hécula stays with him, so too do all the dreams and terrors which Hécula represents, and so also does another aspect of the symbolism of oppression, namely, death. All the deaths witnessed by Pepico were to remain inseparably with the narrator all through his life:

> Aún ahora, pasados los años y por más que he querido alejarme del pueblo, y de todo, aún ahora siento que caen sobre mí en catarata los muertos todos, como en aquellas noches de mi enfermedad, como si ellos llegaran a formar parte de mí y nunca más pudiera dejarlos atrás, olvidarlos, llegar a una separación total, cosa imposible. (p.166)

2. Death

The association of Hécula with death is seen first of all in a certain susceptibility to suicide among the villagers and witnessing such an event was to create a lasting impression upon the child. Then we are told that the boy's father died when he was very young and so, according to the Spanish tradition, his mother was destined to be dressed in black as a sign of her widowhood. That aside, the death of the father in itself seemed to have a devastating effect on a young child, although there is also a hint that Pepico might have been too young to fully understand what was going on. In any case, Pepico himself was obliged to wear mourning dress for the funeral at least. Added to that there are the funerals of all the villagers who died and the accompanying black of mourning worn at some time by everyone. Then there are the individuals we have already seen whose occupations were essentially linked to the notion of death, especially Andresico, the gravedigger, and doña Cesárea, the spiritualist. Another individual death which left its effects on Pepico was surely the death of Susto, his cat, which he witnessed being torn apart by some unidentified wild beast. Last of all, there is the procession of the 'auroros' to the dying through which Cirilo introduced the child to the agony and pains of terminal illness. So, even when death was not present, Pepico was taken to see those on the point of death and thus found it impossible to escape from the subject. Just as Pepico was surrounded by the morbidity of death, so too all the other children of the village were affected in a similar way, as is reflected during the time of Pepico's illness when death seemed very close:

> Ay, cómo me cercó la muerte en aquellos días de mi enfermedad, cómo se me echó encima en forma de procesión implacable en la que iban apareciendo, sin que yo tuviera la menor posibilidad de ahuyentarlos, todos los muertos que había visto en mis cortos años, que habían sido muchos, porque en un pueblo como el mío los niños viven las muertes, mueren las muertes, sufren y padecen las muertes,. porque son las muertes lo más importante que acontece en el pueblo. (p.163)

Associated with the subject of death and mourning is the memory of blackness in the mind of the adult narrator. Whenever there is a picture of Hécula in his mind it is often filled with images of people dressed in black who seem resigned to misery and grief. For the narrator, the black of the outer garments of the villagers was also a reflection of their inner condition:

> Negrura insondable en las conciencias, negro pecado en la cola de los confesonarios, pecado negro en la cola de los prestamistas, pecado negrísimo en la de las comadronas, luctuoso e inacabable negror en la caravana del cementerio, pavor de los pavores de la ciudad que se vestía de luto riguroso para sus fiestas. (p.101)

It seems that this exaggeration of black is a sign of the narrator's frustration and resentment towards a culture which imposed the gloom of mourning on him at a very early age. Since the death of his father, the child was gradually incorporated into the cult of mourning, and the associated black attire was always the external manifestation of grief:

Y recuerdo que por aquel tiempo yo seguía con un babero negro,
luto, siempre luto, no ya el luto por mi padre sino lutos que venían
de todas partes, luto que se cernía sobre mí, sobre mi alma
infantil. (pp.109-110)

The obsession with black is discussed by Ramón Jiménez Madrid who
sees the dimension of colour as fundamental to the symbolic interpretation of the
novel. While black is associated with Hécula and the past, the novel also alludes
to other colours such as green and blue which are clearly opposed to black and
imply notions of optimism and liberation. Nevertheless, it is black which tends
to dominate the novel as Jiménez Madrid indicates:

La avasalladora presencia de lo luctuoso que permite denominar
de 'funeraria' buena parte de la producción del autor, tan sólo es
mitigada por las alusiones a dos nuevos colores: el verde y el
azul.[4]

As well as the greenness of the north and the blue of the sea being considered
positive symbols, we could also include along with black the colour red, both as
a negative symbol of heat and landscape in Hécula and also as the symbol of
blood which will appear to a greater degree in the latter sections of the trilogy
with the outbreak of the Civil War.

One of the points the adult narrator makes about the people of Hécula is
that their attitude towards death is often somewhat sadistic and unnatural:

Quizás todos los pueblos tenían algo de infierno pero éste más que
ninguno, y lo más raro es que ellos parecen felices con su terror
y sus eternales abismos, no como los pueblos del contorno que
viven con un pie en la vida galana y el otro en el irremediable
purgatorio, un poco como por aquí. (p.106)

A similar attitude is found in an earlier novel *Con la muerte al hombro* which
deals with a young man, Julio, coming to terms with an illness, tuberculosis, that

has destroyed most of his family. The novel is also concerned with Hécula and the peculiar obsession with death among the inhabitants who saw the death of another individual as an opportunity to gloat over tragedy:

> Más horrible que morir es ver morir a los demás y, por eso, cada vecino quisiera que este acto se realizara, para poder gozarlo plenamente bajo los focos fosforescentes de un teatro prodigioso.[5]

The nocturnal practice of the 'auroros' is also presented in *Con la muerte al hombro* as further evidence of this morbid obsession and also as a means of expressing this fascination of the villagers with another's demise rather than being understood as an activity with the sole purpose of bringing peace and consolation to the dying:

> Su fe y su religiosidad son de signo tétrico, como los cantos de "los auroros", cofradía de penitentes que recorre de madrugada las calles heculanas, entonando unas melodías fúnebres y quejumbrosas.[6]

The constant fascination with death could suggest that the people of Hécula actually enjoyed witnessing another person's misfortune but, according to Gemma Roberts, the 'heculanos' of the novel *Con la muerte al hombro* focus on the death of another in order to avoid thinking about their own death.[7] It would appear that their own death holds such fear that the only way to combat this is to expose the problem as widely as possible:

> Toda preocupación de Hécula con la muerte está encaminada a privarla de su sentido personal. Los heculanos exorcizan la muerte, pensando y hablando constantemente de ella.[8]

This would also explain why the whole town gathers together in a show of general grief whenever someone dies, since by creating a "universal" sorrow the 'heculanos' are able to avoid the acute trauma of the individual tragedy. In other words, in a collective mourning the individual can escape from the fear of personal death:

> La muerte de que se habla en Hécula es siempre, naturalmente, la muerte del otro, como manifestación social, que oculta evasivamente el sentido de la verdadera angustia ante la propia aniquilación.[9]

These comments on *Con la muerte al hombro* could also be applied to this novel since there are many similarities in the behaviour and attitude of the inhabitants of Hécula towards the subject of death. The apparent obsession with mourning dress and the ritual of the 'auroros' would then be seen in a different light since what appears to be a bizarre fascination could be nothing more than an external disguise in order to escape the personal confrontation with death.

If this explanation is accurate, then what is being disguised is fear and this fear of death, though common, is really out of place in a culture which presumably claims to be Christian. In a town where every procession and celebration was based on Christian tradition it seems unusual that the townsfolk should collectively be governed by the fear of death since one of the fundamental beliefs in Christianity is that of the resurrection. In Christian tradition, death has always been regarded as an evil which has been overcome by Christ, as St Paul explains:

> The dead will be raised, imperishable, and we shall be changed as well, because our present perishable nature must put on imperishability and this mortal nature must put on immortality ... then the words of scripture will come true: Death is swallowed up in victory. Death, where is your victory? Death, where is your sting?
>
> I Corinthians 15.52-55

It seems paradoxical that while death for the Christian means transformation, for the people of Hécula it appeared more like annihilation. It must be assumed, therefore, that the Christianity of Hécula was not truly a religion of freedom, but rather a religion of enslavement and fear. Since very few seemed capable of changing the situation, apart from the protagonist's mother who did protest against her son's initiation in the 'auroros', the religion of Hécula appears somewhat misguided and misunderstood where religious practices and beliefs were demonstrated without any understanding or conviction. This is illustrated in the effects suffered by young Pepico who, instead of finding compassion and consolation, was soon turned into an insecure and frightened individual.

It must be noted, however, that the adult narrator does not judge the behaviour of his native village on any religious grounds but rather from a philosophical viewpoint. We have seen earlier how the author displays attitudes in his writing which are in common with existential thinking and it is on this basis that the author/narrator makes judgements on the human condition and views the problem of death from a human perspective. An example of this can be seen when the narrator examines the attitude of people and relatives towards the deceased. So much care and attention was given to their appearance in the coffin yet none of this is for the benefit of the deceased:

> De un lado están los histerismos, los gritos, los lloros, la desesperación, los afanes de todo tipo, que le pongan una medalla, que le traigan muchas coronas, que le lean la bendición de Su Santidad, y el muerto, nada, ojos y oídos ciegos y sordos, sabiduría o burla total, cuerpos que sólo pesan hacia el vacío como piedras náufragas en el río de la nada. (pp.170-171)

While the bereaved are often displaying great sorrow and despair there is total disinterest in the expression of the deceased:

> Sonrisa helada y heladora de indiferencia total para llantos y gritos, desprecio impertérrito para el dolor de deudos y amigos, enrealidad qué cosa tan vulgar, tan fácil y sencilla, tan corriente, monótona y repetida esto del morir, todo se queda en continente, liviano y grave, natural en su trascendencia, pero sin pizca de

contenido. (p.170)

For the narrator, the notion of what lies beyond death is not an issue but rather what is visible is a corpse devoid of any life or movement, and which thus displays no feelings whatsoever, unlike the ones left behind:

> A un muerto no le duele nada, eso se nota, que en eso está seguramente la majestad de la muerte, una raya divisoria bien clara en cualquier velatorio. (p.170)

These views clearly belong to the adult narrator and could be regarded as cynical in comparison with the general attitude of the 'heculanos'. Quite different from these views are the fears and anxiety shown by Pepico especially during the ritual of the 'auroros'. Pepico had been assured by his uncle Cirilo that taking part in the procession of the 'auroros' would be his first step on the way to manhood. But from what Pepico would see in the behaviour of adults around him, becoming a man was hardly desirable:

> Yo no quería hacerme un hombre, que yo tenía horror a ser hombre, porque ser un hombre era morir, como mi padre, era pecar y morir, era ser como tío Cirilo y otros, magros, desdentados y tristes. (p.128)

Although the boy's mother protested that her son was too young to witness such distressing scenes, Cirilo was adamant that the time was right for Pepico to assume the responsibilities of adult Christians. The adult narrator confirms that the innocence of childhood was all but consumed on that first experience of the 'auroros':

> Yo no sé si comencé a ser hombre, pero dejé de ser niño, y si me hice hombre no fue un hombre para la vida sino un hombre para la muerte y la muerte se me quedó pegada como una camisa de

132

fuerza, como una segunda piel imposible de arrancar. (pp.162-163)

The effects which a morbid experience such as the 'auroros' would have upon a young mind are evident throughout the rest of the novel, especially during the time of illness when all the visions of death and the dying tormented Pepico as he lay suffering:

Tumbado en mi cama de colegial sin colegio, de muerto sin sudario, estuve seguramente semanas sin otro horizonte que recordar persistentemente a los moribundos y a los muertos que pesaban sobre mí como una losa de impotencia y de abulia total. (pp.174-175)

The nightmares of death were so persistent that Pepico was trapped between life and death. Indeed, at times there was the sensation that the child had actually entered the realm of the dead:

Yo ya creía que yo mismo había abandonado este mundo de los vivos y estaba para siempre en la compañía de aquellos que habían traspasado el umbral de la agonía. (p.163)

Here the narrator recalls the early signs of alienation from the world, a feeling that remains during the remainder of childhood in this novel and, in fact, seems to be a very serious concern to the adult narrator. He now feels that the problem of alienation which still affects him has its roots in experiences such as the 'auroros' with the unnecessary witnessing of so much death:

Ahora recuerdo muy bien que los muertos que se me aparecieron aquellos días fueron los que más me habían impresionado, y ahora estoy seguro, como si propiamente hubiera resucitado, como si toda mi niñez y mi juventud hubieran sido muerte, como si hubieran transcurrido en otro mundo, que todo lo que me pasa es por efecto de aquella muerte o aquellas muertes. (pp.163-164)

The experience of death in Hécula, then, seems to have had disturbing consequences for the narrator who confesses to a strange sensation of non-being even as an adult:

> De repente no estoy donde estoy y entonces me pregunto que dónde estoy yo o si soy yo, o si no seré un fantasma de mí mismo, porque me palpo y no me encuentro, y entonces vuelvo a sudar frío, como en aquellas noches que siguieron a los 'auroros'.(p.164)

It is as if the narrator were witnessing now the things of the world from another sphere which is totally alien. In this way, he compares this strange sensation to perhaps the same way in which, for instance, the dead might view the world:

> Si no estaré viendo todo esto desde otro mundo que no es el de los demás, que ya me ha pasado de verlo todo sin interesarme por nada, y cuántas veces tengo que disimular y hacer como que estoy en el ajo, como todos, pero en realidad, ¿estoy o no estoy?, y muchas veces me he preguntado también cómo se sentirán los muertos estirados y amortajados. (p.165)

The revelation of this personal psychological trauma is echoed at varying intervals throughout the trilogy and often the validity of the accounts of the narrator's past and present is questioned by the narrator himself in the same manner as above. In other words, what appears to have happened in reality is suddenly considered to be possibly a dream or illusion and vice versa. The narrator often displays certain uncertainty between reality and fantasy and this appears to be a reflection of the psychological problem. The frustration caused by the confusion between dream and reality can be seen especially in the final part of the trilogy, *Conocerás el poso de la nada*:

> Reconoce que a veces te vengas inventando algo, porque hay un pasado que no sucedió pero que pudo suceder, y para mí como si hubiera sucedido, que a veces no estoy seguro de nada y no me es

fácil deslindar lo que sucedió de verdad de lo que fue sueño
acariciado   y hasta alucinación necesaria, tergiversación no
buscada. (p.56)

In the first part of the trilogy, the narrator seems to be suggesting that all of this
could be related to the disturbing experiences of childhood in Hécula:

Es que muchas veces me he preguntado por qué me pasa a mí esto
que me pasa, y si no será por todas aquellas muertes que pesaron
encima de mi débil, enfermiza, atormentada niñez. (p.164)

Since the narrator's psychological condition could have its roots in the
over-indulgent attitude towards death in Hécula, and since the accounts of
individual deaths continue from the novel on to the second and third novels of the
trilogy, it would appear that the subject of death is central to the entire trilogy.
Death is the ultimate negative symbol which governs not only the memories of
the past but even the condition of the narrator in the present.

3. Cirilo and Cayetano

If, as has been suggested, the 'auroros' were responsible for illness and
fear in the narrator's childhood, and were also the source of unlimited
psychological trauma for the adult narrator, then we must assume that much of
the blame lies with Cirilo, who encouraged and persuaded Pepico to attend the
ceremony. The negative role of Cirilo is not just confined to the 'auroros' but
indeed the narrator attacks his uncle's oppression at every opportunity. When
Cirilo is introduced early on in the novel, the narrator leaves the reader with little
doubt as to his bitterness and resentment:

Una tortura, mandón, fiscalizador de todo, más fanático que el tío
cura cien veces, más chupado que un caramelo, más tieso que un
pararrayos, más magro que la mojama. (p.20)

Before the reader is able to see any negative action on the part of Cirilo, the narrator tells the reader exactly what he thinks of his uncle so that we know Cirilo is a negative character. Hence, the reader will only expect the character to act negatively and oppressively whenever he appears in the novel. The narrator also reveals that as Cirilo more than Cayetano represents religion, so both Cirilo and his version of Catholicism will be presented negatively:

> Voz chillona y atiplada de contundencia terrible, siempre con invocaciones, jaculatorias y salmos, y siempre el mismo consejo a punto: 'Lo mejor sería enviarlo al seminario o al noviciado', la salvación eterna del alma, guerra a Lucifer, la vida son cuatro días y estamos hechos para el cielo, *amén*, muerte a los enemigos de la religión. (p.20)

The narrator objects strongly to the excessive attention given to external observance such as religious obligations and practices in Cirilo's interpretation of Christianity. Mechanical observance seemed to have more of an impact on Pepico than any Christian virtues of mercy, charity or tenderness. The lack of charity was particularly noticed in the manner in which the boy's mother was treated by both Cirilo and Cayetano:

> El caso es que estos dos crueles varones que no usaban más que palabras de paz, resignación, conformidad y bienaventuranza, no eran ningunos benditos y yo, desde la distancia que da saberlos muertos, no tengo más remedio que reventar, porque al final a la pobre de tu madre prácticamente la dejaron en la estacada e hicieron de sus ahorros lo que les dio la gana. (p.28)

Instead of a faith based on love, Cirilo imposed a religion obsessed with the workings of the devil and the fight against sin. The threat of evil was everywhere in the town and talk of individuals who were possessed really frightened a young mind:

> Mientras pasábamos por delante de la casa de doña Cesárea, él me
> susurró al oído 'aquí vivió un endemoniado', y a mí se me
> erizaron los débiles pelitos de las piernas. (p.130)

Cirilo even claimed that one could tell from the smell of a house whether it was evil or not and notions like this were presumably found in the literature which Cirilo had on the subject of the devil. Clearly this kind of attitude and emphasis on evil was not the proper way to attract a young boy to religion, since the general reaction of Pepico was one of fear. And Cayetano was also guilty of this obsession with the devil as he demonstrated in his superstitious behaviour:

> Siempre haciendo la señal de la cruz para espantar al demonio,
> rociando de agua bendita la casa hasta el último rincón. (p.33)

As Cayetano believed that all women were a source of temptation they were thus regarded as nothing more than the incarnation of Satan:

> Estos niños necesitan alguien siempre vigilante, no pueden
> juntarsey menos que se acerquen a las niñas, eso es lo peor, son
> el demonio,se sabe, nos lo han dicho, no puede fallar, son el
> demonio. (p.103)

If the opposite sex were to be regarded in this way then not only would girls be seen as evil by Pepico but also sexual attraction would be understood as an instinct contrived by the devil. Consequently, any sexual feelings whatsoever would be wrong and so begins the torment of a young life filled with guilt about sexuality. This seems to be the origin of sexual repression which was examined in *Como ovejas al matadero* where Alfredo was the victim of a similar attitude towards sex.

The problem of sex becomes more apparent in the second novel of the trilogy *El amargo sabor de la retama* which is concerned with the period of puberty and adolescence, but already we can see that both Cirilo and Cayetano are chiefly responsible for offering Pepico a misguided education which unites sexual feelings with the sense of sin and guilt. An example of the mentality of Cirilo is seen when the narrator reflects that nudity was not even acceptable on medical grounds:

> Ni siquiera al médico le dejaba que me desnudara para examinarme aquel dolor de la ingle, oh la vergüenza de las vergüenzas, por si alguien se crecía viéndose las partes genitales o por si alguien que había visto otros se creía atrofiado, mezcla conjunta de impotencia y desprecio, mejor no saber nada, todo oculto, terror y ciega ignorancia a la fuerza. (pp.102-103)

It was not just forbidden for the doctor as Pepico himself was also under the impression that he could not even look at himself. Any curiosity regarding his sexuality was considered dangerous and sinful and this was the general attitude of the clergy in Hécula:

> Y el confesor siempre lo mismo, que cuanto menos mirar y tocar, mejor, que era preferible cortarse las manos, y no había que curiosear por esos sitios del cuerpo. (p.168)

What a contrast exists between the above attitude and the contemporary situation in Britain, for example, where GPs are urging parents to discuss sexuality with their children at an early age in order to avoid misunderstandings and the problems of unwanted pregnancies. There would be remorse too whenever Pepico became curious about the female body as he had been taught that female sexuality was something shameful and forbidden, and yet again the attraction would have to be admitted to the priest:

> Siempre con el miedo de que tan pronto amaneciera había que ir corriendo al confesonario y el confesonario era la purga y la liquidación, el balance constante y la continua misericordia. (p.98)

The adult narrator saw the constant, unhealthy feelings of guilt experienced by young Pepico as the beginning of a dangerous repression, but the religious uncles did not see things in that way. He reflects how one of the major effects of the instruction offered by Cirilo and Cayetano was to feel guilty always and everywhere. Above all, in the practice of religious rituals like the 'vía crucis' with all its genuflecting and beating of breast the overall intention seemed to be to create an enormous sense of guilt. In this way, young Pepico would possess the notion of guilt before he had ever even thought of doing wrong, and this feeling was to have a lasting effect upon the narrator who remains totally confused as to why feeling guilt was so important:

> Y yo pedía perdón, pedía perdón por todo y por todos, porque todos éramos culpables de todo y de nada, pero alguien tenía que ofrecerse como víctima y también porque uno era culpable ciertamente. (p.98)

Guilt, of course, is a feeling understood by everyone and not just confined to Catholics and, indeed, some psychologists maintain that guilt can be a good thing in that it prevents individuals from committing further offensive actions. To promote, however, a sense of guilt where nothing wrong has really been done cannot surely be healthy or beneficial to a young child. Further evidence of this enforced guilt complex is found in *Conocerás el poso de la nada* where the narrator continues to relive the experiences of the 'vía crucis' with Cirilo and questions why he should always be made to feel guilty:

> Y había que pedir perdón, una y otra vez, y ahora me pregunto por qué teníamos que pedir tanto perdón, pero entonces yo no me preguntaba nada, solamente obedecía y pensaba que había que pedir perdón sólo por estar allí, por vivir, por tener la osadía de vivir y seguramente había que pedir perdón por haber tenido alguna alegría en la vida. (P.21)

It is this sense of opposition to the enjoyment of life which the narrator remembers most of the education offered by Cirilo. In other words, what seemed to be important were the things that he was forbidden to do rather than being encouraged to enjoy the things which any child would like to do. All that was positive was crushed by everything negative. All that he learned from Cirilo and Cayetano was awareness of death and the danger of sin. By knowing about death, he learned about fear, and through being aware of sin, he discovered the sense of guilt. Hence Cirilo and Cayetano will always be remembered for destroying the wonder of life and the joy of childhood:

> No había más camino que el de la hermosa resignación cristiana, la obediencia, el camino abierto por el fatalismo supersticioso, la represión supersticiosa, la aureola de sentirse los defensores de la religión a costa del aborrecimiento de toda idea de progreso, de disfrute, incluso de alegría, porque la alegría es mala, lleva hacia tentaciones peligrosas. (p.130)

It is clear that both Pepico and his mother were victims of this antagonistic attitude to life and we shall see how the mother stands out against the negative images of her brothers.

The critic José Blanco Amor, commenting on the novel shortly after its publication, affirms that the notions of oppression and suppression come over strongly in the experiences of the protagonist, but what is even more acute is the sense of fear:

> La represión moral y mental del niño es absoluta, y se necesita conocer la magnitud de sus visiones mediante declaraciones explícitas. Pero el miedo que la criatura tiene en el alma ya no se lo quitará nadie.[10]

While many children are permitted a certain amount of innocence and wonder before being affected by the harshness of reality, it seems that Pepico was not even allowed to have any childhood. Childhood is generally recognised as one of the happiest periods of one's life, a paradise of innocence but, as Blanco Amor suggests, Cirilo and Cayetano were able to destroy any remnant of paradise in Pepico's life:

> Se suele decir que la infancia es el paraíso perdido. El niño de Castillo-Puche ha vivido en el infierno y nunca le permitieron soñar con el paraíso.[11]

So we can see how many of the problems of life have their origins in infancy. A narrator who admits to psychological problems as well as insecurity and fear returns to the very beginnings of his existence in order to sort out the good things from the bad and possibly discover the source of his troubles. What he discovers is that oppression is the principal cause of a miserable childhood and many of his present ills. From his childhood up to the present, the narrator has been unable to let go of these negative elements of Hécula, death and guilt which still form part of his present existence. Thus the revelation of these memories will hopefully provide some liberation just as he will be somewhat refreshed by recalling those lesser elements of liberation which were also a fundamental part of his childhood.

B.   SYMBOLS OF LIBERATION

Before proceeding to examine any symbol of liberation it is important to note, first of all, that there is a technique to which the narrator often resorts during times of tragedy and intensity, namely, the use of humour. In the same way that the author seeks solidarity with his other self at difficult moments, so there is also a tendency to alleviate the seriousness of the novel through the introduction of a humorous episode or remark. The curious thing about this use of humour is that it is often found to be associated with the use of 'tremendismo' to describe some tragic event. In other words, the author frequently combines grotesque and graphic descriptions with comical inserts. Examples of this can be found in two distinct sections of the novel, both describing a series of tragic disasters and unusual deaths in Hécula:[12]

> De todos los casos, el que me dio mayor susto fue el de aquella mujer que le llamaban 'la blanca' y que estuvo muerta y bien muerta, porque lo demostraban hasta las moscas que venían a posarse encima, pero que debió de asustar a la misma muerte porque, de repente, movió una mano y luego otra, y todo el mundo dando gritos, y anda que si la llegan a enterrar. (p.169)

The use of 'tremendismo' has been seen in earlier works of Castillo-Puche. In *Como ovejas al matadero*, for example, the madness of Alfredo is described in such morbid detail which could only be classified as 'tremendista'. Other examples are found in the description of the Padre Espiritual in *Sin camino* and in the practice of the lashes in the same novel. As Castillo-Puche has already been considered to be within the category of existential writing in Spain, it is also worth noting that 'tremendismo' has often been associated with Spanish existentialism. This relationship is examined by Oscar Barrero with particular reference to the use of 'tremendismo' by Castillo-Puche as well as by other Spanish writers such as Enrique Nácher, José Suárez Carreño and Darío Fernández Flórez.[13] Yet although there are many examples of the author's tendency towards 'tremendismo' in previous novels there has never been so much evidence of black humour as there is in *El libro de las visiones y las apariciones*. In 1985, the author confessed to an inclination towards crudity in his writing but denied the charge that his novels were thus too serious and negative:

> Mi expresión novelesca se mueve siempre entre el esperpento y el lirismo; pero además, y esto no me lo puede negar nadie, está el humor.[14]

The humour found in *El libro de las visiones y las apariciones* often provides relief from the coarseness and realism of the events, but in *Como ovejas al matadero* the use of humour is limited in comparison. This would suggest that humour must be linked to the notion of liberation from the narrator's point of view and not the protagonist's. In other words, the aims of both novels are different and the severity of Alfredo's plight could not be presented humorously since this is one of the central points of the novel. The humour found in *El libro de las visiones y las apariciones* is the black humour of the adult narrator and, in any case, very rarely refers to Pepico but rather to other minor characters in the novel. And since the central theme of this novel is liberation, and most of all the narrator's personal liberation from the oppressions of his past, then the liberal use of humour fits in with this purpose, and is not out of place.

Castillo-Puche admits that often the reader will be surprised by either a humorous interruption or conclusion during the account of some tragedy but he claims that the introduction of humour is not planned in advance:

> Y otra cosa que me viene dada es el encontronazo, a veces inesperado con el humor, un humor que, como hemos dicho antes, deriva hacia el esperpento y que a veces puede ser macabro incluso, pero que tampoco es calculado por mí, sino que se me impone por el giro chusco o chocante que puede tener la existencia aun en sus momentos más agónicos, pirueta que acaso viene a salvarme y a salvar a mis lectores de la ridícula seriedad que se pretende imponer a la vida.[15]

The author is saying, then, that humour is, on the one hand, a reflection of the bizarre nature of human existence and, on the other, a source of liberation for himself and the reader from the often sordid details of human experience. Although, in this novel, there are often humorous descriptions of the disasters and the state of the injured or deceased, it seems that the comic emphasis lies with people's reactions to disaster:

> Y el pobre Serafín parecía un cangrejo rebozado en chocolate,

algo que se estiraba inverosímilmente a pesar de que estaba
hinchado, y decían que el olor que despedía tiraba para atrás a los
de la Cruz Roja y ahora, cuando se pasa por aquellas pozas aún
seguirá diciendo la gente 'aquí fue lo del Serafín'. (p.59)

More surprising is the example found in *Como ovejas al matadero*, which offers
little relief during the disturbing episode of Alfredo's breakdown, where once
again the humour is found in human reaction:

> - Pero ¿qué pasa? ¿Pasa algo? - pregunta el del bar. El doctor ha
> hecho el gesto de atornillarse la sien y ha contestado, simple y
> sencillamente:
> - Se fue al traste la chaveta - respondió.
> - No será el obispo ...
> - Que va: un pobre muchacho que ya veremos quién lo arregla.[16]

In the trilogy, humour seems to form a natural part of the open-ended
style which claims to reflect the illogical and unexpected nature of human
existence. Humour is as much a part of life as tragedy and one cannot be isolated
from the other since this would not be a true reflection of human experience. For
the author, humour is seen as something which can be shared with everyone and
through which many can find a source of relief and liberation, and thus it could
also be an indication that the adult narrator is overcoming his problems:

> El humor para mí no sólo es diversión, sino liberación, la
> unicaactitud coherente y verdaderamente seria que podemos
> adoptar, aunque esto parezca una paradoja; el signo más
> convincente de salud vital y de solidaridad humana.[17]

Although humour represents liberation, it cannot properly be regarded as a
symbol in the novel since it is more an attitude of the writer than a particular
character or element. Of the characters and features which represent liberation,
the two most important are Pepico's mother and water, the latter being associated

both with the north of the present and also liberation from Hécula in the past. Among the lesser elements of liberation are his sister Rosa, who was remembered for her courage and caring attitude; Rafael and Agustina, identified with the happiness found in the country; and also Susto, the pet cat, with whom Pepico established a reliable friendship. However, in the dry and torrid environment of Hécula, it is water which appears as a powerful symbol of contrast expressing the desire for liberation.

1. Water

As a symbol of liberation, water appears in the novel as a source of refuge and comfort amid the misery and bleakness of life in Hécula. When the situation in Hécula seems utterly overpowering, then the narrator promptly reminds himself that he is now safe in the refreshing surroundings of the north. However, the narrator does not always return to the present to find liberation since in Hécula itself lay an undiscovered supply of water which was soon to appear. While recalling the oppressive atmosphere of the 'auroros' in the village the narrator suddenly seeks refuge in this unknown source of salvation:

> Y aquel pisar que aterrorizaba en lo profundo de las losas de los portales y todo el pueblo dormido estaba viviendo y estaba muriendo entre mantas y sábanas la muerte del día siguiente, pero había una consolación y era que por debajo del pueblo corría un río, que algún día aparecería, cuando el pueblo quizá estuviera a punto de morirse de sed. (p.139)

This is a reflection of the adult narrator who understands that water is so important to an area such as Hécula and who infers here a collective sense of liberation. But while the adult narrator indulges in the wealth of water and greenery in the north, young Pepico was desperate to find the sea, no matter how inaccessible this was to him:

> Y siempre se hablaba del mar, se seguía hablando del mar, pero
> el mar cada vez estaba más lejos, y con lo feliz que yo era
> saliendo simplemente a las eras, o a las balsas, o a los pozos, o a
> las fuentes o a las ermitas que había en las afueras, la obsesión del
> mar y de un viaje se hizo para mí una fiebre constante. (p.112)

There is a sense both in the views of the adult narrator and the young protagonist that the sea or water was not just liberation from heat and desert landscape but that everything oppressive would be consumed by its immensity. Even before witnessing the sea for himself, Pepico was under the impression that everything about the sea was powerful:

> Ay, el mar, como el lomo de un colosal caballo encabritado
> cuando se le acercan los tábanos, el mar fiero y pacífico a la vez,
> el mar que decían que también a veces era liso como el camisón
> azul de una muchacha, el mar como una enorme pupila ciega,
> como un vientre redondo a punto de parir, la anchura azul y
> blanca. (p.129)

But the mighty power of the sea itself is never more in evidence than at the end of the novel when Pepico and his mother come face to face with it on the beach and Pepico's fears appeared to be extinguished:

> Y quién sabe si todo aquello sucio y revuelto en el oleaje no eran
> los pedazos rotos de las almas y los monstruos que rondaron tus
> pesadillas, el demonio al fin vencido y ahogado en la inmensidad
> del mar grande y fuerte. (p.205)

All through the novel Pepico displays the anxious yearning for the sea and often the sea is associated with distance and travel. In the same way travel represents a means of liberation though not as powerful as the sea. At times of oppression in Hécula, especially from Cirilo and Cayetano, we see Pepico longing to be as far away as possible from their control:

> Me arrancaba de la realidad siniestra de los tíos mandones para transportarme al ensueño de un viaje, cuanto más lejos mejor, pero sobre todo un viaje que tenía al fondo las quietas y deformes rocas donde termina el mar, acaso donde comienza el mar. (p.121)

To escape from Hécula was an incredible sensation of liberation and travel seemed like a kind of beginning of a new life, leaving behind all the terror identified with Hécula:

> Era la primera vez que iba en tren y lo que quería era ver pasar los campos y dejar atrás el pueblo, y esto me daba un desasosiego especial que era como renacer, como surgir hacia lo nuevo entre esperanza y sorpresa. (p.202)

This sense of new birth is even more vigorously reflected in the image of the sea where the old existence is not only left behind but is actually destroyed:

> Inmensidad indefinible, siempre cambiante y siempre la misma, como un comienzo de vida nueva y para siempre donde los demonios de mi infancia, todos los demonios, los interiores y los externos, se iban a meter y ahogar en la corriente rumorosa y batida. (p.204)

It was the sea, above all, that represented the greatest hope for transformation. A young child whose mind was darkened by the experience of death was, for the first time, discovering life and this life seemed to transform him both mentally and physically:

> Y creí ver que mis ojos tenían una luminosidad nueva, contraria a la muerte, por primera vez despreocupada de la muerte, como si el solo presentimiento del mar fuera vida, sensación de vida. (p.200)

In a world with very little evidence of water and vegetation, young Pepico naturally finds himself entranced by the sight of the vastness of the sea. It could be supposed that water is a logical element of liberation in such a landscape where the scarcity of cultivation could reflect the lack of vitality among the people of Hécula. Indeed, the novel is littered with comparisons between the 'heculanos' and the arid geography of Hécula and it is natural that water or the sea should be considered both as a means of transforming desert into pasture and also death into life. The healing power of the sea is further enhanced by the presence of Pepico's mother who always appears at moments of peace and happiness in the novel.

2. The Mother

From the beginning of the novel, the mother is frequently presented as a source of consolation and protection. Surrounded by the oppression of his uncles and his nightmares, Pepico always finds liberation and peace through his mother, who seems to be the only person able to dispel his fears. In the same way that Hécula becomes part of the narrator in the negative sense, his mother is also inseparable from him since she forms an essential part of the narrator's childhood and this union is further demonstrated in the similar use of the second person:

> Y en ese momento, antes que el enemigo de tu alma, apareciste tú, madre querida, ahuyentando una vez más al bicho acechante de mis angustias interiores y para colmo me traías una jícara de chocolate con torrijas y un libro nuevo de Julio Verne, qué maravilla. (pp.19-20)

Like water, the mother also represents life when everything else seems fatalistic and she alone seems certain to bring joy and hope to Pepico in the midst of seriousness and gloom. We saw earlier how Cayetano and Cirilo had imposed a form of Christianity which suggested that even happiness was a dangerous condition since it could lead to temptation. If happiness was contrary to sound religion in the eyes of his uncles, then it is no surprise that the mother's attitude is at odds with her brothers. The narrator recalls that often Cirilo and Cayetano tried to suppress his mother's happiness:

> Y repito que entre tío Cirilo y tío Cayetano, rodaba mi madre como una pelotita menuda de colores, porque ella tenía un alma alegre, pero no la dejaban manifestarse, nunca la dejaron hacer más que servir a los otros. (p.113)

Clearly the mother is just as much a victim of oppression as Pepico was and the narrator remembers how she often suffered in silence under the authority of Cirilo and Cayetano. However, what is admirable about the mother is that there were occasions when she demonstrated the courage to stand up against their tyranny. This is seen particularly during the positively presented period of peace and convalescence in the country-house which was interrupted by Cirilo:

> Cuando se encontró con mi madre se portó tan irracional, insultándola y todo, porque yo según él estaba abandonado, y tanto fue que mi madre, cosa tan rara en ella, le llamó tirano y salvaje, cosa que nunca yo le había oído, y le dijo que yo era hijo suyo y que estaba harta de abusos y de imposiciones, y tuvo que ser tío Cirilo el que se fue dulcificando. (pp.193-194)

But despite these rare displays of defiance, the integrity of the mother was never strong enough to resist the oppression of Cirilo and Cayetano and the narrator remembers how his mother's strength was gradually weakened by the continuous abuse by her brothers:

> Tío Cirilo no sólo mandaba en su casa sino en la nuestra, implacable, con todo lo menudo que era cerraba los puños implorando al cielo o daba puñetazos en las mesas o en las paredes y lo peor era que en todas partes veía al demonio y a las brujas, y mi madre en pos de la armonía, aunque a veces se plantaba y cómo me gustaba esto a mí, ella tan sana y vivaracha, se iba convirtiendo en un cadáver viviente, blancura de carne de

nieve. (p.27)

It appears that the narrator is not just stressing the difference in character between his mother and his uncles but that in this novel the clash is more between two contrasting interpretations of Christianity. In this sense, the humility and gentleness of the mother is contrasted with the obsessions and strict observances of Cirilo. The narrator presents their case to the reader and questions the desirability or attractiveness of two different attitudes towards religious standards. In other words, the narrator appears to be implying that the way an individual treats other people is far more important than the fulfilment of religious duties. Similarly, the practical care shown by the mother has left a much greater impression on the narrator than the dictates of Cirilo. It is this love shown by the mother which leads the narrator to exalt her above all the rest:

> Más arriba que mi padre todavía tiene que estar mi madre, porque sufrió y amó más que todos ellos juntos, y si el cura Cayetano se ha salvado y si tío Cirilo ha tenido perdón o será por mi madre o por mi tía Teresa. (p.97)

Compared to the reputation that Cirilo and Cayetano had in Hécula, the mother was nothing more than a simple housewife and servant. Her role was never dramatic like her brothers, but it was precisely in this insignificance and humility where the narrator saw a more accurate reflection of God:

> Cada vez el rojo ardiente de sus mejillas la consumía más y estaba más delgada y daba crujir de dientes verla vivir hacia dentro, que ella sí sabía lo que tenía que ser Dios y no ellos, aunque tío Cayetano tuviera fama de santo y tío Cirilo fuera algo así como el campeón de la rectitud y la austeridad. (p.28)

Although Pepico was not aware of it so much at the time, the adult narrator rejects the God presented by Cirilo and Cayetano and equally the God of the 'heculanos' in general. In the same way in *Sin camino* when Enrique

renounces the concept of God as presented in the seminary, so the narrator fails
to recognise God in the very individuals who are supposed to represent God. Just
as Enrique desired to associate God with the world and with life, so the adult
narrator recognises God more in the vivacity of his mother than in the fatalism
of his uncles and of Hécula. It is this contrast in the presentation of God which
makes Pepico realise that a person's behaviour is a reflection of the presence or
absence of God within that person. That is to say, that God is not some distant
reality but that he is indeed to be found in people's hearts:

> Y yo desde aquel día comencé a pensar que lo invisible, fuera
> Dios o el demonio, era algo de dentro de nosotros mismos, y cada
> uno llevaba dentro su dios o su demonio, según, algo interior.
> (p.195)

This could be interpreted as meaning that Cirilo and Cayetano, by their actions,
showed that God was not present in their lives. Consequently, as the narrator
associates any notion of God with the virtues of kindness and humility, then
individuals who behave in this way are the truly religious people:

> Porque no era posible que el Dios de mi madre y el de tío Cirilo
> fueran el mismo, o el de Agustina, tan pacífica, sonriendo siempre
> o cantando, con sonrisa de boba, pero daba paz y daba alegría
> verla. (p.195)

If the narrator's understanding is to be accepted, then God exists in those
who suffer and in those who care about other people. In addition, according to the
narrator, God will be found more in insignificant and ordinary individuals than
in those who claim religious privilege and authority. However, the narrator does
not convert this understanding into the conclusive issue of the novel. For, just as
in *Como ovejas al matadero*, when the virtues of Ramiro and Fulgencio were
overshadowed by the failures of Alfredo, so the goodness of the mother gives
way to the victory of oppression. This God of peace and gentleness seems to be

defeated by the God of fear and control who governed the souls of Cirilo and Cayetano:

> Por qué te has escondido Dios de los niños y de las madres, por qué hacía falta el terror, que había que estar siempre obedeciendo a alguien, que te mandaba acostar, que te mandaba rezar, que te prohibía mirarte a ti mismo porque era pecado. (p.206)

The narrator shows his despair on reflection that injustice has always seemed to prevail in the end. Yet despite the power of liberation in the symbols of the mother and water, the novel concludes with the familiar sense of defeat. The narrator clearly does not understand why God should abandon him, and not act in the face of injustice to protect the humble and innocent from unlawful oppression. Both the young Pepico and the adult narrator seem unable to share in the mother's privilege of close union with God. Instead of inner peace and integrity which were evidently present in the mother, Pepico was left frustrated by his efforts to find God:

> Una voz de lo alto tenía que venir y no acababa de llegar, y tú te impacientabas y quizás por ello, en castigo, no podía ser más que un castigo, te llegaban en cambio aquellos ruidos, murmullos, risas siniestras, que te hacían taparte la cabeza con las sábanas... (pp.206-207)

The pessimism is further illustrated when, while sitting happily on the beach, Pepico becomes aware of the frailty and mortality of his mother:

> Y tú entonces, mirándola, tuviste el presentimiento de algo irremediable y fatal, de que la pálida frente, como de mármol, pudiera hacerse tierra. (p.205)

This sudden awareness of the proximity of the mother's death is significant in that it marks the beginning of Pepico's transition from childhood to early adulthood.

As one of the major sources of happiness will soon disappear, so too, Pepico realises, will any sense of childhood hope or wonder.

NOTES

1. Pablo Corbalán, "Los demonios de J. L. Castillo-Puche." *Informaciones* 10 de noviembre de 1977.

2. Marcelino Peñuelas, "Denuncia y protesta. *El libro de las visiones y las apariciones* de J. L. Castillo-Puche." *Revista Iberoamericana* 47 (1981), 248.

3. Peñuelas, 248.

4. Jiménez Madrid, 101.

5. *Con la muerte al hombro* (Yecla: Ateneo Literario, 1995), 54.

6. *Con la muerte al hombro*, 59-60.

7. See Gemma Roberts, *Temas existenciales en la novela española de postguerra*, 2nd. ed. (Madrid: Gredos, 1978), 240-246: "La muerte como alienación: la visión de un pueblo."

8. *Temas existenciales*, 242.

9. *Temas existenciales*, 242-243.

10. José Blanco Amor, "Nuevos rumbos de la novela española." *La Nación* Buenos Aires, 26 de febrero de 1978.

11. Blanco Amor.

12. There are two distinctly humorous sections concerned with tragedy and disaster from 55-60 and 166-169.

13. See Barrero Pérez, 263-282: "Existencialismo y tremendismo."

14. American lecture (1985).

15. American lecture (1985).

16. *Como ovejas al matadero*, 246.

17. American lecture (1985).

CHAPTER 6
El amargo sabor de la retama

The second part of the trilogy could be considered a virtual continuation of the first: the adult narrator still sees Hécula from his secure haven in the north and young Pepico continues to endure the oppressive elements of Hécula. The principal difference between the two works lies in the age of the protagonist which is considered to be between six and nine years in *El libro de las visiones y las apariciones*[1] and around fourteen years in *El amargo sabor de la retama*[2]. If this is the case, then we are dealing with two distinct periods in the process of growing up where the first part is concerned with the innocence of childhood and the second part with the sense of awareness and change associated with adolescence. But just as Pepico's innocence was marred by the terrors and traumas caused by the environment of Hécula, similarly the consciousness of change during adolescence is tainted with the sense of guilt, and social awareness becomes an introduction to a world of corruption and injustice.

The first part of the trilogy was set mainly during the time of childhood in Hécula interposed with brief interludes in the Basque country of the present. In the same way, the time in the second novel is divided principally between the period of Pepico's adolescence and that of the older adult narrator. However, it becomes clear in the second novel that the narrator is not limited purely to the memory of one period in the past, that of adolescence, but that experiences belonging to other periods of his life are also introduced at different stages. If the narrator's experiences are linked to historical events, then the period of adolescence in Hécula when don Jerónimo controlled the water supply belongs to the immediate pre-Civil War period since the death of don Jerónimo coincides with the outbreak of hostilities shortly after the election victory of the Popular Front in February 1936. Although most of the events in the novel are concentrated around that period, the narrator also recalls other childhood experiences as well as memories of wartime and the post-war period. At the beginning of the novel, for example, the narrator recalls a recent visit to his native town just two months before the time of writing. This recent visit revives in turn memories of early childhood:

> Y andando por el pueblo de mi niñez algo como una sarna interior me picaba y me desazonaba, y comenzaban a resucitar los fantasmas de mis noches febriles, aquellos aparecidos que se descolgaban de las casas cerradas. (p.11)

After some brief references to the visions and apparitions of the first novel, the narrator returns to the details of his recent visit, describing the post-war situation in the neighbouring town of Turena:

> Y todavía había muchas camisas azules y pistolas que no sacaban billete para viajar, mientras los otros se pudrían en los campos de concentración y en las cárceles, y ya se habían reparado o estaban entre andamios algunas iglesias incendiadas. (p.38)

There are moments also when the narrator cannot avoid returning to the scene of the Civil War itself recalling the confusion and chaos which prevailed especially in the southern half of the peninsula:

> Que allí se dieron el gran festín, sangre y agua bendita a partes iguales, montones de plomo y de calaveras, variadas tapias de ejecución y vestimentas de insospechados carnavales, muertes a lo conejo y pleamar de brazos en alto, puños cerrados bajo la tierra y campanas repicando a *Te Deum*. (p.27)

It is evident from the way in which these memories of different periods in the past intrude upon the basic plot of the novel that the narrator is not concerned with a strict chronological order of events. Furthermore, it is not unusual at times to find the narrator wondering why he has deviated from the story as in the case of the above interruption concerning the Civil War:

> Y para qué enredarme con la guerra, tú estabas hablando de aquel soponcio absurdo que te dio en el portal de un banco de Turena. (p.27)

Yet although the narrator often seems apologetic for confusing the reader, the disorderly fashion in which the novel is presented is seen by Gemma Roberts as an intentional ploy of the narrator to give the reader a true representation of the unpredictability of the function of memory:

> Castillo-Puche demuestra dominar a plenitud el modo de estructurar una narración basada en las fluctuaciones esquivas de la memoria. Sabe que recordar es divagar, situar hechos y circunstancias en el desorden propio en que funciona la memoria.[3]

I would not agree that this was merely a talent or ploy used by the author but rather that this could also be a manifestation of the nature of the author. In the same article on this second part of the trilogy, Gemma Roberts suggests also that the free-flowing narrative, which is evident throughout the entire trilogy, contributes further towards an accurate reflection of the indeterminate nature of the memory:

> El tono repetitivo, la ausencia casi total de punto final y la trayectoria a saltos responden, con toda naturalidad, a la dificultad de revivir el pasado en su integridad y reflejan el fenómeno evanescente del olvido.[4]

So Gemma Roberts affirms that chronological order is not only impossible in a novel of this sort which is based on memory but that neither is it important since she feels the aim of the structure is to reveal precisely the confusion and instability of the narrator-protagonist:

> El autor sabe que ninguna rememoración puede presentarse en un riguroso orden cronológico, y por eso procede con los requeridos desquiciamientos espacio-temporales que revelan la ineludible fragmentación de la memoria, y la tensión que él establece entre el querer recordar y el querer olvidar. La estructura novelística se convierte de esta manera en la clave para apreciar la conmoción psíquica del protagonista de *El amargo sabor de la retama.*[5]

Five years after this article was written, Castillo-Puche himself echoed the view that the technique of the trilogy was adapted to suit the function of memory:

> En mi *Trilogía de la liberación* fue muy celebrada la técnica a base de retrocesos, reiteraciones, vacilaciones o borbotones, porque se trataba de plasmar el funcionamiento de la memoria.[6]

However, the main reason offered by the author for the irrelevance of chronological order is to do with the principal aim of the novel itself. Since the author regards the novel as an exploration of the mystery and complexity of the workings and development of the human mind, he feels that this purpose will not be advanced by any logical structure:

> Queda claro que este intento totalizador de conocimiento del hombre a base de hechos y sueños, de vivencias y experiencias, de pesadillas y recuerdos, de recreaciones y fantasmas, no puede hacerse con una técnica lineal. Por eso la técnica lineal en la novela está desfasada y en desuso.[7]

But despite the claims of the author and the observations of Gemma Roberts, the basic chronological order of the trilogy from childhood to early manhood remains intact. While the memory of the adult narrator is free to move from one period to another, young Pepico's experiences in each novel conform to the period depicted by the novel. In other words, the chaos proceeds from the adult narrator since he is the one responsible for the deviations and interruptions to the story. Judging from the author's comments, we must presume that these interruptions are intentional in the development of the novel as a whole but the title of each novel of the trilogy is related mainly to the age and particular period of the narrator's life. Similarly, this second novel of the trilogy concerns the adolescence of the narrator and this is evident from the amount of pages dedicated to that period including the sections about don Jerónimo, the storm in Ciriza, the spell in Murcia and later in the country-house in El Algarrobo.

In this second novel there is a sense of continuity in the theme of oppression, as Cirilo and Cayetano are still in control, and the atmosphere of the first novel continues to prevail in Hécula at least in the earlier parts of the novel. Similarly, Pepico continues to find refuge in the mother, and water is still very much an element of salvation. However, we can observe some alteration to the symbols of oppression and liberation in *El amargo sabor de la retama*. There is a shift, for instance, in the emphasis within Hécula when political conflict takes over from religious fanaticism and the theme of water is linked with the notions of social injustice and the thirst of the 'heculanos' not only for water but for justice. In both cases, the conflict and injustice are realities experienced by the adolescent Pepico along with other elements associated with that particular period such as sexual awareness and the notions about a religious vocation. However, there are other factors involved in this novel which do not strictly belong to the precise period such as, for example, the experiences of later parts of the war and the post-war period along with experiences in the seminary which obviously appear at a later stage in Pepico's life and of which young Pepico would have no knowledge. In this way, we can distinguish between the perspectives of Pepico and the adult narrator and determine which elements confront Pepico at the time and where the voice and feelings of the adult narrator are introduced. Of course, these distinctions are not always so simple, as often the feelings of the adolescent are confused with those of the adult, as can be seen during the storm sequence:

> Tía Matilde estaba loca, eso estaba claro, pero no siempre estaba
> claro para ti en aquellos momentos, que cada vez que estallaban
> los relámpagos, tú mismo pensabas que aquella tormenta era un
> castigo, un castigo para todos nosotros. (p.102)

But whether the feelings expressed are those of the adult narrator or of the adolescent, what becomes evident as the novel unfolds is that this is a work about feelings. That is to say, everything which takes place in the novel and all the views expressed can be related to how the protagonist reacts emotionally to the surrounding environment. Each character and element tends to provoke either positive or negative sensations in the narrator/protagonist and the entire novel can be interpreted on the basis of four very different and powerful feelings. The first and most significant feeling to be conveyed to the reader will undoubtedly be the sense of thirst. The others are guilt, happiness and depression.

A. THIRST

Important though it was in the first part of the trilogy, we find that water has an even more powerful role in this second part. While retaining its capacity to provide refreshment and liberation water assumes much wider implications since its presence is relevant in all the different locations of the novel. In Hécula, water is associated with the notions of abuse and social injustice while in Ciriza the deluge is connected with the sense of guilt and divine chastisement. It is mainly in Murcia and in the country-house at El Algarrobo where water reaffirms its role of symbol of salvation and purification. But quite apart from the individual and social relevance of water, there is also an attack on the injustice of nature itself which has deprived certain regions of the earth of such an essential element. In this way, the symbolism of water, as Gemma Roberts indicates, assumes also a metaphysical dimension:

> Más allá de lo psicológico y lo social, el motivo del agua en esta novela comporta un acento metafísico al comunicar el desequilibrio cósmico, el inquietante absurdo de la injusticia y desigualdad de la Naturaleza, el capricho incomprensible de la Creación que ha privado a algunas tierras de sustancia tan esencial a la vida.[8]

This unequal distribution of water has already been suggested in the difference between the arid conditions of Hécula and the humid environment of the Basque country. And as water is so fundamental to life and growth, it is of no surprise that the absence of water in Hécula is reflected in the behaviour and attitude of the people. Since this precious element is so scarce in Hécula, so the people must live in constant thirst. The injustice of nature is accentuated by the social injustice of Hécula which permits the exploitation of the thirst of an entire town by one wealthy owner of the water supply, namely, don Jerónimo.

The collective thirst of the 'heculanos' is reflected in the individual thirst of the narrator who, from the very beginning of the novel, cannot separate the memory of Hécula from the sensation of thirst:

> Lo primero que me acude a la memoria son sus secas torrenteras, sequedades de árbol fosilizado con las raíces al aire, y todo ello, aun ahora mismo, me produce sed, sed aun en el recuerdo, una sed hiriente como si se me hubiera taponado un estropajo en la garganta. (p.9)

The notion of thirst is particularly relevant to the adult narrator as he recalls how he himself was employed by don Jerónimo to operate the water supply. In other words, the protagonist was directly involved in the unfair exploitation of the townspeople who had to jostle and queue for their ration of water. He remembers how the intense thirst of Hécula was reflected in the faces of the women:

> Que parecía que fueran a apagar un fuego que estuviera

consumiendo la ciudad entera, y ciertamente en la ermita, que
estaba al lado de la fuente, la palabra que más podía escuchar
san Cayetano, era la de agua, agua, agua para una garganta
colectiva ya reseca, para todas las gargantas agrietadas por la
sed. (p.60)

Although many of the townspeople were aware of the injustice of the situation,
no one dared to confront don Jerónimo, and thus one person was able to control
the whole water supply and every ration had to be paid for. The only one to voice
her opinion was the boy's mother who complained to Cirilo and Cayetano that the
water should belong to everybody, and not be held exclusively by anyone. But the
failure of don Jerónimo to heed the growing resentment and unrest among the
people was to lead eventually to his tragic end:

En fin, que el agua, la sed del pueblo, llevaría a don Jerónimo al
pozo seco de la cal, que es verdaderamente un final triste para un
hombre que tenía al pueblo en un puño, sujeto por la sed, por esa
cosa tan clara que es el agua. (p.65)

So the primary notion of thirst originates not only from the landscape of
Hécula, but from the 'heculanos' themselves who were physically deprived of
water. This experience of thirst and injustice belongs to the adolescent period of
Pepico, yet the physical sensation still remains with the narrator. It is the adult
narrator, in retrospect, who realises how unfair the situation was in Hécula with
don Jerónimo holding so much power that the entire municipal authority seemed
to be under his control. Just like the previously mentioned attack on nature and
the unjust distribution of water, the narrator also attacks through don Jerónimo
the unequal distribution of power and wealth:

Que aquí, en la vida, unos han venido a mandar y a gozar un poco,
aunque sea gozar contando las perras, una a una, pero los demás
a jorobarnos de la mejor manera posible. (p.71)

In this way, it could be said that don Jerónimo is yet another symbol of oppression and, judging by the description of him in the novel, he plainly manifests all the trademarks of a typical Spanish 'cacique'. The description offered by Gerald Brenan of the privileges and power of the Spanish 'cacique' seem to conform with that given by the narrator in the novel:

> In most parts of Spain (the Basque provinces alone excepted) they were practically omnipotent. They appointed the mayors in the small towns and villages, controlled the local judges and public functionaries and through them distributed the taxation. Their fiscal principle was a simple one: to excuse themselves and their friends from paying taxes and to charge their enemies double or treble. They also usurped common lands, pastured their cattle on other people's arable and diverted their neighbours' irrigation water to their own fields. If anyone tried to stand up against them, lawsuits were brought against him and he was ruined.[9]

It is of no surprise, then, that the authority of don Jerónimo went unchallenged by the local people who had no alternative but to pay up. The adult narrator admits in the present that water is no longer administered with such unfairness, but his anger is demonstrated still in the frequent references to the fate of don Jerónimo, one of the first victims of the peasants' revolt:

> Y el primero, el amo del 'líquido elemento', que más le hubiera valido que hubiera dejado los grifos abiertos y que cada uno bebiera cuando le diera la gana. (p.74)

When the news of his death came to Pepico's family in Pinilla it was evident from the manner in which he died that this was not simply an act of retribution, but rather an example of poetic justice:

> Nos contaron con pelos y señales cómo don Jerónimo había sido echado al pozo de los tejares, y luego echaron encima cal y agua para que se quemara vivo, y también tiraron grandes piedras, porque no quisieron matarlo sino que se consumiera vivo poco a

poco, ardiendo en la sed de todo un pueblo hecha fuego justiciero
de cal viva. (p.89)

Once the revolution had started, however, the thirst for water in Hécula
was transformed into a craving for justice. After so many years of oppression and
injustice, Pepico knew that the time had finally arrived for the peasants to exact
vengeance, and the fair distribution of water was only the beginning:

> Ahora el pueblo en vez de agua pedía revolución, justicia, cabezas
> por el suelo, sangre, y estas voces revolucionarias parecían
> bañadas en cal y salitre, en odio y en hambre, que los campesinos
> habían dejado la viña, el olivo y el pasto, la almazara y la bodega,
> y andaban desparramados por el pueblo con caras afiladas por los
> muchos años de sed y de necesidad, y sobre todo de sed de
> justicia. (pp.108-109)

These thoughts do not only proceed from the mind of the young protagonist, or
from the adult narrator. The powerful rhetoric and symbolism are an expression
of the author's own feelings on the issue as he expressed in his own words:

> La sed del agua no es solamente sed del agua. Hay también una
> sed de justicia y especie de venganza y una sed de libertad en el
> pueblo.[10]

The way in which don Jerónimo is disposed of also has biblical implications as
the author implies in the same conversation:

> Es totalmente como un castigo bíblico y como una especie de
> ejemplaridad, y va a ser la ejemplaridad de que este hombre es, en
> la guerra civil, como el odio.[11]

By comparing the death of don Jerónimo to a kind of biblical punishment, the
author appears to be suggesting that his death was an example of divine justice
and that, indeed, God was supporting the rebelling peasants.

Another figure to be connected with water and thirst is undoubtedly the most significant symbol of salvation in the entire trilogy, namely, Pepico's mother. The principal reason for the association between water and the mother lies in the discovery of an underground water stream at El Algarrobo at the end of the novel. This discovery is the culmination of the adolescence of Pepico and is probably the greatest event of liberation ever experienced by the protagonist. The significance of water is underlined by the colourful descriptions used which denote the sense of salvation and transformation not only of the inhabitants but of the landscape also:

> Agua gozosa y cantarina, agua soñada y presentida para el abrazo
> con la tierra sedienta, que había de convertir 'El Algarrobo' en
> rumorosa tierra de acequias y verdores. (p.207)

It is further implied that the prosperity of Hécula in the present owes much to the mother's intuition:

> Y aquel manantial ciertamente fue el presentimiento de las
> humedades que hoy han trasformado esta tierra. (pp.39-40)

While the transformation of the arid land is important the narrator also underlines the relevance of the timing of his mother's discovery which coincides with the chaos and destruction of the political situation:

> Ella que quería librarnos del desierto, precisamente cuando en
> Hécula la revolución lo había dejado todo arrasado como una pala
> vacía a la puerta del horno y con más sed todavía de vida que de
> agua. (p.39)

It is not clear here what the term 'revolution' actually refers to but since the action coincides with the immediate aftermath of the elections of February 1936, it could be assumed that the narrator is not referring to the Civil War itself but rather to the Socialist-backed peasant revolts which took place during the spring and early summer of 1936. These revolts occurred in response to the new government's plan for the redistribution of land and took place mainly in southern and central Spain. Though landowners were subject to violence and destruction of their property, Stanley Payne points out that in these areas, at least during that period, actual murders were relatively rare:

> Though there were comparatively few political murders in the rural areas of southern and central Spain, the wave of anarchy, regularized only to the extent that the revolutionaries were actually beginning to take over local authority in some areas, had the rural middle classes in a state of absolute panic.[12]

However, it seems more likely that the narrator is referring to the situation just after the military uprising when the previous restraints had been removed by the official outbreak of hostilities. As Paul Preston comments in his book *The Spanish Civil War 1936-39*, the situation in the southern rural areas of the country was particularly horrific:

> In the rural districts, the local *braceros*, fervent supporters of the Republic, were usually able to overpower small Civil Guard garrisons. Cruel reprisals were then often taken, both against the landowners not rich enough to have removed themselves to the safety of Seville or the south of France, and against the priests who had legitimized the tyranny of the *caciques* and *latifundistas*.[13]

Judging from these descriptions of the historical situation, the death of don Jerónimo seems to have been inevitable and the flight of Pepico's family, which had so many links with the clergy, appears quite logical under the circumstances.

It is interesting to note how the symbolism of thirst has shifted from the original physical need of water to the eventual thirst for social justice and then, in the midst of such death and violence, to the further dimension of the thirst for life. It is this thirst for life which still plagues the adult narrator as he contemplates how the green pastures of the north had at least satisfied his initial thirst for water:

> Aquí sí que hay agua, a veces demasiada agua, a veces al principio yo creía que me iba a volver rana, pero ahora los días pasan monótonos, iguales, en la indiferencia de los verdes, las neblinas y las lluvias, sedante catarata de casitas en la erupción de los verdes precipitados. (p.43)

While the physical sensation of thirst had been eased by the narrator's escape to the north, it was the spiritual or psychological drought that still remained. The psychological thirst is caused by the effects of his miserable childhood in Hécula at the hands of Cirilo and Cayetano and it would seem that this thirst is the most difficult to satisfy. On the train journey from Hécula to Madrid, the adult narrator contemplates this dilemma as he views the passing landscape. As in many other instances in the novel, the narrator compares his own situation to some detail of the world around him:

> Todavía sentía la sequedad de los años mozos e igual que los solitarios arbolillos yo no había tenido garganta para cantar sino solamente noches de delirio en aquella cambra de cal y tinieblas. (p.49)

An interesting comparison can also be made here in the use of the term 'cantar' since there are references in other parts of the novel to the singing sound of the water, 'agua gozosa y cantarina', as we have already seen, and 'las voces cantarinas' of the people of Murcia. Both Murcia and the water are presented very positively in the novel and both are associated with the notion of singing which is probably why the narrator connects the thirst with the inability to sing. On seeing his own drought reflected in the surrounding landscape of la Mancha the narrator searches in vain for some evidence of water:

> Y mirando el desierto de la Mancha pensaba en una fuente o en un
> río cercano, y no aparecía nada para mis labios de sediento
> perpetuo. (p.49)

It is as if his whole life has been a desert existence ever since his appetite for life

had been crushed from his early childhood by the limitations imposed by his

uncles and by the oppressive presence of death:

> El inmenso campo en rastrojos era como el símbolo de mi vida,
> un sueño de fuente prohibida, una fiebre delirante con los labios
> resecos, la pesadilla del luto sobre mis piernas y mis brazos, un
> andar cansino como de fierecilla cohibida por los palos y los
> gritos. (p.49)

We can see how the narrator is transforming the image of water, the fundamental

element of life, from the physical necessity of Hécula to the symbolic purification

and liberation from the desert of his existence. In this way, the thirst for water is

just as real and desperate as the thirst of the people of Hécula for social justice as

well as the thirst of the narrator for life and meaning. The sense of thirst, then, is

fundamental to the understanding of the experiences of Pepico and the ultimate

condition of the narrator, and perhaps, according to Javier Del Amo in his article

on the novel, to the understanding of the author himself:

> El manantial de agua ... es tanto el símbolo de la sed milenaria del
> pueblo heculano como la de las criaturas que aparecen en el libro
> - la sed de la existencia - y, en definitiva, la ineludible sed del
> autor, sed de la que nos participa, vibrante y dolorosamente.[14]

The theme of water, however, cannot be dealt with fully without

considering its links with the notion of guilt. This connection is never more

poignant than at the end of the novel, just after the discovery of the well. Joy

turns to guilt as the family's conscience is stirred by the envious glances of the 'heculanos' and a reminder of the inscription above the well of don Jerónimo:

> Que nos miraban como si por el hecho de haber encontrado agua
> fuéramos culpables, o éramos nosotros quienes nos sentíamos
> culpables, y acaso era el recuerdo de don Jerónimo lo que nos
> hacía más culpables, y hacía más culpables las miradas, y no
> bastaba con ofrecernos y ofrecer el agua, que 'el agua es de
> todos'. (pp.208-209)

Just as the memory of Hécula creates the sensation of thirst in the narrator at the beginning of the novel, so the novel ends with the images of drought and desolation:

> Aquella Hécula de la sed ha quedado para siempre en el alma de
> tu paisaje y en el paisaje de tu alma, y tu alma sigue teniendo sed,
> una extraña e interminable sed. (P.209)

Since water and thirst are inevitably identified with the figure of don Jerónimo, so Pepico's association with this person must involve a certain degree of guilt. However, Pepico's sense of guilt is not confined to isolated episodes but is, in fact, related to most of the experiences of his adolescence.

B. GUILT

It was noted earlier in the novel *Sin camino* how every calamity and disaster, no matter how great, was associated with the protagonist's fear of divine vengeance or chastisement. For Enrique, anything that went wrong was interpreted as a punishment for some misdemeanour and the most eccentric example was shown during the episode of the great fire in Santander. The eccentricity lay in the fact that Enrique was identifying the disaster of Santander with his individual misconduct with the prostitute and the subsequent behaviour displayed by Enrique was a reflection of a very profound and unhealthy guilt complex. Similarly in this novel both the outbreak of hostilities at the start of the Civil War and the ferocious thunderstorm in Ciriza are also interpreted, especially by the young protagonist, as the inevitable divine retribution and punishment of sin. If these disasters are to be related in this way, then it must be assumed that sins have been committed either by the protagonist himself or by his family or by other individuals either in Hécula or in the area as a whole. Sometimes the guilt is attributed to an individual, either the protagonist or another character in the novel, and in other instances, the sense of guilt is more collective.

As don Jerónimo is a major symbol of injustice a lot of the blame is attributed to him. One of the elements associated with the exploitation of the people and the abuse of the water supply is the metal box that was used to collect the payments for the water, and this metal box is also associated with the notions of guilt and injustice. However, the metal box is not just related to don Jerónimo, it becomes also for Pepico a significant symbol of guilt as he recalls his part in the unjust administration of the water supply:

> La caja de hierro que yo llevaba sobre mi conciencia, todo el peso que había sentido en mis manos pequeñas de aquella caja que tantos males había traído al final. (p.142)

There is a sense that Pepico knew that it was wrong for him to be associated in this way with such an individual who could exploit the poverty of the peasants, but it seems that it was the fate of don Jerónimo that finally brought the message home:

> Yo mismo me consideraba cada vez más culpable por haber cargado con aquella caja, que yo creo que recibí también una buena lección, porque desde entonces aprendí que no hay que estar al lado de los poderosos que venden a los pobres lo que es de Dios y debe ser de todos, pero quizás lo había aprendido demasiado tarde. (p.145)

The narrator is evidently establishing a link between the sense of guilt and the relationship with don Jerónimo and there follows a discourse between the adult narrator and the young protagonist as to the validity of the feeling of guilt. In the first place, Pepico begins to suspect a connection between his employment with don Jerónimo and the flight of his family:

> A veces pensaba si no sería por mí, por haber servido a don Jerónimo en el grifo y por haber llevado aquella caja negra de hierro, por lo que estábamos huyendo. (p.145)

Pepico also wonders if the family's present predicament has anything to do with the money collected by the Church:

> ¿Si sería también por el cepillo de San Cayetano por lo que íbamos huyendo? ¿Es que había alguna relación entre la caja negra de don Jerónimo y el cepillo que pasábamos en la misa de domingo en San Cayetano? (p.145)

But both of these connections are analysed and rejected by the adult narrator. In the first place, the adult narrator recalls that he often never charged the customers when don Jerónimo was absent and also the people knew that none of the profits went to Pepico. In the second place, it was wrong to imagine that the people were in any way forced to contribute to the upkeep of the chapel:

> No había ninguna relación ni tampoco parecido, ni podía haberlo, porque la limosna para San Cayetano era voluntaria, y se daba lo que se quería y eso no era poner precio a la devoción, y el que no quería no daba. (p.145)

There is a clear distinction here between the mind of the young protagonist and the more mature mind of the adult narrator. While young Pepico's thoughts are filled with fear and guilt, the adult narrator now sees a lot of this worry as

irrelevant and illogical. On the evidence of this, it appears that with the exception
of the guilt attached to the vocation, the sense of guilt in the novel is experienced
more by young Pepico than by the adult narrator. Furthermore, the guilt can be
identified with three main features in the novel, namely, the political conflict, or
the revolution, as the narrator refers to it; sexuality; and the religious vocation.

1. The Revolution

The episode covering Pepico's experience of the revolution sees his family
fleeing from Hécula to Pinilla and Ciriza, and then to Murcia. However, it is their
accommodation in Ciriza with a wealthy acquaintance which provides the sense
of fear and guilt when a ferocious storm is accompanied by the ranting and raving
of his deranged aunt Matilde. While the whole family are obviously affected by
the severe atmospheric conditions, it is an opportunity for Matilde to relate the
situation to the manifestation of God's anger and the fulfilment of apocalyptic
omens:

> Tía Matilde comenzó casi a delirar y decía que el cielo se abriría
> de un momento a otro con gran estruendo y después, como abejas
> de un panal, descenderían los ángeles de la cólera divina y no
> dejarían piedra sobre piedra. (pp.92-93)

The frantic remarks of Matilde and the prayerful movements of Cayetano and
Cirilo begin to impress upon the boy the feelings of being trapped in a deadly
situation:

> Y tú pensaste, recuérdalo bien, que efectivamente estábamos
> atrapados, toda la familia, sin saber por qué ni con qué objeto, y
> empezaste a pensar si no sería el fin, un fin merecido, inevitable,
> puesto que éramos una familia de bufones siniestros, payasos de
> la muerte. (p.107)

Following the line of thought of young Pepico, the reader can begin to detect a gradual change in the boy's attitude which increases in tension and fear as the storm worsens and gives more credence to the warnings of Matilde. The predicament in Ciriza makes Pepico begin to question the reasons for being there at all and as the boy begins to question his own values very seriously the collective sense of guilt which Matilde is insinuating is gradually reduced by Pepico to that of his own family who alone seemed responsible for the distressful predicament:

> ¿Quién nos había conducido allí sino nosotros mismos?, peregrinos del miedo y de la locura familiar, de nosotros mismos era de quien huíamos, de nuestra pintoresca familia, la que debería sufrir un castigo ejemplar, y por eso no saldríamos más de allí. (p.107)

Pepico seems to suggest that in the same way that don Jerónimo was taught a lesson for the way he treated the people, so his own family might suffer a just punishment for all the terror and fear which they helped to promote. As the individual sense of guilt is transferred to the collective guilt of the family, the narrator also offers a new dimension to the narration by introducing a temporary period of first-person plural narrative, especially during the storm sequence when the term 'nosotros' is just as much in evidence as the 'tú' and 'yo'. This is seen when Pepico examines the possible causes for his family's plight and concludes that religion must be related to the problem:

> Pero entonces la religión, ¿era algo malo, o era algo tan bueno que había que merecerlo sufriendo intensamente, pasando miedo, mucho miedo, sufriendo persecución?, y en este caso, ¿estábamos nosotros, en aquel momento, sufriendo persecución, como los mártires de los libros? ¿o estábamos simplemente haciendo el ridículo, como tía Matilde? (p.102)

If, indeed, his family were being persecuted for their religious activity and devotion, then the situation becomes yet more confusing for Pepico, since he could not regard religious devotion as something sinful. What is more, most of the people in Hécula were involved in religious devotions, yet suddenly all these practices were considered wrong:

> ¿O es que sería pecado cuidar de san Cayetano, poner aceite, en su lamparilla, cuidar de que estuvieran almidonadas y limpias las sabanillas del altar, si san Cayetano era un santo popular en Hécula, un santo que llevaba una camisilla corta con puntillas y al Niño Jesús en brazos, y rara sería la casa que no tuviera su estampa o su imagen detrás de la puerta o encima de la tapa del amasador? (p.112)

Here is another example of the different attitudes of the young protagonist and the adult narrator. While Pepico seems confused about the reasons for the conflict and the attacks on religion, we can observe the adult narrator in the post-war period launching attacks on the atrocities committed in the name of religion. To put it another way, the young protagonist, a victim of the situation, seems to be against the unjust persecution of religion, while the mature narrator, having experienced the later events of the post-war period, is apparently protesting about the persecution of the non-religious population. From his present situation in the north, the adult narrator recalls the executions that were carried out with the Church's approval, comparing them to the senseless atrocities that are still going on in the name of religion:

> Qué ignominias se hacen en nombre de Dios y de la caridad, qué tormento para la fe y la esperanza son a veces estos intermediarios de la tiranía, yo lo estoy viendo en esta tierra, donde todavía permanecen el castigo, la persecución, la eliminación más brutal y bárbara, y naturalmente siempre con el nombre del santísimo Dios por delante, por Dios y por España. (p.23)

Comments like these are seen by Jiménez Madrid as a personal statement of the author. In earlier works of the author there are many indications of the author's criticism of the superficiality and pretentiousness involved in religious institutions, but here the attack is directed at the whole concept of Spanish Catholicism. As this novel is written in the post-Franco era, it is likely that previous restraints have all but vanished:

> Aquí cabe señalar la presencia de una condena del nacional catolicismo con una contundencia nunca tan manifiestamente expresada.[15]

In private conversation, Castillo-Puche has expressed concern about the interpretation of Catholicism in Spain while recognising that the problem lies in the Church's control over political life:

> Esto es una constante tradicional de España, que en el fermento casi constitutivo de la nación ha entrado tanto la Iglesia, y entra el catolicismo casi como la esencia misma del ser.[16]

The relationship is so close that, at times, it is difficult to distinguish Spanish nationality from Catholicism:

> No se puede ser incluso buen ciudadano o buen patriota sin ser católico.[17]

The concept of national Catholicism can be traced back to the sixteenth and seventeenth centuries when the Church was involved in all aspects of social and political life in Spain. At a time of no real political unity among the various kingdoms, the Church played a major role in keeping the nation together, as Gerald Brenan observed:

> But if the Church so affected and penetrated the State, the latter also reacted upon the Church. It was essentially a national Church. A Spanish army captured and sacked Rome and humiliated the Pope. Both Inquisition and King were often at

sharp variance with the Vatican.[18]

This unity, however, was not permanent as from the eighteenth century onwards the State had intermittently tried to distance itself from the Church. The close working alliance between them throughout most of the nineteenth century was due mainly to the Concordat of 1851 which regulated the powers and spheres of responsibility of Church and State in order to prevent conflict between them. This was no less true in Franco's time when the Church had regained much of the influence lost during the Second Republic. Yet even then the Church began to distance itself from the regime in the 1950s when, as we saw in our discussion of social justice in *Como ovejas al matadero*, the clergy began to associate more with the lower classes. After Franco's death, the Constitution of 1978 introduced more secularisation and declared once again that the State had no official religion. So although there was a definite sense of national Catholicism in the great age of the Reconquista and Empire, it must be said that the unity between Church and State since has been anything but solid.

As this novel was published in 1979 just after the new Constitution, it is possible that the author is reacting to the forty years of Franco's regime when the Church was at least "officially" recognised as being at one with the State. A few years later, Castillo-Puche gave the impression that he is not attacking the association between the Church and State but rather the traditional Spanish version of Catholicism which had always seemed so narrow and oppressive:

> El catolicismo aquí ha sido entendido de una manera muy cerrada, muy intransigente, muy feroz, totalmente despótica - yo diría que ancestral, un catolicismo muy levítico, casi heredado de la Biblia, pero no del Nuevo Testamento, sino del Viejo.[19]

Judging by previous comments by characters like Ramiro and Fulgencio in *Como ovejas al matadero* about the need for social justice and a greater solidarity between the Church and the working-class, we could assume that Castillo-Puche's political affiliation does not lie with the Right:

> Todo el mundo está colocado a la derecha que se cree en la
> posesión del Reino de Dios, y que ellos son los elegidos, y para
> ellos está hecho ya el sitio en el Reino de los Cielos. Creo que es
> una equivocación, creo que, a veces, son muy ignorantes y, sobre
> todo, son muy hipócritas y muy conservadores en el sentido de
> que les va muy bien rozar aquí la tierra un poco, y después tener
> casi garantizado el cielo, me parece que es una hipocresía
> maestra.[20]

And a similar opposition to the politics of the Right is reflected in the views of

the adult narrator in this second part of the trilogy. It is not just the activities of

the Church which come under attack but also the attitude of the Nationalist

victors who were determined to carry out vengeance on anyone associated with

the Republican side during the war, as was demonstrated during the

interrogations which took place at the numerous trials:

> Y el que había estado en el lado rojo, fatal, por fuerza tenía que
> ser un asesino, y el que había estado en los dos lados, cuidado,
> averiguación al canto, que en esta guerra ha habido muchos espías
> y traidores, y las brutalidades pasadas no tenían nada que ver con
> las que estaban pendientes y se estaban cometiendo. (p.42)

This is probably a direct reference to the executions and courts-martial

that were carried out in the immediate post-war period. Thousands of Republican

prisoners were executed at the end of the war in various parts of the country, most

noticeably in Madrid, as Paul Preston indicates:

> The British consul in Madrid reported that by June there were
> 30,000 political prisoners in the city and that twelve tribunals
> were dealing with them at breathtaking speed. In proceedings
> lasting only minutes the death penalty was invariably demanded
> and often granted. British consular sources estimated
> conservatively that 10,000 people were shot in the first five
> months after the war.[21]

But the executions continued well beyond 1939, and those Republicans fortunate enough to escape the death penalty were usually sent to labour or concentration camps where they were forced into the work of rebuilding the country:

> The hundreds of thousands of prisoners were formed into 'penal detachments' and 'labour battalions' to be used as forced labour in the construction of dams, bridges and irrigation canals. Many were hired out to private firms for work in construction and mining. Twenty thousand were employed in the construction of the Valle de los Caídos, a gigantic mausoleum for Franco and a monument to those who fell in his cause.[22]

The adult narrator is plainly critical of the post Civil War regime, however there are instances in the novel when he is horrified by the Left's behaviour, particularly their treatment of the clergy:

> Los fueron sacando de las casas y arrastrándolos en una fila escalofriante, y los llevaron hasta la cárcel, dándoles golpes y poniéndoles el pie para que se cayeran. (p.88)

This criticism of the actions of those who sided with the Left in the novel is reflected in the author's own comments when he displays disillusionment with the Spanish version of the Left:

> Las izquierdas en España tampoco son unas izquierdas muy liberales, muy generosas sino que actúan también en un odio dogmático que es la propia negación.[23]

Similar criticisms of both the Right and Left of Spanish politics have already been seen in *Como ovejas al matadero*.

Perhaps a more significant demonstration of how this work rises above the particularisation of history and politics and makes the appeal to universal values, applauded by Wayne Booth, is seen in its symbolic dimension. As well as expressing the plight of the victims of the political war, the novel seems to suggest that the protagonist was also a victim of another kind of war, a war imposed by his family:

> Porque ellos siempre han vivido interiormente en guerra, guerra
> contra el cuerpo principalmente, guerra contra la naturaleza y
> contra el espíritu, y tú eras un producto típico de esa guerra. (p.78)

By extending the notion of war to include the protagonist's education and upbringing, the narrator here suggests the symbolic significance of the Civil War. Although the Civil War with its implications of guilt and punishment is important, this internal war with the impulses of nature is much more significant with regard to feelings of personal guilt.

2. Sexuality

The theme of sexuality is significant in a novel which deals with the period of adolescence and its related problems. As Pepico associated the storm with notions of guilt and punishment, so his sexual feelings are related to a similar sense of sinfulness and remorse. This can be seen in the first physical encounter with the opposite sex in the wine cellar of 'tía Juana'. It was this episode with Santi which was to provide release for his curiosity and which was also to signal the end of his childhood days:

> Y un alacrán me había mordido en el cuerpo que ardía y no era
> veneno lo que paladeaban mis labios que ella había mordido sino
> un gusto áspero pero dulce a la vez en lo más recóndito y
> conforme mi inocencia se diluía entre torpes esfuerzos como cae
> la miel sobre un trozo de pan del campo. (p.35)

The idea of crossing the frontier between innocence and knowledge which has been seen already in the novel *Sin camino* is also associated with Pepico's first sexual experience. As Enrique realised that he had entered a different world when he became acquainted with the prostitute, so the meeting with Santi was the turning-point for the adolescent Pepico. That episode in the wine-cellar, then, remains significant in the memory of the narrator and Santi will forever be associated with the narrator's introduction to the sensual world.

The subsequent anguish of the protagonist is displayed through the fear of being discovered by tía Juana and, ultimately, by his uncles and his mother. In addition, the immediate sense of guilt is shown in the way Pepico contemplates the difficulty and shame of confessing such an incident to a priest. It seems inevitable that the initial release of the sexual urge would bring confusion and remorse to a young adolescent but, as Gemma Roberts indicates, the negative attitude and backward education in Hécula would have done little to help the adolescent to understand his sexuality and so alleviate the sense of guilt:

> La práctica sexual significa, sobre todo, para el protagonista, una insoportable y angustiante conciencia del pecado, originado por las recalcitrantes enseñanzas del clero heculano, que hace imposible la vida sana y libre, no sólo del cuerpo, sino del espíritu.[24]

Examples of this repressive education are seen in the attitude of Cirilo and Cayetano towards women and sexual attraction. As already seen in the first part, sex was considered dangerous and a threat to the boy's well-being, and consequently these dangers had to be avoided. As a result, the inevitable signs of his sexuality were to be suppressed and any sense of pleasure would be considered sinful.

Gemma Roberts has suggested that it is the Catholic clergy in Hécula who are responsible for promoting this attitude towards sex, but in the novel it is mainly Cirilo, the married uncle, who is particularly obsessed with the dangers of sex. However, it is clearly an attitude of the Church, but how Catholicism came to adopt such an attitude needs to be examined further.

It is certainly true to say that the concepts of chastity and celibacy have always played an important part in the history of the Christian Church, but the Scriptural basis for celibacy and purity is not as manifest as later Catholic doctrines appear to assume. In the Gospels there is no commandment enforcing celibacy, although those who aspire to it are usually assumed to be doing something worthwhile:

> There are eunuchs born that way from their mother's womb, there are eunuchs made so by man and there are eunuchs who have made themselves that way for the sake of the kingdom of heaven. Let anyone accept this who can.
>
> Matthew 19.12

In his first letter to the Corinthians, St Paul urges his fellow Christians to seek and encourage chastity but this is by no means to be made obligatory, as he says:

> This is a suggestion, not a rule.
>
> I Corinthians 7.6

St Paul recognises that celibacy may be a worthy state, but admits it is not always practical in view of our nature as sexual beings:

> There is something I want to add for the sake of widows and those who are not married: it is a good thing for them to stay as they are, like me, but if they cannot control the sexual urges, they should get married, since it is better to be married than to be tortured.
>
> I Corinthians 7.8-9

It is clear, then, that there is nothing sinful about sexuality and St Paul is merely upholding the virtues of celibacy for those who are able so that they would not be tied to the responsibilities which married life entails. Furthermore, he stresses that celibacy is not a divine recommendation, but a state that he personally has found to be beneficial:

> About remaining celibate, I have no directions from the Lord but give my own opinion as one who, by the Lord's mercy, has stayed faithful. Well then, I believe that in these present times of stress this is right: that it is good for a man to stay as he is. If you are tied to a wife, do not look for freedom; if you are free of a wife, then do not look for one. But if you marry, it is no sin, and it is not a sin for a young girl to get married.
>
> I Corinthians 7.25-28

Celibacy remained a voluntary ideal during the first three hundred years of Christianity until it was made obligatory for clerics by Canon Law at the Council of Elvira, as stated in canon thirty-three:

> We decree that all bishops, priests, and deacons, and all clerics engaged in the ministry are forbidden entirely to live with their wives and to beget children: whoever shall do so shall be deposed from the clerical dignity.[25]

While the Eastern Orthodox Church eventually forbade the marriage of bishops, priests and deacons were permitted to marry before ordination, but not after, and the same rule still applies. In the Catholic Church, however, the ideals of priestly celibacy were reinforced by the decrees of Pope Gregory the Seventh in the eleventh century, but were later opposed by Calvin and the Protestant Reformers. At the same time, the Council of Trent (1545 to 1563) upheld the laws on celibacy while stressing, nevertheless, that it was an ecclesiastical rule and not a divine decree. Since that time until the present, the Catholic Church's stance has remained unchanged with regard to celibacy and the freedom it purports to allow the ministers to perform their duties, and this position is confirmed by the teachings of the Second Vatican Council:

> Through virginity or celibacy observed for the sake of the

kingdom of heaven, priests are consecrated to Christ in a new and distinguished way. They more easily hold fast to Him with undivided heart. They more freely devote themselves to Him and through Him to the service of God and men. They more readily minister to His kingdom and to the work of heavenly regeneration, and thus become more apt to exercise paternity in Christ, and do so to a greater extent.[26]

In all this it should be remembered that it is possible to be both a Christian and be married, and that these recommendations are solely for those involved in the ministry.

What seems to be so unfair in the novel is that Pepico is being prepared and disciplined for a celibate way of life which is not totally of his own choosing, but which rather is being imposed upon him by his uncles and his family. While most of the children in Hécula are likely to have experienced a similar kind of education, Pepico may have been singled out for a particularly oppressive version due to his close connection with the clergy and the Church. But if so much guilt can be linked to sexuality, then the religious vocation must also be associated with guilt since the fundamental condition of the vocation was the renunciation of sex for a greater ideal.

3. The Vocation

As Cirilo and Cayetano were anxious to nurture this ideal of the religious vocation, they went to every extreme to make sure that this ideal remained intact. Cirilo, in particular, became so obsessed with the idea of protecting his nephew from corruption that often the only solution was to isolate the child from any possible danger, as the narrator recalls:

Que nada valía la pena en comparación con ser un gran misionero, pero sobre todo un santo, y yo fui alejado del parque los sábados y los domingos, y ni podía montar en los caballitos ni en las

> barcas, porque en esos sitios había niños muy golfos. (p.67)

We can observe how the adult narrator tends to refer, at times, to the years before adolescence when seeking out the source of his later problems. As the adult narrator's memory moved from childhood to adolescence in the first novel so here we see that the narrator's mind wanders backwards to childhood once more in order to emphasise a particular aspect of his early life. In this case, it seems that young Pepico was unaware of the abnormality of his isolation from the other children and it is the adult narrator who now sees how cruel and unhealthy the attitude of Cirilo was:

> Y ahora te das cuenta de que no has jugado ni has salido de paseo como otros niños, que no has tenido infancia ni nada parecido, aunque simplemente fuera ir a San Francisco a comprar cascarujas, regaliz, piñones o turrón, que siempre tenías que ir de la mano de tío Cirilo. (p.68)

In the first place, then, this preparation for the priesthood imposed by Cirilo filled Pepico with the notion of being different from the other children and also with a sense of loneliness.

It was the repressive upbringing to which Pepico was subject which made so desperate his thirst for life, to which we referred earlier. Although both Cirilo and Cayetano saw their restrictions and control as something positive and beneficial, the fact that the adult narrator continues to suffer as a result shows how damaging certain individuals' interpretation of religion can be:

> Y como estaba destinado al altar y como todo el pueblo ya esperaba el seminario o el noviciado para mí ni podía ir a un cine, ni podía fijarme en una muchacha, ni ver un periódico o una revista, condenado a ir detrás de él, todos los días, a la ermita de San Cayetano, rezando las estaciones del Vía Crucis, o eschuchando vidas de santos. (p.49)

In this instance, the restrictions imposed on early childhood are seen to continue into adolescence where the isolation seems all the more oppressive bearing in mind the increase in the variety of distractions as the child gets older. But the narrator now sees no justification for such continuous control:

> Todo tortura del alma, agarrotamiento de los pulsos de la vida, inmolación en la cual mi madre sufría tanto como yo. (p.49)

The longer this kind of repressive education continued the more lasting the effects became, and the enforced sense of isolation and being different from the rest was to remain with the narrator in adult life after the failure of his vocation:

> Y entonces vino la ruptura total con todo, el caos y la soledad entre los hombres, y ya nada te importó, solitario como un faro entre rocas y espumas. (p.78)

The adult narrator remembers how vulnerable he was to the suggestions and persuasions of the people around him, letting others decide his future for him:

> Tú tenías que ser, por lo visto, un gran apóstol, un misionero o si acaso obispo, que a eso se te había destinado desde siempre, a eso conducían las súplicas de tu madre acabada, a eso conducían los consejos y orientaciones de los Jesuitas que se metieron por medio, y tú eras el único que no tenía voz ni voto en la decisión. (p.77)

Considering how he never had the right to decide his own future as well as the chance to make friends with other children and adopt a healthy attitude to life, the narrator now seems unable to comprehend how the religious vocation could be considered fruitful:

> Ellos seguían queriendo hacer de ti un santo, qué santo desde la negación, la humillación y el desarraigo, qué santo podías ser a costa de la identidad, de la paz y de la aniquilación, un santo de

palo únicamente. (p.78)

When we take into account the feelings both of the adolescent Pepico and the adult narrator we find that the sense of guilt is related to the religious vocation in three ways. In the first place, the guilt is seen in the young protagonist when he finds his natural impulses and desires are seen as sinful, in the eyes of his superiors. Since the religious vocation meant the annihilation of these urges so Pepico would feel unworthy every time he failed to control his human nature. The second sense of guilt is felt more by the adult narrator concerning the sincerity of his vocation. What was supposed to be a call from God is now seen by the narrator as nothing more than escape from a world that seemed too difficult to cope with. In this way, the narrator appears to be admitting that his vocation was completely false and thus confesses his guilt:

> Y teniendo como excusa para ti mismo la presión familiar, tuviste
> que enrolarte en aquella quimera de vocación, en el fondo una
> fuga, otra fuga más en tu vida, una cobardía para no enfrentarte
> con la realidad que tu juventud y tu sexo te imponían, un fraude
> total, porque aquella entrega hipócrita y falsa al ciego misterio
> había de ser frustrada y vana, vana para todos. (pp.77-78)

The third sense of guilt is related to a later stage in the protagonist's life when the time came for him to abandon the seminary. Although the adult narrator admits that his vocation was not genuine, there is still a sense of guilt attached to the notion of failure:

> A partir de entonces todo fue muy duro, lo tengo que reconocer,
> y qué triste y lamentable se te hizo, por ejemplo, volver al pueblo,
> fracasada la vocación, cuando en Hécula todavía corría un río de
> sangre sobre el páramo. (p.82)

The guilt associated with his failure to become a priest is further illustrated in the view that some kind of curse attends those who abandon the religious life. The curse appears to exist in the context of the ex-seminarian being unable to assume a fresh identity. In other words, the narrator feels that the religious life marks a person for life and can be detected even in the physical appearance:

> No sé por qué, y es que eso del sacerdocio deja marca en las personas, que yo con el tiempo llegaría a distinguirlos entre miles, y en el autobús, en una cafetería, en la fábrica, en el frente, donde fuera, yo decía 'ése es un ex-seminarista' y acertaba, que no lo podemos negar y se nos conoce a la legua, y a lo mejor tienen razón los que dicen que pesa una maldición sobre cualquier exclaustrado. (p.138)

Despite the falseness of his vocation, the narrator remembers that at least the seminary had offered a kind of identity and security. But when the decision was made to abandon the seminary, there was a tremendous sense of emptiness and loss:

> Y te saliste del seminario vacío como un saco que se pone a andar por la calle, como una cáscara de hombre, y comenzó el engaño mayor, la mayor mentira de todas, la de ser un hombre más, un hombre libre que busca trabajo, que busca amigos, que busca ... (pp.81-82)

Accompanying this sense of displacement is a curious sense of freedom. The decision to leave, because it is personal, signals the beginning of a different life that could be of his own making. But when one's life has been controlled so much by others, the determination to start deciding for oneself will inevitably be a difficult process. In one sense it is easy to remain in a secure establishment under false pretences but it is more difficult to be sincere with oneself and step away from the control of the system:

> Y menos mal que tú te agarraste a tiempo a tu liberación personal, puesto que la otra, la Liberación con mayúscula, había resultado

> una farsa, tú el primer farsante, y entonces fue cuando diste el
> paso de tu propia redención, la redención con minúscula también.
> (p.82)

The liberation, then, is to do with the protagonist searching for self-fulfilment, something which he feels could not be achieved while under the control either of his relatives or the religious establishment. Thus the term 'liberation' in the title of the trilogy can be interpreted as not just referring to the adult narrator being liberated from the past but also to the protagonist's continuous desire for personal liberation. It is not just a case of the individual reacting against the mass but, almost like an echo of the attitude of Enrique in *Sin camino*, young Pepe renounces the salvation offered by the seminary in order to find his own salvation in the world. It must be noted also, however, that the difference between Enrique and Pepe in this novel is that here there is no mention of him searching for God in the world.

C. HAPPINESS

As in the first part of the trilogy, the character of the mother and the element of water are introduced in this novel to denote the sense of liberation and salvation. This is particularly the case during the discovery of the well at 'El Algarrobo' when both mother and water join together in one of the happiest moments of the narrator's life:

> Y yo creo recordar que aquella noche del agua inundando los
> bancales fue la noche de más gozo de tu vida, porque parecía que
> el agua todo lo lavaba, todo lo alegraba. (p.205)

However, we must also take into account the geographical situations in this novel since they are relevant in that they distinguish the good times from the bad. For instance, both Hécula and Ciriza in the first part of the novel are remembered for their associations with conflict, injustice and death which culminated in the massive storm which trapped the entire family. But as the family continue to escape the troubles they eventually decide to travel to Murcia and it is in Murcia where the narrator recalls experiencing one of the greatest periods of happiness:

> Y tengo que decir, ahora, desde el recuerdo, que para mí aquellos días en Murcia, aparte el nerviosismo político que lo mismo nos hacía aparecer ante nuestros propios ojos como desterrados que como conspiradores, y aparte de todo esto del visiteo de curas y gente rica, fueron días felices. (p.164)

There are various reasons for associating the Murcia region with the sense of happiness. Apart from the liberation experienced in escaping from the area of Hécula, there is a parallel between the adult narrator's present experience in the Basque country and the younger protagonist's experience in Murcia. The principal link between the two is the presence of water and with it the similar sensation of vitality and renewal:

> Porque en la huerta el agua anda cerca y anda suelta, el agua brinca de un huerto al vecino, el agua tiene su música, una música adormecedora, y aquella espuma que no era la del mar pero era una espuma que hacía presentir los frutos, donde se ve claro que el agua es la vida y que sin agua los espíritus se vuelven atormentados y fieros. (p.141)

While in the north the narrator is refreshed by the surrounding greenery of the landscape, so also he recalls the impression created by the abundance of vegetation in Murcia:

> Una región de la que siempre se hablaba como de algo entrevisto en sueños, miel colgante del melocotón o frescura del melón casi escondido en la tierra, cima prometedora de la palmera con su oro en racimo y tupido bosque del naranjal con el azahar como una joya de pureza embriagadora. (p.149)

By means of these vivid and colourful descriptions filled with imaginative comparisons, the narrator succeeds in transmitting not only the beauty of the region but, more importantly, that personal sense of wonder which has rarely been experienced before. In a similar way to the Basque region, the transformation of the countryside also signifies a different lifestyle among the local people. So in Murcia the people come across as more content and relaxed compared to the mournful and aggressive attitude of Hécula. The narrator offers another powerful description of the city of Murcia itself and continues to indulge in comparisons as he shows how both the inhabitants and the landscape contributed to the atmosphere of peace and happiness:

> Vida de modorra y también de felicidad vegetativa que se revolvía como la verde y moviente cama de los gusanos de seda, vida sedurmiente arrullada por las voces cantarinas entre el vaho soporoso de la huerta y las campanadas lentas y profundas que hundieron mis catorce años en un nirvana de ensueño y felicidad torpona. (p.165)

In real life too when Castillo-Puche travels to Murcia he is filled with a sense of wonder and admiration. Although he is well travelled and has written much about life in other countries, no description can compare with that of Murcia and its surroundings of colour and vegetation, as found in his book *Mosaico de Murcia*.[27]

The sense of renewal found in Murcia is also related to the initial signs of manhood in the young protagonist. Earlier we saw how puberty was often associated with a sense of guilt on account of the awful attitude of Hécula towards sexuality. However, the positive atmosphere of Murcia seems also to have transforming effects on the understanding of adolescence, giving new meaning to the experience of puberty and the beginnings of manhood:

> Y es que, de hecho, aquellos días murcianos habían despertado mis sentidos hasta el enervamiento y me sentía, creo que por primera vez, un hombre, y me salía a pasearme con cualquier

pretexto por las calles empedradas o asfaltadas y gozaba de mi
soledad como quien se bebe un néctar a escondidas. (p.165)

Another contributory factor towards the happiness of those days was
undoubtedly the mother who is always associated with any moments of
brightness and hope. Despite the uncertainty of the political situation, the
protagonist's mother seemed unthreatened by the dangers and made the most of
the opportunity in Murcia to create a new kind of lifestyle. The narrator
remembers even greater happiness with his mother when the two of them had left
Cirilo and Cayetano in Murcia in order to return temporarily to Hécula. In the
absence of those forces of control, the mother became a different person as she
seemed stronger and more confident:

Y los dos éramos felices y nos brotaba la alegría como cuando se
va de excursión o de jira campestre y se espera que todo sea
espontáneo. (p.170)

The special relationship between the protagonist and the mother is based
on trust and hope. During the previous storm sequence when surrounded by so
much calamity the boy turns to his mother for refuge and protection since she is
the only one in whom the boy confided. Despite the abnormality both of the
circumstances and the behaviour of her relations, the mother continued to act as
if everything was normal:

Y tu madre, por eso, se había puesto a tejer, a pesar de la
tormenta, y esto era tranquilizante para ti, y permitía pensar en un
futuro con jersey nuevo. (p.120)

This apparently indifferent and unflinching attitude in the face of chaos and
disaster is demonstrated also during the period of refuge in Murcia:

> Bendita madre, 'alegría quiere el Señor aun en lo más doloroso de
> la persecución', decía y era verdad que ella parecía no abatirse
> con nada. (p.157)

Her approach to danger was such a consolation to Pepico and further showed the

difference in faith between the simple goodness of the mother and the so-called

religious authority of Cirilo and Cayetano who displayed clear signs of worry and

fear. But the greatest achievement of the mother was undoubtedly the discovery

of water at the country-house in defiance of the opinions and pressures of her

brothers. It was fitting that the element of purification should be found by the

only person who offered hope and it was appropriate also that the mother's name

was Clara, since the purity of her soul was comparable to the clarity of water:

> Y a ti te gustaba que a tu madre la llamaran doña Clara, porque de
> verdad era clara, clara como el agua que brotaba del pozo nuevo,
> todo el mundo, al menos los que queremos, tienen el nombre que
> se merecen, y clara con la claridad del nombre tenía tu madre el
> alma, y lo había demostrado contigo, llevándote poco a poco al
> reino de la luz cuando tantas tinieblas turbias te envolvían de
> pequeño. (p.205)

It seems that the presence of the mother is symbolic along with the water

in this novel just as in the same way she appeared in the first part of the trilogy.

There were several brief references to the mother in *Sin camino* and in association

with Alfredo in *Como ovejas al matadero* where her influence on the proceedings

was significant. Judging from the author's comments in 1985, it would appear that

the figure of the mother is indispensable in all the author's novels:

> La madre ha sido un elemento, el nudo, el más importante que ha
> habido en toda mi novelística.[28]

While most of the other elements in the novels are identified with pessimism and oppression such as Hécula, his uncles, the Civil War, and death, the author claims that the mother always stands out as a symbol of hope and joy. Furthermore, she is usually present at times of danger or threat as the sole redeemer of a hopeless situation and the author claims that whenever she appears it is not only the protagonist but the whole atmosphere that appears to be transformed by her presence:

> La madre ha sido siempre el elemento feliz, dichoso. Todo que en mi novela es tétrico, ensombrecido, terrible, apesadumbrado, hosco, en el momento de aparecer la madre hay una dulcificación, el ser se enternece, la naturaleza vibra, y todo es recuerdo e invocación.[29]

What the author claims here is certainly true about the trilogy and her role in this second part is clearly defined by Castillo-Puche:

> La madre va a ser el núcleo central de esta novela.[30]

At the same time we must recognise that, although the narrator often excuses his mother's influence, both in this novel and in the concluding part, a lot of pressure concerning the religious vocation is due to the mother's ideal. This is also the case in the previous novels of *Sin camino* and *Como ovejas al matadero* where the pressure both on the character Enrique and the character Alfredo could hardly be considered beneficial. Furthermore, in both of these earlier novels, the respective mothers never really appear as symbols of redemption but rather as obstacles to the possible abandonment of the seminary. Hence the author's statements regarding the role of the mother cannot be applied to all other novels by the author while remaining more or less valid in the case of the trilogy. However, despite this redemptive power of the mother and water in this novel, and the happiness of Murcia and the country-house in La Magdalena, the bright periods are short-lived and fail to hold any dominant role in the novel. Instead, all the happiness experienced by the protagonist must finally give way to melancholy and depression.

D. DEPRESSION

Considering the abundance of negative forces in the novel, it is of no surprise to find the narrator feeling depressed about the way his life has been suffocated by external oppression. The narrator is depressed by Hécula with its people and landscape, by his religious education, by the conflict which divided an entire nation, and ultimately by the constant presence of death. The depression seems almost obsessive and inevitable as Ramón Jiménez Madrid observes when describing the novel's possibilities of entering a new period of optimism at the country home of El Algarrobo:

> Tras una primera lectura cabría hablar de un moderado contento que se advierte en la ausencia de los típicos matices despectivos. Sin embargo, una mayor atención nos advierte que lo sombrío es parte fundamental. Una escueta relación de muertos - el culto o la erótica funeraria perdura - bastaría para evitar esa primeriza sensación jocunda.[31]

Connected to this period is, of course, the death of Andresico, the water diviner, which comes on top of the death of tía Matilde at the end of the storm sequence and the death of don Jerónimo. The death of Andresico is a sudden interruption to this period of happiness and also causes some distress to the mother, but, more significantly, it revives the fascination of the locals with the subject of death:

> Porque en seguida empezaron a hablar de muertos, de otros muertos, de todos los muertos vecinos y conocidos, porque en Hécula se habla mucho de los muertos, y las muertes son las noticias más fruentes. (p.190)

Even before the death of Andresico, the sight of Hécula in the distance only served to remind the narrator of the negative elements at work in the town:

> Un pueblo donde siempre se luchaba por algo y siempre se
> hablaba del espíritu pero sin inteligencia, con rutina y odio,
> siempre pensando en la muerte, siempre odiando la vida, donde
> todo heroísmo consistía en exacerbar lo siniestro, matando la
> sencilla alegría de cada amanecer. (pp.172-173)

Earlier the death of don Jerónimo was symbolic of the hatred and vengeance of the peasants. Similarly, the death of Matilde seemed to be the inevitable outcome for a character so clearly identified with notions of fear, retribution and death:

> Sus signos eran signos que podían muy bien descifrarse como
> símbolos de la muerte y de lo divino, la guadaña de la muerte, la
> cruz encima del féretro, el momento en que la caja entra en el
> nicho, cosas todas en las que yo no podía dejar de pensar al
> mirarla, porque había en sus gestos y en su mímica resonancias de
> ultratumba. (pp.116-117)

For Pepico, the mysterious actions of his aunt seemed to conform so much to the extreme atmospheric conditions that his young mind began to feel that both were essentially related. The boy was already tormented with the experience of so many deaths that this episode only served to nurture his obsession even further. The chaotic experience also had depressing effects on Pepico's family, which compounded its effect on him:

> Estábamos todos como pegajosos de sudor y tristeza, una tristeza
> que probablemente estaba en el aire, una especie de opresión y
> desconsuelo que nos envolvía impalpable, pero pesadamente,
> como un manto negro del que uno no podía zafarse y no sabíamos
> qué hacer. (p.126)

There appears to be no escape from death and depression and the timing of the death of Andresico illustrates how death will attempt to destroy any possibilities of happiness and hope. But it is the death of Pepico's mother, as we shall see in the final part of the trilogy, which has the greatest impact of all, and the thought of which even here leads the narrator to consider how short-lived every happiness in life must inevitably be. Since every period of hope is followed by disappointment and tragedy, the narrator reflects that the pain of tragedy is even more severe when preceded by a state of bliss:

> Porque ya todos los recuerdos, aun los más alegres, son dolorosos, punzantes, y cuanto más alegres más lancinantes, porque vivimos alegremente muchas veces los acontecimientos más proclives a la tragedia, aquellos que en la cumbre de la euforia insensata y la esperanza más ilusa nos están conduciendo inexorablemente a la mayor desolación. (p.172)

We can understand here the severity of the narrator's depression where any moments of joy are viewed with caution and suspicion and, because of the frequent occurrences of tragedy in his own life, the narrator sees these inevitabilities as a general rule of life. In this way, the narrator attempts to give his personal depression and pessimism a universal value that applies to every individual. In other words, he is sure he is not alone in possessing such a negative attitude as he appeals for solidarity and universal understanding of his plight:

> Que poco duran los sueños, que lo aprendiste entonces y no tienes que olvidarlo, sueños que uno desearía que pudieran continuar, pero que rara vez se consigue atar ese nudo dichoso que enlaza ideal con realidad, y si dura poco la felicidad bajo el techo del pobre, también dura poco la ilusión en la cabeza del soñador. (p.171)

Here the narrator appears to suggest that his depression and pessimism are not only based on the experience of tragedy and death but equally on the loss of the ideal. Perhaps in this sense the narrator can apply his experience to a wider audience, that is to say, that it is a universal truth that many individuals do lose their dreams and ideals as they go through life. Probably the greatest ideal of the narrator's own experience was that of becoming a priest but, as we shall see, this ideal also falls victim to reality.

However, the ideal of the priesthood remains far from being straightforward since the sincerity of the vocation is questioned by the narrator already in this novel and to a greater degree in *Conocerás el poso de la nada*. On the one hand, the vocation is regarded at times as nothing more than an escape from the world, in which case the narrator must assume personal responsibility. On the other hand, the whole idea of the seminary is blamed on his uncle Cirilo and other relatives along with the wishes of his mother, in which case the responsibility lies with others. Whoever is responsible, it is unquestionable that with the loss of the religious ideal comes a great sense of personal failure despite the irregularities and imperfections discovered in the seminary. It is the mere fact of failure itself which haunts the memory of the narrator so inclined to dwell on misfortune. The confusion around the sincerity of the vocation is complicated further by the narrator's admission to being a victim of other people and circumstances as, once again, the narrator tries to give his own experience universal validity:

> Y me pregunto también quién tiene la libertad de actuar, que yo nunca la he tenido, y ahora mismo que cualquiera puede creer que soy libre, que ni siquiera familia que me ate, yo siento que nunca hago lo que querría hacer, sino lo que me marcan las circunstancias, o los demás, ataduras invisibles de las que uno no puede liberarse. (p.199)

This lack of freedom is associated with the notion of passivity, an attitude which was already seen in the novel *Sin camino* and which reappears in the final part of the trilogy. In *Sin camino* there is enough evidence to suggest that Enrique's predicament was in the hands of other people and external circumstances but, at least, he eventually made a personal decision and exercised his own free will. The next part of the trilogy is full of examples of this indecision and passivity as the narrator tries to come to terms with the sincerity of his vocation.

In this second novel, as well as the circumstances and events surrounding the adolescent period of Pepico, we have examined the perspective of an older and more mature narrator who has often viewed things differently from his younger self. Because of the narrative style, it is possible at times to witness two versions of the same event with the impressions of the younger boy interchanging with the reactions of the adult narrator. An example of this was seen especially during the storm when the terror of Pepico was in sharp contrast with the calmness and understanding of the adult. The adult narrator is also in the privileged position of introducing other experiences from both earlier and later parts of his life. Most of these experiences are related in some way to the period of adolescence and are often just as painful as the experiences of Pepico. If this second novel is to be considered part of the narrator's journey of self-exploration, then these painful experiences must be revealed and thus exorcised from the narrator's memory. It is only in this sense that the novel can be included in a process of liberation, a process that must allow the memory to flow, regardless of time or space. Memories of Hécula and the revolution both produced sensations of thirst and guilt and these feelings were shared by the adult narrator and his younger self. Other memories brought sensations of joy and depression but it seems that most of the joy remained in the memory and was something experienced solely by Pepico. The depression, on the other hand, seems peculiar to the adult narrator who attributes the cause of this both to his early experiences and to his own personal sense of failure.

NOTES

1.   According to the author in private conversation (1985).

2.   See p.165 of the novel.

3.   Gemma Roberts, "Con el pasado al hombro: *El amargo sabor de la retama de José Luis Castillo-Puche.*" *Cuadernos Hispanoamericanos* 361-362 (1980), 374.

4.   "Con el pasado al hombro." 374.

5.   "Con el pasado al hombro." 374.

6.   American lecture (1985).

7.   American lecture (1985).

8.   "Con el pasado al hombro." 376.

9.   Brenan, 7.

10.   Conversations (1985).

11.   Conversations (1985).

12.   Payne, 191.

13.   Paul Preston, *The Spanish Civil War* (London: Weidenfeld & Nicolson, 1986), 54.

14.   Javier Del Amo, "La amarga necesidad de la sed." *El País* 22 de agosto de 1979, 18.

15.   Jiménez Madrid, 113.

16.   Conversations (1985).

17.   Conversations (1985).

18.   Brenan, 39.

19.   Conversations (1985).

20.   Conversations (1985).

21.   Preston, 167.

22.   Preston, 170.

23.   Conversations (1985).

24. "Con el pasado al hombro." 373.

25. J.D. Douglas, *The New International Dictionary of the Christian Church* (Exeter: Paternoster Press, 1974), 206.

26. The Documents of Vatican II, 565-566.

27. See J.L. Castillo-Puche, *Mosaico de Murcia* (Madrid: CajaMurcia Obra Cultural, 1995), 16-28

28. Conversations (1985).

29. Conversations (1985).

30. Conversations (1985).

31. Jiménez Madrid, 111.

CHAPTER 7
Conocerás el poso de la nada

In this final part of the trilogy the narrator, still writing in the Basque country, moves on from the period of adolescence to introduce the reader to the experiences of early manhood, another crucial stage of Pepico's life. The story is mainly concentrated on the events surrounding this period but, as in the case in the earlier parts of the trilogy, the plot is frequently interrupted by the older narrator who is distracted either by some later experience, like his relationship with Herminia, or by personal reflection and emotional response. Of course the earlier part of the novel is mostly dedicated to the protagonist's experience in the seminary and this experience does not follow chronologically from the events of *El amargo sabor de la retama*.

We have seen in the second part of the trilogy that the age of the protagonist was fourteen years and that the historical setting was some months after the election victory of the Frente Popular in February 1936. This same election victory is included once more in *Conocerás el poso de la nada* and is said to occur while the protagonist is present in the seminary:

> Vivíamos secuestrados, como presos, dentro de aquellas paredes de espesor inquisitorial, y todo lo de fuera era pecado para nosotros, aunque también había pecado y pecados dentro, vaya si los había, pero no queríamos o no sabíamos verlos, y en aquellos días, recuerda, con el triunfo del Frente Popular, todo eran novenarios sobre la Gran Promesa y la Gran Confianza, la gente estaba asustada y en nuestros paseos todo eran recomendaciones. (p.57)

Following on from this we have the outbreak of hostilities later in the year and it seems that the Civil War made it necessary for young Pepe to abandon the seminary along with most of the other students since the seminary was in Murcia and Murcia was in the Republican zone:

> Y fue verdad que la llamada a filas se produjo pero tú, recuerda, te hiciste el loco porque esperabas que la guerra se terminaría de un momento a otro, que eso era lo que se decía todos los días, y tú te pusiste a trabajar en unos laboratorios, porque del seminario hubo que salir, que aquello fue la desbandada. (p.104)

This obligatory abandonment of seminary life in the novel conforms to the real-life experiences of Castillo-Puche who entered the seminary of San Fulgencio in Murcia in 1929. After seven years of attendance at the seminary, his studies were brought to a halt by the outbreak of war:

> Al estallar la guerra civil, en 1936, tiene que abandonar el seminario y trabaja en un laboratorio privado para atender a los gastos de su familia, en Murcia.[1]

In real life, the author was seventeen years old at the start of the Civil War whereas in *El amargo sabor de la retama* we are told that the protagonist was a fourteen year old adolescent when conflict broke out and his family sought refuge in Murcia. The chronological order is altered further in *Conocerás el poso de la nada* when the protagonist is considered old enough to be recruited by the military:

> Yo me pasaba los días con mi bata blanca metido entre orines y esputos y mierdas, y tratando de conseguir un certificado para pasar por servicios auxiliares de segundo grupo, y efectivamente fui pasando de miedos y de peligros, porque estaba visto que a partir de los diecisiete años te declaran apto para morir y para matar pero yo seguía en mi condición de camuflado. (pp.104-105)

It would appear from these variations in the age of the protagonist that the author is not concerned with an accurate and logical account of his early life which complies with the historical order of events at the time. There is no doubt that the Civil War is significant and this is shown by its continuous presence in almost two thirds of the trilogy. Similarly, it could be said that the vocation is essential to the adult narrator's self-exploration and understanding. In other words, the experience in the seminary cannot be omitted from the quest for identity and neither could it be left out of a novel which culminates in the death of Pepe's mother, since, as we shall see, the mother becomes the driving force behind the religious vocation. It is important, therefore, that the seminary experience and the abandonment of the vocation should be included in this final part of the trilogy along with the disappearance of the mother.

However, although the mother is understood as the inspiration behind the vocation, she cannot be viewed as the sole reason for the inclusion of the seminary experience. It would seem that the seminary forms an essential part of the protagonist's early life because it also represents a time of hope and idealism. But these positive aspects of seminary life are often overshadowed in the novel by the notions of routine and deceit among the seminarians. There is also the sense of falsehood and deception connected with Pepe's vocation which is sometimes related to his mother:

> Sólo el miedo, la indecisión y el recuerdo de tu madre que reverenciaba tu camino, tu futuro, tu santidad plenamente admitida y venerada, te pudieron retener y obligar en el sacrificio, el engaño y la aniquilación. (p.39)

This novel is full of self-accusation concerning the sincerity of Pepe's vocation; just as in *El amargo sabor de la retama* the narrator similarly regards his desire to become a priest as fraudulent. There are further examples of this acknowledgement of insincerity in the novel *Sin camino* where the protagonist Enrique is often aware of his inability to succeed. And if we go back to the 1983 preface of *Sin camino* we can find evidence of a similar recognition in the author's own life:

> Pero yo no tardaría en confesarme a mí mismo la falsedad de mi vocación, que acaso había sido solamente un invento personal para sublimar mi soledad o quién sabe si una fuga inconsciente de la lucha por la existencia para la que no estaba ciertamente preparado.[2]

So all of this seems to indicate that neither in the novels we have studied nor in the author's own life was there any shred of evidence to support the sincerity of the religious vocation. However, if we examine the novels a little closer we will discover that the accusation of falsehood cannot be entirely justified.

In *Sin camino* the heroic ideal of the priesthood had been with Enrique since childhood. The use of terms such as 'sueño', 'anhelo' and 'ideal' would suggest that the priesthood was something desirable. Also in *Como ovejas al matadero* there is plenty of evidence of the personal desire to become a priest in all four main characters. Only in *El amargo sabor de la retama* is there no mention whatsoever of any heroism or sincerity surrounding the religious ideal. Instead, the adult narrator seems excessively critical of his apparent deceitfulness and fully recognises the falsehood of his own vocation. But if the narrator was so convinced of this, then why did he believe that some kind of curse fell upon those who had abandoned the religious vocation? Surely to believe in a curse would be to suggest a punishment for doing something wrong. But if his vocation was such a fake, then why should he have to suffer for being honest about it?:

> No es que yo me saliera a tontas y a locas, que lo pensé muy bien, y entonces, ¿qué tendría que hacer? ¿seguir con las sotanas a pesar de todo, sin saber bien lo que quería o no quería? (p.139)

It seems from this that the narrator is not so certain about the wisdom of his decision to abandon the seminary and, although the narrator would like to think that the whole issue has been justly concluded, there is still a suggestion that the question of his vocation remains unsolved:

> Que allí dentro uno debe estar seguro de lo que quiere y de dónde está y para qué está, y otra cosa es engañar y engañarnos bobamente, que no hay manera de simular lo que no se es, y del mismo modo, lo que uno es imprime una huella no sólo en el carácter de la persona sino hasta en su físico, pero yo no estoy arrepentido, porque nunca tampoco estuve seguro de nada. (p.139)

This uncertainty still continues in *Conocerás el poso de la nada* where the adult narrator launches further attacks upon his own inadequacy and yet manages, at the same time, to suggest the possibility that the priesthood was also a personal ideal. It is for this reason that so much space is given to the problem of the religious vocation in this novel to show that it was an ideal both encouraged by his uncles and his mother and, as we shall now see, desired by the narrator himself.

A. THE IDEAL

One of the principal motives behind the religious vocation of Enrique in *Sin camino* was the need to discover a more authentic way of life. There is a sense in *Conocerás el poso de la nada* that the young protagonist was also in search of a higher form of existence:

> Necesitabas una experiencia más mística, más entregada, necesitabas una huida total, romper todos los lazos con el mundo, creías que así escaparías a los miedos, a las cobardías, pero todo estaba dentro de ti, no hubo huida posible, allí menos que en ninguna parte, allí todo fue peor, allí comenzó el verdadero fraude. (pp.88-89).

The adult narrator now recognises that fear and escape were also fundamental reasons for entering the seminary while recalling, at the same time, how he was attracted to the noble ideals of Christianity with its concern for mercy and social justice. Although the narrator seems still aware of the sincerity of these ideals, he now confesses the reasons for being unable to pursue these ideals:

> Eras un ser demasiado sensible, acaso enfermo de terrores y de sueños que sentía de una manera apasionada y trémula el choque de la belleza, el amor y el misterio de la vida, y aunque me había sentido en cierto modo atraído por el riesgo de dar a mi vida entera un carácter de mística sublimación, al final tendría que ser barrido como escoria de un volcán. (p.24)

While the notion of sacrifice appeals to Pepico the narrator knows that it was others who had impressed this notion upon him and so attempted to persuade him that he was different from his brothers Manolo and Pascual whose vocations had failed:

> Tú no podías ser como tus hermanos, que también habían ido por delante al seminario pero se volvieron como habían ido, en medio del gran escándalo y del gran disgusto de la familia, pero tú no, tú eras seguramente el elegido, todo hacía creer que eras el elegido, desde el principio, alguien tenía que sacrificarse por todos, y ese eras tú. (p.17)

With the pressure and preparation all around him, the narrator realises how difficult it would have been to back out of his commitment. The effects of such hopes and expectancies of Pepico's family and relations are emphasised by the sudden introduction of direct speech into the narrative:

> Pero él sí, 'este sí que lo hará', 'este será feliz y nos hará felices a todos', 'nos salvará a todos', no hay otra salvación que la del cielo, 'este ha acertado', y era como una herencia impuesta. (p.17)

The use of direct speech to describe the pressure upon Pepico offers the reader the sensation of directly experiencing the atmosphere and the same technique is applied when the boy is being counselled by his uncle Cirilo:

> Y tío Cirilo seguía con su retahíla, 'cuando un día te veamos en el púlpito de la Iglesia Nueva, predicando, y como habrás estudiado tanto, nos tendrás a todos con la boca abierta y tu madre, mi hermanica, verá que yo tenía razón, porque yo no quiero más que tu bien'. (p.23)

There is the suggestion here that Cirilo more than anyone else was responsible for promoting the ideal of the vocation, but the adult narrator is plainly indicating that there is a very thin line between encouragement to pursue an ideal on the one hand and deciding for someone the path he should choose on the other. In this sense, the narrator now realises that his uncle went well beyond the exercise of simple encouragement:

> Que hoy pienso que aquellas manos fueron para mí las más férreas ataduras que un niño puede soportar. (p.23)

The fact that the adult narrator is now aware of all the external pressure to pursue his vocation does not diminish the sincerity of the young protagonist's desire to dedicate his life in a special way. In the first part of the trilogy we saw how Cirilo had always tried to separate Pepico from the other children and from any bad influences in the village and now we see the results of such an attitude. Young Pepico not only felt isolated from other people but also had the sensation of being different, as was illustrated during the bus journey to the seminary:

> Allí en aquel autocar, separado, marginado de todos, apartado de las gentes, acaso acababas de ser apartado incluso de tu familia y de tu pueblo, sí, como un apestado, como un elegido, no lo niegues, te sentías elegido, predestinado. (p.31)

But for the young boy it was not just a matter of being different, for example, from the other passengers on the bus, but along with this came a sense of superiority over the rest:

> Y tú los sentías de otra especie, de otra raza, de otro mundo, te sentías ajeno, dentro de ti bullía el vértigo de lo inefable, de lo celestial. (p.32)

It is also at this point when we witness the protagonist's declaration of the independence of his own vocation. While the other passengers were commenting on the unfairness of his predicament, Pepico reacted by asserting his own self-determination:

> Estaban equivocados, yo sabía más de lo que creían, yo marchaba convencido, no iba empujado por nadie ni por nada, 'voy porque quiero'. (p.32)

There is a distinction, however, between the convictions of young Pepico and the later hesitant attitude of the narrator:

> 'No sabéis nada de nada', no sabéis que yo he elegido un camino, o el camino me ha elegido a mí, otra vez los elegidos, pero qué otra cosa podía pensar entonces. (p.33)

The adult narrator appears to be recognising the existence of a personal ideal but now admits that this ideal has long disappeared. It would seem also that the intended audience of this novel should also be convinced of the futility of this ideal since the narrator is apparently apologetic for even having such an ideal. However, this attitude could also be related to the narrator's guilt tendency. In other words, since the narrator is seen constantly attacking and criticising himself either for his actions or his inability to act, it is not surprising that he should also show remorse for ever having considered the possibility of the priesthood. But to recognise now the vanity of such an ideal does not invalidate the fact that the ideal was once treasured.

We cannot really discuss the notion of the religious ideal without considering the powerful influence of the protagonist's mother. From the very beginning of the novel it is evident that the ideal of the priesthood was also linked to the fulfilment of the mother's dream of having a priest in the family and this is illustrated when the decision was finally made for Pepico to enter the seminary:

> Cumplido el sueño de su vida, el sueño de tu destino, 'será sacerdote', y su rostro se iluminaba, y te lo pedía y te lo había pedido con lágrimas en los ojos, y no era necesario porque no se lo hubieras negado nunca, no se lo podías negar, no se lo negarías por nada del mundo. (pp.16-17)

Later in the novel when the protagonist's ideas began to change and the ideal was becoming less of a possibility it was the fear of disappointing his mother that made Pepico endure the lifestyle from which he was becoming more and more alienated. In a sense, this is the moment when young Pepe's integrity is threatened for as the ideal was beginning to wane, it was only his mother's dreams which sustained his continued presence in the seminary:

> Aunque sentía que por mi madre yo haría milagros, si había que hacerlos, sobre todo, y el primero el milagro de hacerme sacerdote, que sería un milagro si llegaba a cantar misa, y tanto, como que nunca llegó ese día, y menos mal que ella no pudo ver mi deserción. (p.93)

Since the primary reason for his abandoning the seminary was the outbreak of war, his mother still believed that her son would return to the religious life. However, the protagonist knew that with the death of his mother the religious ideal was meaningless though he would never upset his dying mother by admitting this. Instead, we find the mother insisting that her son should continue:

> Entonces me llamó y ahogándose me dijo 'ahora es cuando hacen
> falta buenos sacerdotes, hijo mío, y tú serás uno de ellos', y
> seguía 'prométemelo', 'prométemelo' y qué no le hubiera
> prometido yo en aquellos momentos. (p.126)

In almost an echo of the remarks made by the mother of Alfredo in *Como ovejas
al matadero* the narrator's mother puts emotional pressure on her son to the last.
But the young protagonist knew that it was now an impossible dream and refused
to commit himself to an oath:

> Pero yo eludía prometer nada, diciendo 'lo más importante es que
> te cuides tú' y 'nos iremos a Murcia enseguida, madre', 'nos
> iremos a Murcia', y con esto evitaba toda promesa, todo
> compromiso, porque cómo decirle todo lo que fallaba en mi
> interior, cómo confesarle que mis sueños iniciales se habían
> venido abajo. (p.126)

It is not just a matter of the protagonist feeling guilty about disappointing his
mother: young Pepe is also aware of being a failure to himself since he plainly
admits here to having a personal dream about the priesthood. It is important to
note that the mother's ideal is significant enough but we must not forget that
young Pepe also has some responsibility in the decision to enter the seminary.

It appears that the protagonist's own ideals began to wane during his time
at the seminary and, as we shall examine later, his initial enthusiasm and
commitment were gradually reduced to indifference and false conformity. After
his own ideals had vanished, there were times when young Pepe considered the
vocation to belong more to his mother than to himself:

> Acaso estaba dolida de cómo yo interpretaba y resolvía su
> vocación sacerdotal, porque mi vocación era la suya, obviamente,
> irremediablemente, y estaba claro también que yo no interpretaba
> bien su deseo, su ilusión, sus exigencias místicas. (pp.63-64).

The problem here is to what extent the mother is responsible for putting pressure on her son to become a priest since we have observed above that Pepe could not bring himself to tell his mother that his ideals had vanished. Consequently, if the mother is not aware of her son's unhappiness, then she could hardly be held responsible for encouraging him to persevere. The protagonist is clearly responsible for his lack of honesty with his mother and for pretending that his vocation remained sincere. In this way, the mother's encouragement could not be regarded as damaging to her son's interests since, as Gemma Roberts indicates, she probably thought she was doing the right thing:

> El narrador no recrimina, ni puede recriminar a su madre, por su propio fracaso. Si ella había anhelado para su hijo una vocación sacerdotal, a la cual éste no podía entregarse de corazón, no hay duda, sin embargo, que la buena mujer pensaba con sinceridad y actuaba de buena fe, víctima ella también del ambiente opresivo de la casa de sus hermanos y de los prejuicios de su sociedad.[3]

This notion of victim was seen in *El libro de las visiones y las apariciones* when the narrator considered the control exercised by Cirilo over both his mother and himself and it was only on a rare occasion when his mother showed the courage to defy him. Indeed, one of the most surprising displays of defiance by the mother was seen at the country-house at the end of the first novel when Cirilo was insisting that Pepico should be attending the seminary. The fact that the mother argued against the possibility of sending him to the seminary shows a completely different picture of the woman who later pleaded with her son to become a priest:

> Y tío Cirilo volvió a hablar del noviciado y dijo que yo ya tendría que estar allí, si no fuera por ella, que me estaba echando a perder, echando a perder la obra de Dios, la voluntad de Dios. (p.195)

The earlier disagreement in the same novel about the wisdom of introducing

Pepico to the practice of the 'auroros' also suggests that it was not the mother who was fanatically pushing her son into the religious life but rather Cirilo. In *Conocerás el poso de la nada* the narrator once again refers to this notion of victim and thus exempts his mother from any blame with regard to his failed vocation. The mother was merely a victim of his uncles' regime and Pepico, in turn, became a victim of his mother's hope:

> Su vida de víctima permanente, primero de un marido enfermo, después de los dos tíos mandones e intransigentes, y yo sabía que su única esperanza era yo, y era también mi sacerdocio, y esto me privaba de toda iniciativa, de toda resolución propia, yo era una víctima más. (p.72)

It seems that the narrator wants to accuse his uncle Cirilo more than any other person of exerting too much pressure and influence on Pepico's destiny while much of the blame is also directed at himself for his weakness and insincerity. However, there is still a hint in the novel that the mother's pressure was somewhat excessive when, as we shall later examine in the discussion of the abandonment of the ideal, the narrator questions the right of anyone to impose a destiny on someone else.

When all those external agents and circumstances are stripped away, we discover a young boy filled with hope and excitement about his future in the seminary. We find an innocent boy who personally wants to do something special with his life in contrast with the mature adult narrator who now views it all as an illusion. In a life of misery and emptiness, the adult narrator recalls the great ideals of his early days and wonders how life can change so dramatically while recognising that the outcome was inevitable:

> Ahora mismo yo me asusto del abismo que hay entre aquella quimera soñada de salvar almas, convertido en un san Francisco Javier, y la vida estúpida de bacanal y vacío, de abandono y olvido de todo, pero me era necesario -sí, sí, no te disculpes-,

había vivido entre el terror de la muerte, el miedo supersticioso,
el fanatismo de la religión heculana, una religión *sui generis*.
(p.88)

The narrator now admits that his ideals were doomed to fail simply because his early education had done so much damage that it would have been impossible to heal the pain caused by those years. In other words, since the paradise of childhood had always been denied him, it was never likely to be discovered. In a way, the decision to enter the seminary could be regarded as an attempt to find that paradise, but the realities of human experience even here were enough to overcome the slightest hope.

B. THE REALITY

There are a number of factors involved in the destruction of the religious ideal but there is little doubt that the seminary environment itself was a major blow to Pepico's hopes. The routine of seminary life together with the attitude and behaviour both of the other seminarians and the superiors were all responsible to some extent for the gradual erosion of his boyhood dream. The first disappointment was in the discovery of insincerity and vulgarity in the conversations and actions of the other seminarians and this was noted in his first encounters with the older seminarians in Hécula:

Entre ellos uno no tenía más remedio que aguantar bromas, devociones y juegos que siempre llevaban el sello de lo falso, lo amansado, rebañil y vulgarote, y yo lo notaba, y todo concluía en largos rezos, rezos que comenzaban con caras contritas pero que muchas veces terminaban en risas. (p.26)

Once inside the seminary the protagonist was surrounded by individuals from a whole range of different backgrounds and with such a wide variety of temperament it was clear that a certain degree of caution was required in forming relationships:

> Había compañeros y compañeros, los había relamidos y los había zafios, los había limpios y los había zarrapastrosos, había los silenciosos, demasiado, y los bullangueros, los tristes y los potreadores, los reservados y los pícaros, los maliciosos y los inocentones. (p.37)

It is likely from the number of negative elements here that young Pepico would find only limited solidarity with some seminarians and there are further indications that Pepico eventually considered it necessary to withdraw completely from any real association with the rest:

> Fue la soledad, la soledad del seminario, la que me fue empujando hacia dentro de mí mismo, hacia la necesidad de acorazarme y defenderme de 'los otros'. (p.23)

The adult narrator now feels that the reason for the vulgar behaviour in seminarians lies with the fact that they had not entered the seminary for the sake of an ideal but rather only to flee from the harshness of life outside:

> Porque no había sentido de nada, ni auténtica devoción ni conmoción ni mierdas, éramos los elegidos -¿elegidos de qué?-, elegidos de mierda, leva forzosa de unos seres que sólo buscaban escapar de la penuria, la sordidez o la asfixia pueblerina. (p.26)

It is interesting to note the contrast between Pepico's innocent sense of being chosen and the adult narrator's angry attack at the misuse of the term to include those individuals whose presence in the seminary, according to the narrator, had no connection with the will of God. Perhaps it could be said that the narrator has no right to pronounce judgement on other individuals' decisions but from the descriptions we have observed above it would appear that many seminarians did not display any Christian attributes.

There was also a considerable amount of negative behaviour among the superiors and the 'teólogos' who are also criticised by the narrator for their part in promoting a system which was obviously damaging to the development of the young seminarians. An example can be seen when the narrator recalls the time he was sexually abused by the Spiritual Director, don Crisanto, in the infirmary. The narrator found it impossible to liberate himself from the memory of the incident:

> Jamás pudiste evitar que de repente, en cualquier circunstancia, a veces cuando estabas con tu madre, a veces cuando estabas incluso a punto de recibir la comunión, porque la imagen de don Crisanto, los olores, sus manoseos de aquella tarde quedaron grabados como un punzón en tu memoria, algo que aflora en los momentos más inesperados, barrena perforadora del alma, que jamás te abandonó. (p. 54)

The narrator later reveals with great indignation a further episode involving yet another homosexual cleric, padre Eladio, at the country-home of El Algarrobo:

> Y ¿qué hacer con estos débiles que resultan fuertes como robles en hacer la puñeta a los demás?, porque no hay nada más temible que estos seres débiles, coño con los débiles, que nos hacen víctimas a todos de sus debilidades, al diablo con ellos, al diablo con el padre Eladio. (p.122)

Although these incidents were relatively serious, the narrator confesses he had only ever confided them to his journal. He certainly did not reveal them to his mother since she was under the illusion that anyone in a clerical habit would be a saint. But the narrator now knows differently and one of the purposes of the novel, it seems, is to expose these negative aspects of the religious life and the seminary since, as Gemma Roberts points out, they were so important to the narrator's understanding of himself:

> Junto al análisis en profundidad de la conciencia en esta novela
> corre el deseo de denunciar los falsos valores de una sociedad y,
> en particular, un ambiente eclesiástico de hipocresía y corrupción
> que tanto contribuyó a la simulación y deformación del carácter
> del protagonista.[4]

Also relevant here is the difference between the mother's understanding of the clergy and the reality experienced by her son who previously had similar ideas to his mother. As his mother was clearly unaware of the truth, there is even less reason to criticise her for encouraging her son to endure, yet ironically it was precisely that truth or reality which helped to destroy the ideal.

Apart from the failings of the priests and the other seminarians, a third factor which contributed to the loss of the ideal was the militaristic seminary routine itself:

> Y allí, junto a los ventanales enrejados y carcelarios, pasábamos
> todo el tiempo que no estábamos en la capilla o en clase, días y
> horas en que todo era reglamentado por la campana, una campana
> que tenía algo, o mucho, de toque de corneta. (p.49)

In a life divided between study and prayer the fact that every individual's life was totally organised meant the absence of any personal initiative or development and so each day became a continuation of the same rudimentary system. In addition to this was the almost total absence of the intellect since no-one was allowed to investigate or analyse anything. It seemed that the superiors exercised strict control on this matter and the inability to act led further to an attitude of resignation and passivity:

> Unos te alentaban como protectores, pero otros te recriminaban la
> espontaneidad, la originalidad, los brotes de ideal o de poesía, y
> terminabas acostumbrándote a todo, renunciando a ti mismo,
> dejándote llevar, y así cada día iban siendo menores y más
> escasos los efluvios de mística arrobadora. (p.58)

From the control of Cirilo outside the seminary, Pepico has passed to a realm of equal control, and an individual who is persistently deprived of self expression will eventually react with hostility against those agents of control, as the narrator is now showing. While the protagonist continues to endure the seminary, however, we discover that the reality of seminary life was not only destroying the ideal, but was actually damaging the protagonist:

> Todo era desafío al que había que responder con altivez interior
> y afectación externa, y todo iba creando el lecho de la deserción,
> el fingimiento, la alienación total. (p.59)

The fourth factor that must also be taken into account in examining the effects of the seminary reality upon the protagonist's ideal is, of course, the problem of sexuality. In common with the earlier parts of the trilogy, the narrator returns to this fundamental aspect of human nature which was given so little attention by the religious authorities. Indeed, there was as much taboo surrounding the subject of sex as there was surrounding the reading of literature. Yet although both literature and the opposite sex were out of bounds to the seminarians, there were limits to the authorities' control:

> Los libros entonces comenzaron a ser un refugio, tantas veces
> prohibido, igual que mirar a las muchachas, 'no las mires', 'no las
> mires', 'los ojos en el suelo', pero hasta en las losas hallabas su
> imagen, y sus risas, y su olor, no hacía falta mirarlas porque las
> tendrías dentro mismo de los ojos, dentro de tu alma. (p.27)

However, externally young Pepe did try to conform to the advice of his superiors and totally ignore his sexuality, bearing in mind that the ideal depended on this victory over the body. But this struggle against nature was impossible and also proved damaging. The narrator recalls a painful sense of defeat later on:

Después del desgarrón final no quedarían más que sombras amedrentadoras en torno, y no sabría decir si un resto de libertad inútil, libertad sin esperanza y sin ilusión, que eso fue todo lo que quedó de aquella batalla mil veces más aniquiladora que las de la guerra. (p.25)

So it is ironic that the very place in which the religious vocation was meant to flourish was actually effecting the gradual and complete destruction of the religious ideal:

Tú no sabes decir hoy cómo pudiste aguantar tanta tortura, tanta comedia, tan sistemática y dolorosa destrucción de los sueños, de los auténticos sueños, que tan a menudo eran sueños de ideal, pero había que desgarrar los sueños en aras de un júbilo falso, de una devoción convencional, de una ficticia consolación, y todo se fue haciendo poco a poco ridículo, tristísimo, vacío y abochornante. (pp.38-39)

All in all, the narrator presents a grim picture of the reality of religious life. It would appear from the adult narrator's sense of anger and resentment that the experience of the religious institution has served him no purpose whatsoever but rather has caused him more harm than good. The blame seems to lie both with the regime of the seminary and with the failings of human nature. In the case of the seminary regime it is likely that many areas of religious life were badly in need of reform and the narrator suggests at one point that the Catholic Church in general was aware of certain shortcomings and that the authorities were in the process of creating a revised structure of the seminary system. Major changes did come about with the Second Vatican Council and we observed in the prologue to *Sin camino* how Castillo-Puche had recognised this fact.[5] However, whereas the changes to the system then would no doubt have been welcome, it does not necessarily follow that human nature would improve as a result. Insincerity and hypocrisy are not going to be eliminated by a healthier approach to the religious vocation and it is mainly this side to our human nature which troubled Castillo-Puche so much in his own experience of the seminary:

> Es toda la peripecia del contagio alrededor en el cual se mezclan los pequeños vicios, incluso las pasiones camufladas: la hipocresía, la falta de lealtad, la mentira, y en el caso del seminario, esta especie de homosexualismo enmascarado.[6]

The negative side of human nature will inevitably be present in any institution, religious or otherwise, and wherever there is a group of individuals in community there will be weakness and failure. However, the religious vocation is essentially based on the concepts of self-denial and self-sacrifice and the author knows from his own experience that it is the unwillingness of individuals to live up to these ideals that poses the greatest threat to the religious establishment. Consequently, if there is no-one setting any standards, then the religious ideal will gradually become meaningless and the individual vocation will not be advanced:

> Para que un individuo la pueda salvar dentro de sí, tendría que encontrar una sublimación en el ambiente y en las circunstancias que le rodean de mucho sacrificio, mucha entrega, mucha abnegación, pero lo que encuentra es mucha comodidad y mucha atracción al futuro. Entonces se desvirtúa porque uno está dispuesto a entregar todo hasta la vida por un ideal y uno encuentra que el ideal prácticamente no existe.[7]

It is important to note that we are not talking here of a problem that was peculiar to the Catholic Church in Spain. Karen Armstrong, who had some experience of life within a convent in England just prior to the reforms introduced by the Second Vatican Council, describes some of the traditional practices in the convent which were so degrading to the individual:

> Every fortnight we were expected to do a 'refectory penance'

during meals for faults against the Rule, but during the retreat these penances were more severe. We had to look back over the past year, pick the fault we had failed most in and publicly accuse ourselves, asking the forgiveness of the community for all the disedification we had given.[8]

Many of these religious practices, Karen Armstrong recalls, led to a continuous feeling of guilt and self-disgust and this could hardly be regarded as promoting a healthy understanding of Christianity. Also noticeable here is the notion not only of the surrender of the will but also of the intellect, a requirement that the protagonist in the novel we are examining found so difficult to accept:

One of the things that had to die was my mind. We were being trained in Ignatian obedience, which aims to break down the will and the judgement of a religious so that he unquestioningly accepts the will of God as it is presented to him through his superior. It is the obedience of the professional soldier that Ignatius was before his conversion.[9]

Yet despite all the apparent criticism of the religious institution, Karen Armstrong, in a similar way to Castillo-Puche in the prologue to *Sin camino*, still considers the religious vocation a worthy ideal:

The ideal of the religious life is still, I think, a beautiful one. But only a few of those who undertake it are capable of it. My most crucial mistake was the overvaluing of the will.[10]

It would appear in the novel that Pepico was also guilty of over-valuing the will and, at the same time, of overestimating the commitment of the other seminarians. It must be said that the young protagonist was far too impressionable and vulnerable for his personal ideal to survive. The only way to maintain the ideal seems to lie in the assertion of the will in order not to be affected by the behaviour of others as was suggested in our study of *Sin camino*. But there is a paradox here in the sense that a strong personal will was not encouraged by the regime and yet the lack of it meant being contaminated by the behaviour of the rest. The problem for young Pepe lay in his needing to find support for his ideal within the seminary and, since this was clearly not the case, his own religious ideals collapsed and faded leaving him forever hurt and resentful about a failure that was still to trouble him in his later years.

C. THE IDEAL ABANDONED

The Civil War was finally to force Pepe out of the seminary, but long before that his vocation had collapsed and he remained there purely out of a desire to please his mother and out of fear of disappointing her. At the same time he very much wished he could have been truer to himself:

> Y ahora yo deseaba ardientemente volver a la playa con ella, y allí, ante las olas, le diría la verdad, que no podía ser, que mi vocación estaba rota, y ella allí, frente al mar inmenso, el mar que iba y venía con el ritmo de un corazón eterno, incansable, ella allí lo entendería. (p.64)

However, with his mother already burdened with the scandal of his sister Rosa's elopement, there was no way Pepico could inflict more pain on his mother by telling her the truth:

> Y así, una vez más, te quedarías sin decir a tu madre que estabas de más en el seminario, la verdad era que estabas de más y de menos, pero cualquiera se atrevía a hablar en aquel momento de una posible retirada, hubiera sido una puñalada más en el pecho escuálido y deteriorado de aquella madre. (p.77)

Consequently, he had to remain in the seminary observing a way of life which no longer held any interest for him. Out of this tremendous care and respect for his mother, young Pepe refused to give up the struggle yet he secretly hoped that an external force would bring about change for him:

> Sólo a veces en lo íntimo había la esperanza de la revolución
> inminente como detonante de escapada posible, igual que los
> locos de una cárcel pueden pensar en un incendio que los librara
> de las rejas, lejos del propio terror, de la propia atonía, del propio
> desprecio. (p.87)

By comparing the seminary to a prison, he is plainly demonstrating how miserable his life inside had become and how much damage his dishonesty was causing him.

By confessing his own inner cowardice and dishonesty, it is as if the narrator was trying to turn the reader into a kind of therapist to whom he appeals for sympathy and understanding. The narrator seems to be saying that the time has come for the truth to be told instead of continuing to endure a life of deception:

> Es que la vida está montada, sin remedio, sobre la mentira,
> mentiras llamadas piadosas, pero mentiras cochinas, sucias
> mentiras, mentiras para medrar o para sobrevivir, mentiras para
> poder seguir mintiendo, que así he llegado a esta orilla harto de
> mentiras y proponiéndome no mentir más en la vida. (pp.129-130)

This deception was directed mainly, of course, at the protagonist's mother and the narrator now resents the fact that he never allowed his mother to know him as he really was:

> Ojalá tú hubieras afrontado la responsabilidad total, diciéndole a
> tu madre todo lo que sentías por dentro, todo lo que había dentro
> de ti. (p.130)

This is a crucial point in young Pepe's life for it seems that up to this point there was a certain degree of self-determination in the religious vocation. However, once he realised that his religious ideal was all but over, he began for the first time in his life to deceive those around him, and it appears that since this time the narrator has never recovered from that terrible mistake of lying not only to his mother, but also to himself:

> Qué remedio había para tanta desolación, cómo transformar casi
> de la noche a la mañana los anhelos románticos, o místicos, en un
> puro companage de subsistencia, en supervivencia ignominiosa,
> mentirse cada día, no sólo a los demás sino a ti mismo, por no
> llegar a ninguna afirmación convincente. (p.127)

Probably the most damaging consequence of these deliberate acts of deception was the effect it had on the concept of identity.

1. Loss of Identity

By trying to maintain this outward display for the sake of the mother, young Pepe was plunging himself ever deeper into an identity crisis. Gemma Roberts points out that the protagonist's attempts to hold on to his religious identity had rendered the treasured relationship with his mother completely false:

> La madre de Pepico sólo puede conocer de su hijo al ser que se
> manifiesta, al que finge y disimula, mientras los anhelos más
> íntimos de éste se encierran en un silencio enfermizo que le
> hostiga y le amarga el alma.[11]

It is precisely the contrast between what young Pepe feels inside and what his mother thinks he feels which is the fundamental cause of the crisis in identity. The identity of an individual cannot be established solely on the basis of personal assessment: it must necessarily include the assessment and opinion of other people. Consequently, if what others recognise a person to be is not in accordance with what that person considers himself to be, then there is a crisis or lack of identity.

Since the sense of identity is so important to the growth and development of the individual, the subject is of special interest to the psychologist John Powell who recognises in his work the importance of identity in human relationships:

> The essential condition of identity is that there must be a sameness or continuity between what I think I am and the picture which others reflect to me (my 'feedback'). My own self image must be validated by the reaction of others to me.[12]

He points out that individuals, especially young people, have a tendency to accept the image imposed by others mainly because they are afraid of being rejected if they do not conform. In the novel, too, there is a sense that young Pepe was afraid to reveal his true feelings for fear of being spurned by his mother:

> Cuando fingías delante de tu madre una devoción, una entereza, una seguridad que no tenías por dentro, que eras pura jalea blanda y cambiante, indecisa y cobarde. (p.130)

Powell believes that this willingness to settle for an acceptable image that is not compatible with one's inner self-awareness is both damaging and dangerous. By seeking to be recognised as someone he is not, the individual is actually rejecting any sense of personal worth:

> In the absence of the essential condition for identity, namely the sameness or continuity between what I am and what others recognise me to be, I am cast into the role of an actor, and all the world becomes a stage, and life becomes a prolonged charade. Only one thing is certain about the life of such an actor: a sense of personal identity and worth will never be achieved.[13]

This view is reflected in the novel when the narrator considers the long-term effects of his attempts to conceal his true self:

> Mi madre me creía feliz allí dentro y yo callaba, y en cierto modo callaría siempre, la vida ha sido tan sólo un silencio continuado

repleto de palabras mudas, de palabras muertas sin nacer, mientras
un río de sinceridad vital se pudría por dentro, como las aguas
estancadas y podridas, como las aguas ciegas y subterráneas,
escuela de silencios, de simulaciones, de contenciones, escuela de
morir poco a poco, de apagarse poco a poco, como una vela sin
oxígeno, rostro cada día más pálido y demacrado. (p.87)

Together with the loss of personal worth, there are two other long-term
consequences of such deceptive behaviour. In the first place, since the narrator
has spent his entire life avoiding any confrontation with his true self, the reality
is now that he is hardly likely to know himself. Even at the beginning of the
novel the narrator seems to acknowledge the inevitable outcome of living the life
of an actor:

Si hay que vivir disimulando, engañándose uno a sí mismo, y por
supuesto engañando a los demás, acaba uno por corromperse, por
envilecerse, y luego viene la necesidad de anulación, de olvido
total, hasta no reconocerte a ti mismo. (p.20)

Yet the narrator also appears to justify his behaviour by suggesting that since he
had never had a life of his own so there would not be anything of real value about
himself worth getting to know. Consequently, he is afraid to confront his true self
because he knows that he will discover nothing, as the title of the novel suggests:

Yo sabía todo lo que había confusamente encrespado dentro de
mí, porque me había pasado la vida hasta entonces
desconociéndome, ignorándome, evitando toda introspección,
porque sabía que allí encontraría, oscuro y vacío, el poso de la
nada. (p.126)

The question remains as to when the narrator initially experienced this
sense of nothingness since by using the term 'hasta entonces' he is implying that
all of his early life up to his mother's death has been a farce. Yet in other parts of
the novel the narrator suggests that the early stages of his life were filled with

meaning:

> No sabrías decir si tú, en verdad, te has recuperado o no, si has
> logrado entroncar con aquellos años que fueron tu raíz y tu
> sentido, el sentido de tu vida, y si queda en ti realmente algo de
> todo aquello. (p.20)

Thoughts such as these conform to the earlier assertion during our study of the
ideal that there was a stage when young Pepe showed sincerity and commitment
towards his vocation. However, once Pepe had entered into the world of
deception, his true self and feelings became suppressed and he found it
impossible to escape from such a world. Powell suggests that once a false image
has been adopted, it can easily become a habit of a lifetime, while the real person
remains constantly suppressed:

> We throw up all sorts of defenses around our aching areas; we
> repaint our masks to keep our pains from surfacing. When the
> habits of our 'games' have become ingrained, there comes a time
> when we don't even know ourselves at all and neither can anyone
> else. We are definitely sidetracked in our pursuit of identity and
> interpersonal relationships. We have forfeited the fullness of
> human life. This is the tragedy of non-identity.[14]

The second long-term consequence of deception is the inevitable
surrender of free will. In his attempts to conform to the image held by his mother
and relatives young Pepe allowed his own life to be dictated by others. Again it
could be said that once his personal will had been surrendered it was difficult to
recover control over his own destiny. We have already seen examples of this
when young Pepe was hoping that the political situation would force him to
abandon the seminary and so it turned out. But once outside the seminary he still
showed no firm commitment to anything but rather allowed himself to be
recruited by the army:

Que tú ya intuías entonces que acabarías dejándote ir a la deriva, dejándote llevar por las cosas y los acontecimientos, como cuando te metieron en aquel camión que iba derecho al frente, y tú sin oponer resistencia, sin desear siquiera otra cosa, que siempre has preferido que te lo dieran todo hecho. (p.130)

The passivity continued:

Ahora también habían elegido ellos, aquel retén de policia militar que me había 'cazado' a la orilla del río, ellos decidieron por mí, otros habían decidido antes, condenado a ser sacerdote primero, condenado a estar en el frente ahora, condenado a tener un fusil en la mano, condenado quizás a matar, condenado a ver morir a todos. (p.204)

Although the protagonist's attempts to deceive his mother lead to the loss of identity, it is the mother's death itself which signifies the end of everything.

2.   The Death of the Mother

We discover that with the disappearance of the mother go also any hopes about the vocation and all sense of purpose or identity. The narrator realises that his existence had been sustained purely by his mother and that she was the inspiration behind everything he did, especially the decision to go to seminary. It is not surprising then that her death was, in a sense, the narrator's death also:

¿Alguna vez has sentido una voluntad definida de algo?, reconoce que no, y ahí es donde está el fallo, que su muerte te dejó vacío y anonadado, como si lo que tú podías ser, lo que tú eras, se lo hubiera llevado ella en su última mirada. (pp.133-134)

It is here especially where we find the tremendous sense of nothingness which Pepe felt after his mother's death. Though he had previously admitted to having lost both his vocation and his personal worth before his mother had died, there was a sense that as long as she was alive then life was still worth living. So with the mother's death, then, what little hope remained was reduced to nothing, and this is the main cause, it seems, of the narrator frequently referring to the nothingness within himself and hence the nothingness of his existence:

> Pero tú andabas aturullado, con una madre reducida a la nada en un día de muertos al paredón, y de esa nada habías provenido tú, y estabas ahora camino de esa misma nada, una nada latiendo en cada pulso, la nada que creía amar la nada, soledad infinita y duelo sempiterno. (P.202)

Similarly, there is another comparison between the effects of the mother's death and the abandonment of the vocation with regard to the notion of self-recognition. Just as Powell has suggested that the lack of identity would lead to the inability to know oneself, so also the narrator is affected in such a way by his mother's death that he became a different person. The pessimistic individual who was the product of that death failed to recognise himself in the previous person, who displayed some sense of hope and purpose:

> Que a veces no eres el mismo que se acostó por la noche cuando te despiertas por la mañana, que hay pesadillas que nos transforman, que nos embarullan hasta el extremo de no reconocernos, y eso te ha pasado a ti con la muerte de tu madre, quizás porque tú mismo no has salido vivo de aquello, más bien has sido ya desde entonces una sombra que vaga de acá para allá, sin fijeza y sin ilusión en nada. (p.110)

We should remember here that the fundamental connection between the mother's death and young Pepe's sense of purpose is seen only through the eyes of the adult narrator. The fact that his dying mother was pleading with her son to continue with the vocation suggests that she died with the illusion that Pepico would still become a priest. Since it is clear also from the way the protagonist had deceived his mother into thinking that the vocation was solid so his mother would have no idea that the religious life was over. In the events of the novel, then, the abandoning of the seminary and the mother's death are totally unconnected. It is only in retrospect that the adult narrator realises how important his mother's influence was on the determination of his own existence and the turning point of his life is now traced to the mother's death. This essential link between Pepico's mother and the religious ideal was recognised by Castillo-Puche when commenting on the novel during private conversation in 1987. For the author the very notion of an ecclesiastical career cannot exist without the narrator's mother although we have already seen in the novel that the vocation was not entirely due to the mother but had also originated to some extent from Pepico himself. However, the author confirms that the link between the vocation and the mother is intentional and conforms to the author's own experience:

> Como la presencia de la madre está ligada a la vocación, la madre desaparece con el abandono del seminario, y eso obedece a la mente del novelista, porque si no la madre estaría ordenando la vida nueva del novelista, estaría diciendo '¿Con quién te vas a casar?' o '¿Qué es de tu vida?' o '¡Vuelve al seminario!' La madre desaparece porque ha dejado de ser el motor de su vida, pero no sentimentalmente. Ha dejado de ser el motor o el inspirador de la idea vocacional.[15]

The significant impact of the death of his mother in the author's own experience is reflected in the attention given to the matter not only in the trilogy but also in other novels such as *Con la muerte al hombro* and *Como ovejas al matadero*. The consistency of this theme of the mother's death in the different novels led me to question the author on the importance he places upon her death and the motive behind her inclusion in the novels. In reality, the author's mother died in 1946 which was well after the Civil War had ended and also after his departure from seminary in 1943. However, Castillo-Puche indicated that the precise date of his mother's death is irrelevant in the trilogy and the other novels and what is of primary significance is the event itself and its effects upon the different protagonists:

> En la trilogía hay varias muertes de la madre. En *Con la muerte al hombro* la madre muere en otra fecha, o sea, la muerte de la madre es flexible. Es un hecho que está enmarcado por un tiempo, pero el tiempo no es un tiempo limitado y concreto.[16]

The author goes on to confirm that the timing of the mother's death normally coincides with the son's vocation when important decisions have to be made by the protagonist:

> En cualquier caso, para él, en la plenitud de la vida es cuando muere la madre. Lo que pasa es que las demás circunstancias pueden variar un poco, pero la madre muere en el momento en que él o va a ser sacerdote y no lo es, o está 'intentando' ser sacerdote.[17]

It seems that the sense of failing his mother by not becoming a priest originates also from the author's personal experience.

The author's mother died of illness after he had decided to abandon the seminary, and the author clearly feels guilty about his failure to fulfil her dreams, a guilt that is reflected in the novel we are studying:

> Está más conforme con la realidad de que la madre espera, después de la guerra, que el hijo vaya a ser sacerdote pero que no lo es y, una vez esto, ella desaparece y él tiene el trance de eso.[18]

Castillo-Puche openly admits to identifying the personal trauma surrounding his own mother's death with that of Pepe in the trilogy and we can easily compare the effects of this event upon the author with those upon the protagonist. Once the vocation was lost and the mother gone, the protagonist in the novel is left without identity, inspiration or purpose. From this state of nothingness came two inevitable reactions on the part of the protagonist, namely, a sense of guilt, and also the need to escape.

D. REACTIONS

It should be said that the notion of disappointing the mother is solely in the mind of the narrator although he is convinced at times that other people are lining up to accuse and condemn him. An example of this can be seen at the mother's bedside in the 'asilo' when Pepe was verbally attacked by the now deranged Cayetano:

> Entonces el tío, furioso se volvió hacia mí y comenzó a barbotar maldades: 'estabas deseando que viniera la revolución para quitarte las sotanas, míralo, es un judas, un prevaricador'. (p.198)

Though these accusations are expressed through the voice of Cayetano, the fact that they include a desire that Pepico had previously admitted to suggests that Cayetano is also used here as a vehicle for the expressions of guilt and condemnation which the narrator directs against himself. There are also examples when, with the use of the second person, the narrator criticises himself for not living up to his mother's expectations:

> Y mira por dónde la defraudaste, no cumpliste con tu compromiso de hijo, no fuiste capaz de llegar hasta el final, no te responsabilizaste con su felicidad. (p.64)

It is evident that it was his inability to fulfil his mother's ideal, much more than his own, that now seems to be the major failure:

> Quizás esto es lo que arrastro toda mi vida como una traición, como una cobardía, como el fallo más grande de mi existencia, el fallo radical, total, y por eso yo nunca he podido levantar cabeza ni ilusionarme con nada. (p133)

At the same time, however, the narrator recognises the problem of destiny and personal free will and questions whether any individual has the right to dictate the destiny of another individual, no matter how close that person might be:

> Cuando llego a este punto me pregunto también con toda responsabilidad, ¿puede alguien, aunque sea tu madre, la madre más querida, disponer de tu destino personal, de tu destino íntimo?, y esta pregunta tengo que reconocer que, por más que he rehuido siempre afrontar la verdad, me la he hecho muchas veces en la vida, y muchas veces me he quedado un poco tranquilo respondiéndome que no, que nadie tiene derecho a imponer un destino a los demás. (p.133)

The fact that Pepe remained silent in the face of his mother's dying wish, then, suggests that he was beginning to take control of his own destiny, yet there was still the dilemma of whether to be honest about this or simply avoid causing more distress to the mother.

It could be said that the narrator shows a natural response to the notion of failure and the abandoning of his ideal by blaming himself for his own shortcomings and for letting other people down. Anyone who had experienced the same situation of not being able to fulfil an ideal would probably react in a similar way. In a sense his reaction could be interpreted as showing just now much the religious ideal meant to the narrator since he is still troubled by this failure at a much later stage in his life. However, on closer observation of the novel, we discover indications that the guilt feelings are far from healthy as the narrator shows indications of a much deeper guilt complex. This complex tends to go beyond the natural sense of remorse about the vocation to include notions of responsibility for other events:

> Acaso los muertos se nos mueren porque los dejamos morir, y esa es mi gran pena, ¿he dejado yo morir a mi madre, o pude hacer algo que no hice?; esta es la cuestión que me tortura y que me ha impedido ya nunca más ser yo mismo. (p.111)

This ridiculous attempt to take responsibility for his mother's death is accompanied by contempt for himself and his own apparent worthlessness, when he and his dying mother were being driven around Murcia looking for a hospital bed:

> Y comencé a sentirme culpable de aquella profanación de una muerte para mí tan sagrada como temida, no había derecho a que ella no tuviera al menos una muerte en paz, en quietud, rodeada de los suyos, como debería ser, y en lugar de eso allí estaba yo, solo a su lado, yo, el más indigno, el más vacilante ser del mundo que ni siquiera sabía a qué atenerme sobre mis propios sentimientos. (p.186)

It becomes clear that this initial sense of guilt soon grows out of all proportion when the narrator feels obliged to carry the world on his shoulders and take responsibility for all the death and destruction of the period in what is sometimes regarded as the Atlas complex:

> Y me sentía culpable, ¿culpable de qué?, pues culpable de todo, culpable de la muerte de mi madre, de la guerra, de todo lo que veía. (p.179)

The narrator's guilt problem is evidently very deep-rooted and goes beyond the seminary experience as was observed in the first and second parts of the trilogy.

We saw earlier how the abandonment of the religious ideal led to the loss of identity and therefore an inevitable consequence of this was to go out in search of a new identity. However, this was an extremely difficult objective since Pepico's life up to that point was dependent upon values and convictions which had sustained him ever since childhood. Once those values had been abandoned there was an awful sense of nothingness and emptiness, especially after the death of his mother. The young Pepe was evidently in need of what Pío Baroja, a writer Castillo-Puche much admires, would have called a 'mentira vital'.[19]

At times, there is the sense of young Pepe being happy about his abandonment of the seminary and the subsequent discovery of freedom:

> Si he de ser sincero, aquellos meses fueron para mí de cierta exaltación, pues aunque no me atreviera ni siquiera a aceptarlo como pensamiento tentador, era evidente que la revolución que invadía las calles ponía a mi alcance por primera vez una libertad personal inesperada, miedo y euforia combinados, terror sacro y al mismo tiempo un cierto vértigo ante la ruptura inevitable y forzosa de todas las ataduras pasadas y quién sabe si de las presentes y las futuras, es decir que, inesperadamente, yo estaba como estrenando un destino. (pp.109-110)

However, these initial feelings of exaltation are normally overshadowed by an awareness of much deeper and more serious consequences:

> Yo sé muy bien, aunque de piel afuera procure disimularlo, que mi vida no es en realidad una vida desarrollada, tendida como un arco hacia un fin definido, abierta y desplegada como una alfombra que se desenrolla, sino una vida en hibernación, al margen de todo. (p.166)

Thoughts such as these conform to the notion that the loss of those values and convictions has proved detrimental to the narrator who evidently found himself unable to adopt another identity. In contrast with the humanist or existential view of writers such as Baroja, the psychologist John Powell will naturally interpret this problem from a religious point of view which associates the rejection of values with the absence of meaning in life and consequently the absence of motivation:

> As the Viennese psychiatrist, Victor Frankl, maintains in his theory of logotherapy, man's most desperate need is to find some meaning in life, and meaning can be built only on certainties andconvictions. The fragmentation and depersonalization of the individual does not lie far beyond the fragmentation and denial of his absolutes, certainties, and personal dedication.[20]

From the evidence in the novel, it would appear that this latter interpretation of the abandonment of values is more appropriate in the understanding of the narrator's problems.

Since Pepico had rarely made any decisions for himself, so now he was dependent upon external circumstances to offer a new kind of life as we just saw with the example of the change brought about by the outbreak of the Civil War. However, he did not seek a new identity within the area of military involvement in the conflict. Instead, he made every possible effort to avoid being sent into battle and, by using his wits for the first time, he experienced a new sense of challenge in his life:

> Mientras duró aquello tuve y sentí la mayor ansia de vivir que había sentido nunca, sin duda no era yo mismo, pero era un hombre, un hombre como los demás, un hombre que quiere vivir, ¿había algo malo en eso?, y a veces me entraba un valor extraño, una especie de desafío loco frente a la vida y al destino, una osadía que nunca hubiera sentido siendo yo mismo, porque la inteligencia no me faltaba y no sólo me salvaba yo sino que ayudaba a salvar a otros. (p.105)

By the use of intelligence, then, instead of faith, young Pepe experienced the sensation of being someone different and this would conform to the idea expressed by Baroja that our will and intelligence will offer new meaning to our existence. However, Pepe was still unable to eliminate his former self and it became obvious that nothing external either would succeed in erasing the past:

> En todo caso busqué el olvido, el olvido del pasado, que sucediera lo que tuviera que suceder, pero que fuera otra cosa, que yo fuera otro ya para siempre, una nueva vida, un nuevo ser, y sin embargo, ya ves, ¿lo has logrado?, seguro que no lo has logrado ni lo lograrás, ni la guerra puede cambiarnos, ni eso tan nefasto, tan horrendo como es una guerra, puede liberarnos de nosotros mismos. (p.105)

The inability to break with his former self seemed to continue through the rest of the narrator's life and is responsible for creating the continual desire to escape, the second main consequence of the abandonment of the ideal. When he first settled in the Basque region, there was an early sense of peace and liberation but his experience of the darker side to the Basque people soon changed his perception. Although in the previous novel the narrator gives the impression that he was eventually accepted into Basque society, the narrator now says that he was never fully admitted into the community since they seem to maintain a certain distance and reserve. Such behaviour only created a sense of further alienation in the narrator who becomes convinced that he will never really belong anywhere:

> A mí me hace pensar que en esta tierra del tiro en la nuca a mí no se me ha perdido nada, y esto me trae una nueva confusión, y pienso que mi destino es ir de un lado a otro sin saber nunca a qué carta quedarme ni si estoy o no estoy en mi verdadero sitio, si es que todos tenemos un lugar en esta vida, cosa que dudo también. (pp.100-101)

While the narrator admits that the rest of his life has been one long continuous flight there is also a sense that this need to escape cannot be confined only to Pepe's experience after the seminary since there was already the suggestion that the seminary too was an escape from Hécula. In the earlier parts of the trilogy the perpetual desire in Pepico to get away from the hostile environment of Hécula shows that the notion of flight has also been the habit of a lifetime:

> No sólo prófugo del ejército sino prófugo de mi propia persona, prófugo también de Hécula y de su viento, prófugo de los míos, de todo lo mío, prófugo de prófugos, una situación absurda que se hizo permanente porque nunca he sabido salir de ella. (p.107)

It was the desertion from the army during the Civil War which symbolised the protagonist's total dissociation from the aggression and hatred of the people around him. By abandoning the combat and entering the river the protagonist performed the ultimate gesture of flight and alienation, with little regard for logic or rationality:

> No tenía conciencia de a dónde me dirigía, sólo quería huir, huir a través del agua, como envuelto en una manta fresca, huir sin saber hacia dónde. (p.205)

As well as providing a means of escape for young Pepe the river has symbolic significance concerning passivity and liberation too. His desire to escape had always been linked to a desperate search for liberation and yet, paradoxically, he appeared now to find liberation in letting himself be carried along not by other people or political events but by the smooth current of the river:

> Me parecía haber encontrado por fin mi destino en seguir la corriente del río, olvidado de todo, enajenado de mí mismo, seguía simplemente el curso del río como una rama arrojada a la corriente. (p.205)

In this way, the passivity which has denied him the use of free will and self-determination is converted into the only alternative means of liberation. Earlier in the trilogy, both the element of water and the figure of the mother had been recognised as the two principal symbols of liberation, and now that the mother no longer existed, the protagonist had only one source of liberation left:

> De momento mi gran amiga, mi cárcel suave, mi portillo hacia un espacio nuevo, imprevisto, inesperado, era el agua, un agua que se veía negra ante mis ojos pero que olía a limpia, a libre, a auténtica, y cuando mis pies tropezaban en alguna piedra y la sorteaba, me decía: 'todavía soy libre', y entonces deseaba que aquel camino de agua se alargara indefinidamente hacia un alba de liberación. (p.208)

The river is also significant with regard to the concept of neutrality which was mentioned during our study of conflict and guilt in *El amargo sabor de la retama*. It was clear the narrator was not issuing any political message but was equally critical both of the Right and the Left. Now at the end of the trilogy the river becomes a symbol of that neutrality as the protagonist makes the point of staying clear of both the right bank and the left bank of the river as he moves along with the current. In our examination of biography and the novel in the introductory chapter to the trilogy, we saw how the brothers of the narrator, Pascual and Manolo, were representative of the two opposing sides in the Civil War. While his mother clearly supported the nationalist cause believing them to be the defenders of the faith, young Pepe did not want to be associated with either cause:

> Porque yo tampoco tenía bando propio, ni mucho menos, ¿el bando de Pascual?, ¿el bando de Manolo? ... yo estaba en el cruce dramático en que ni siquiera era desertor, ni tampoco combatiente, los ideales habían muerto en mí antes de florecer, tampoco era un recluta ni llegaría a ser veterano en ninguno de los bandos. (p.205)

The reader should now be convinced that the narrator does not possess any political ideals or prejudice but appears only to condemn the futility of war. If the war has no political significance for the narrator, then it must be seen to have a purely symbolic role just like the water. In this way, the novel can be seen to dissociate itself from reality for, although the Civil War was an historical event which affected the life of the author, it is converted by the author into a symbol which does not have to conform to any chronological order. This view was supported by the author five years after the novel was published:

> Esa cosa de la guerra es simbólica. No responde a los hechos biográficos. Ese cruce del río es un hecho simbólico, y entonces él no es nadie, no está dedicado a nada.[21]

This symbolic interpretation of the war would help to explain its presence in the last two novels of the trilogy regardless of the age difference of the protagonist. Though the author was not specific as to what the war symbolises, it was suggested earlier that it was symbolic of the war waged by his uncles against nature and life itself.[22]

For the author, the presence of the war in the last part of the trilogy is essentially connected to the notion of maturity, which helps to explain the temporal 'desfase' between the age of Pepico at the end of *El amargo sabor de la retama* and the beginning of *Conocerás el poso de la nada*. In other words, it is the war which accelerates the transformation in Pepico from adolescence to manhood:

> Hay un problema que es el de la guerra civil que ha sido para mí el trauma más grande de todo. Entonces yo he hecho de un símbolo en *Conocerás el poso de la nada* el trauma de ¿hasta qué punto el niño de las dos novelas anteriores se hace hombre? Se hace hombre con conciencia de la sangre, por ver la sangre.[23]

In the novel it is the sight of blood rather than death itself which frightens young Pepe:

> A mí la muerte no me daba miedo, nunca a mí me matarían, lo único que me daba miedo era el ruido del disparo, y la sangre. (p.203)

In contrast with the negative effects of blood is the purifying aspect of the water and, for the author, the symbolism of the water seems to go beyond the realm of reality:

> Y va a ser el problema de la sangre y del agua en lo cual el agua es el elemento purificatorio y es un elemento milagroso, y el agua sigue siendo un mito y el mito sigue siendo una salvación.[24]

Although the water is presented as a vital substance in the novel, the author appears to endow this element with supernatural power. In the same way, the significance of the mother is not just limited to her physical presence in the novel but also pertains to the mythical realm:

> La madre es una necesidad, pero no biológica, no de la tierra sino del cielo, una superación de la tierra, de la muerte. La superación de la muerte está en la madre. La madre para mí es mítica ... es una superexistencia totalmente.[25]

Evidence of this mysterious interpretation of the figure of the mother can be found especially during those final moments before her death when the narrator experienced that strange sense of separation:

> Una especie de quietud suprema, de serenidad inasequible se fue apoderando de ella, como alguien que de pronto comienza a caminar por senderos irreales, por nebulosas imprecisas, todo fuera de tu alcance, de tu comprensión. (p.196)

It is this mythical understanding of the mother which finally puts everything into perspective not only in this novel but in the whole trilogy. Since not only the ideals and the religious vocation, but also every dream and happiness of childhood and adolescence, can be associated with the mother, she alone was the symbol of hope amid the harshness of reality. The reality of life consisted of Hécula, Cirilo and Cayetano, and, above all, the Civil War and it is clear that the narrator did not want to belong to such a reality, but in a way he seems to conclude that this is the only world now left. The death of the mother did not only signify the end of the religious ideal, but it equally signified the end of the narrator's childhood. Once the mother had gone, the narrator had no alternative but to become a man, and this could only be achieved by confronting reality, a task that was undoubtedly difficult for him:

Ahora mismo yo la necesitaba tanto que tuve que salirme al
pasillo para llorar, y recuerda que llorabas más por tu soledad, no
te habías sabido hacer un hombre, no querías hacerte un hombre,
y ahora entrabas en la orfandad total como un niño. (p.199)

By entering into the conflict the narrator had begun the painful process towards
maturity and growth in reality. So with the end of the mother went the end of
everything to do with the spiritual or supernatural realm and the reality that was
left had nothing to offer. The phrase of the title of the final part 'el poso de la
nada' is used in the novel to describe what the narrator eventually finds at the
depth of his being and this nothingness can always be traced back to the moment
of his mother's death.

In the end, it is the narrator's notebook which provides the only source of
liberation since it seems that by writing down all the experiences of early life he
becomes somehow 'liberated' from his torment. In other words, by sharing his
memories with the reader, the narrator attempts to unload an enormous
psychological burden which he has secretly endured for so long. Yet there is still
a sense at the end that his endeavours to find liberation have not been successful:

Reconoce que ni la pureza ni la dulzura del agua te liberaron de
nada, que año tras año habías de purgar liberación tras liberación,
y comenzar siempre de nuevo, todo lo que es mito y realidad,
sueño y desengaño, quimera y desencanto, porque cotidianamente
te has de liberar de ti mismo y de tus demonios. (p.208)

It would appear that the sense of liberation throughout the trilogy is
essentially connected to this notion of self-discovery and self-fulfilment.
Consequently, every move that is made by the protagonist is accompanied by the
hope of finding his true self. The trips to the countryside and the coast, the
decision to enter the seminary and the later move to the Basque country, even his
involuntary involvement in the Civil War, are all linked to this fundamental

search for self. It is ironic at the end that Hécula, the very place where his problems began, should be considered by the narrator to be the only option left:

Allí posiblemente te puedas encontrar a tí mismo. (p.209)

NOTES

1. Curriculum Vitae, 2.

2. Preface to *Sin camino*, 6.

3. "Memoria e identidad en *Conocerás el poso de la nada* de José Luis Castillo-Puche." 101.

4. "Memoria e identidad en *Conocerás el poso de la nada* de José Luis Castillo-Puche." 103.

5. See above, ch.2: *Sin camino*, 10.

6. Conversations (1985).

7. Conversations (1985).

8. Karen Armstrong, *Through the Narrow Gate* (London: Pan, 1982), 162.

9. Armstrong, 155.

10. Armstrong, 28.

11. "Memoria e identidad en *Conocerás el poso de la nada* de José Luis Castillo-Puche." 101.

12. John Powell, *A reason to live! A reason to die!* (Texas: Argus, 1972), 45.

13. *A reason to live! A reason to die!*, 47.

14. *A reason to live! A reason to die!*, 48.

15. Private conversations (1987).

16. Conversations (1987).

17. Conversations (1987).

18. Conversations (1987).

19. See Pío Baroja, *El Arbol de la Ciencia* (Madrid: Alianza, 1967), 131.

20. *A reason to live! A reason to die!*, 51.

21. Conversations (1987).

22. See above, ch.6: *El amargo sabor de la retama*, 172-173.

23. Conversations (1985).

24. Conversations (1985).

244

25.   Conversations (1985).

CHAPTER 8
Conclusion

One common feature of *Sin camino*, *Como ovejas al matadero* and the three novels of the *Trilogía de la liberación* is the sense of uncertainty and inconsistency which surrounds the notion of the religious vocation. On the one hand, the religious vocation is seen as a personal ideal which cannot be fulfilled and which inevitably leads to a sense of failure. On the other hand, the vocation is seen as something imposed by external agents or circumstances in which case the abandonment of the seminary is viewed more as a means of liberation. But whether the vocation is a matter of personal choice or external pressures, there are three main concerns of Castillo-Puche which are dealt with in these novels and which are evidently related to the author's personal experience of the religious vocation, namely, the harshness of reality, man's enslavement to nature, and the need for personal identity.

In comparison with the later novels studied, *Sin camino* appears rather innocent and idealistic. Nevertheless, there is a sense of a world in conflict outside of the seminary along with a sterile environment existing within the seminary. The main issue of the novel is the conflict between the religious ideal and Enrique's passion for literature and the world of the senses which leaves the protagonist in a perpetual state of uncertainty and indecision. In the end it is nature, and mainly his attraction to women, which leads to the abandonment of the vocation. The departure from the seminary does not come across as a failure but rather as a time of liberation and Enrique's future looks promising and hopeful.

Como ovejas al matadero presents a more serious approach to the notion of man's enslavement to nature. With the impending outbreak of the Civil War and the oppressive heat of a Murcian summer, Alfredo is battling against the reality of his own sexuality. The severity of the problem is reflected in the graphic account of Alfredo's subsequent breakdown and madness. In sharp contrast to the feelings of Alfredo is the heroism of Ramiro and Fulgencio and their concern for the poor, which is a clear indication of the influence of Vatican II. However, there is little doubt that the major issue of *Como ovejas al matadero*, as in *Sin camino*, is the irresistible power of man's sexuality, as Alma Amell has indicated in her article on both novels:

> El verdadero protagonista, el héroe que sale victorioso en ambas novelas, es el instinto reproductivo del varón. Si en Enrique dicho instinto se limita a manifestarse en la añoranza y una vaga búsqueda del cariño femenino, en Alfredo se agudiza en una absorbente y enloquecedora obsesión con el indómito miembro viril. Así, *Como ovejas* continúa y elabora el tema de *Sin camino*.[1]

The sexual theme is also dominant in the three novels of the *Trilogía de la liberación*, both in the narrator's attack on the Church's negative attitude to sexuality, reflected in the ideas of Cirilo and Cayetano, and during Pepico's adolescence and seminary experience. The two other concerns of the author are also in evidence in the trilogy as the narrator returns to his past with the aim of self-analysis and self-discovery. The harshness of reality is reflected in all the books under consideration. In *El libro de las visiones y las apariciones* it is there in the landscape of Hécula and the obsession with death; in *El amargo sabor de la retama* and *Conocerás el poso de la nada* it is there in the presentation of the Civil War. The need for personal identity is mostly confined to the final part where it is inevitably linked to the abandonment of the vocation. Although there is a sense of liberation when the Civil War forces a change in Pepico's direction, the adult narrator admits to the difficulty of trying to adopt another form of identity.

There is also the suggestion in the trilogy that the problems of Pepico concerning free will and determinism are universal. The narrator asks if anyone is truly able to act freely, and if not, does anyone have the right to impose a destiny on others? These questions can indeed be related to every individual and they obviously apply to characters like Enrique and Alfredo in the earlier novels. In the novels studied, the problem of free will and determinism is primarily concentrated around the notion of the religious vocation and is essentially linked to the influence of the mother in the different works. In each case, there is a degree of personal choice involved in the vocation since it is regarded as a search for authenticity and a higher ideal, and this is usually accompanied by the full support of the mother. The problem arises when the personal ideal is challenged or begins to wane and the mother's emotional pressure becomes the only driving-force behind the vocation. It is when the vocation gets involved with deceit that the different characters are plunged into all sorts of problems. The only one in the novels to show honesty and courage in this matter is Enrique in *Sin camino* while Pepico in the trilogy had to wait for the Civil War to change things and Alfredo in *Como ovejas al matadero* was destroyed by sexual pressure.

While the mother's pressure is viewed negatively in *Sin camino* and *Como ovejas al matadero*, her role in the trilogy is much more positive in contrast with the oppression exercised by Cirilo, Cayetano and don Jerónimo. With so much emphasis on death and resignation, the mother stands out in the trilogy as a sign of life and hope, who evidently becomes Pepico's only source of purpose. The dependence on the mother is illustrated at the time of her death when all hope seems lost and Pepico is drawn into the thick of the Civil War. The fact that the narrator has felt emptiness and nothingness ever since his mother's death suggests that she is not simply a symbol of hope in the trilogy but that she is the very sustenance of her son's life. This great bond between Pepico and his mother is an evident reflection of the great admiration which Castillo-Puche had for his own mother. This could also explain the optimism of Enrique in *Sin camino* where the mother is apparently still alive and the madness and chaos in Alfredo in *Como ovejas* when the mother had previously died.

The powerful emotions expressed in the trilogy concerning the mother could be linked to the fact that, in reality, the author was not present when his mother died in 1946. There is not only the sense of remorse that the author had failed to fulfil his mother's hopes but also that she passed away in his absence. Castillo-Puche seems to have spent the remainder of his life regretting this fact and attempting to make some form of reparation through his novels, especially in the last part of the trilogy.[2]

Finally, since the vocation of Ramiro and Fulgencio in *Como ovejas* are presented favourably, it appears that the vocation to the priesthood is still considered to be a worthy ideal. In the novels we have studied, we have examined the conflicts between the religious ideal and human nature. While the natural forces often come across as healthy and appealing, there is also the notion that negative behaviour within the seminary like hypocrisy and deception are also obstacles to the fulfilment of the ideal. The constant disillusionment in the trilogy with the oppression and injustice of Hécula, the insincere attitude of priests and seminarians in the seminary, and the destructive effects of the Civil War suggest that the author is evidently disturbed by the evil forces which prevent an atmosphere of peace and welfare among individuals. The key to the author's feelings on the subject can be found in a passage that I quoted earlier from the book on Sender:

> Explicación racional y profunda del fracaso de nuestros sueños de convivencia y de paz; análisis de aquellas influencias nefastas que, en determinados momentos históricos, nos han impedido ser lo que queremos ser.[3]

Although commenting on Sender's work on the Civil War, Castillo-Puche is plainly concerned with the effects of these destructive forces not only upon society but also upon the individual. This personal concern is further illustrated in a letter I received from the author in October 1990 in which he discussed the contradictory elements within human nature:

> La condición humana es precaria de por sí, y aunque el hombre es capaz de mucha grandeza, mucha bondad y mucha belleza, también es capaz de caer en terribles aberraciones y abominaciones.[4]

In the same letter, he appears to be under no illusions concerning the existence of an evil spiritual force at work in the world:

> Hemos de creer en la existencia del espíritu del mal que tiene entablada una lucha en el corazón del hombre, y de ahí el terrible poder de las pasiones que a veces dejan al ser humano maltrecho y arrumbado física y espiritualmente.

Sin and evil, then, seem to be as much a part of our human existence as any positive values. Therefore that is why there is a need for redemption and that the religious ideal is indeed a good thing, but as something active in the world and not separated from it.

The clearest example of man's debasement in the novels is undoubtedly the mental deterioration of Alfredo with its accompanying signs of guilt and paranoia. The psychological problems are also very much in evidence in the trilogy where the narrator is presented as an individual troubled not just by a guilt complex but by the sense of non-being and split personality. It seems that this mental trauma is the result of the actions and behaviour of other people in the narrator's past, whether it is the guilt associated with sexual abuse or whether it is the feeling of non-being related to Hécula's obsession with death. It could be argued that these problems were already inherent in Pepico in the trilogy and in Enrique and Alfredo in the other novels but there is no doubt that destructive forces were also at work and were partly responsible for the characters' predicament.

The fact that Castillo-Puche is still writing about the Church and the religious life almost forty years after his departure from seminary suggests that he is still deeply troubled by the question of his own religious vocation. While also affected by his experience of the Civil War and the memory of his mother, the crucial factor about the religious life was the accompanying sense of identity which has not been easily replaced.

NOTES

1. Alma Amell, "El seminarista en dos novelas de José Luis Castillo-Puche." *Horizontes*, 62 (1988), 39.

2. See above ch. 7, 227 and *Conocerás el poso de la nada*, 111.

3. *Ramón J. Sender: el distanciamiento del exilio*, 83.

4. The letter consisted mainly of the author's comments on the fundamental themes of the human condition, the uncertainty of destiny, and the conflict between nature and the soul.

Bibliography

1. Works by Castillo-Puche

The first editions of the works are listed in chronological order followed, where relevant, by the significant later editions. All page references in my study are to first editions except where an asterisk (*) indicates the later edition.

A. Full Length Novels

Castillo-Puche, José Luis. *Con la muerte al hombro*. Madrid: Biblioteca Nueva, 1954 and Barcelona: Destino, 1972 and Yecla: Ateneo Literario, 1995*.
———. *Sin camino*. Buenos Aires: Emecé, 1956 and Barcelona: Destino, 1983*.
———. *El vengador*. Barcelona: Planeta, 1956 and Barcelona: Destino, 1975.
———. *Hicieron partes*. Madrid: Escelicer, 1957 and Barcelona: Destino, 1967.
———. *Paralelo 40*. Barcelona: Destino, 1963.
———. *Oro blanco*. Madrid: CID, 1963.
———. *Como ovejas al matadero*. Barcelona: Destino, 1971.
———. *Jeremías, el anarquista*. Barcelona: Destino, 1975.
———. *El libro de las visiones y las apariciones*. Barcelona: Destino, 1977.
———. *El amargo sabor de la retama*. Barcelona: Destino, 1977.
———. *Conocerás el poso de la nada*. Barcelona: Destino, 1982.
———. *Los murciélagos no son pájaros*. Barcelona: Destino, 1986.

B. Stories/Short Novels

Castillo-Puche, José Luis. *Bienaventurados los que sueñan*, in *La Verdad*, Murcia, 15 de agosto de 1943 to 1 de octubre de 1943 and republished in Emilio González-Grano de Oro. *El español de José L. Castillo-Puche*. Madrid: Gredos, 1983.
———. *Cartas de amor y olvido* in *La Verdad*, Murcia, 21 de octubre de 1945 and republished in Emilio González-Grano de Oro. *El español de José L. Castillo-Puche*. Madrid: Gredos, 1983.
———. *El perro loco*. Madrid: La Novela Popular, 2, 1965.
———. *De dentro de la piel*. Madrid: Editora Nacional, 1972. - three short stories

and one full-length novel: *El superviviente*. 1951, *Una historia en pedazos*. 1952, *Carta de Judas Iscariote*. 1953, *Misión a Estambul*. Madrid: CID, 1954.

———. *El leproso y otras narraciones*. Murcia: Ediciones Mediterráneo, 1981. - five short stories and four extracts from full-length novels: *El leproso*. 1978, *Y los sueños, sueños son*. 1968, *Una mosca en Manhattan*. 1968, *¡Con lo que cuesta criar un hijo!* 1962, *El superviviente*. 1951. - appeared previously as part of *De dentro de la piel*, see above, 'Los Auroros' - extract from *El libro de las visiones y las apariciones*, 'Tormenta sobre Ciriza' - extract from *El amargo sabor de la retama*, 'La difícil batalla de la liberación personal' - extract from *Conocerás el poso de la nada*, 'Historia de la monja visionaria y toma del convento de las Anas' - extract from *Jeremías, el anarquista*.

C.   Non-fiction Articles and Books

Castillo-Puche, José Luis. *Memorias íntimas de Aviraneta o Manual del conspirador*. Madrid: Biblioteca Nueva, 1953.
———. *América de cabo a rabo*. Madrid: CID, 1959.
———. *Tierra de Campos. Más bien mares de tierra*. Palencia: Diputación Provincial, 1961.
———. *Hemingway entre la vida y la muerte*. Barcelona: Destino, 1968.
———. *Hemingway in Spain*. New York: Doubleday, 1974 - a translation of *Hemingway entre la vida y la muerte*, see above
———. *Francisco Lozano, una mística del paisaje*. Madrid: Rayuela, 1979.
———. *Ramón J. Sender: el distanciamiento del exilio*. Barcelona: Destinolibro, 1985.
———. *Hemingway, algunas claves de su vida y de su obra*. Madrid: Huerga y Fierro, 1992.
———. *Mosaico de Murcia*. Murcia: CajaMurcia Obra Cultural, 1996.

D.   Unpublished Material

Castillo-Puche, José Luis. "Escribir en Murcia.", lecture given by author at the University of Murcia in 1988.
———. "Curriculum Vitae." (up to 1983). Written in the third person. Material supplied by the author.
———. Untitled lecture given by the author at several American universities in 1985. Material supplied by the author.
———. Conversations between José Luis Castillo-Puche and Martin Farrell recorded at the author's home in Madrid during September 1985 and January 1987.

2. *Works on Castillo-Puche*

A. Complete Books

Belchí Arévalo, Cecilia, and María Martínez del Portal, ed. *Estudios sobre José Luis Castillo-Puche*. Murcia: Academia Alfonso X el Sabio, 1988.

Belmonte Serrano, José. *Origen y proceso de la narrativa de José Luis Castillo-Puche*. Murcia: Universidad de Murcia, 1997.

González-Grano de Oro, Emilio. *El español de José L. Castillo-Puche. Estudio léxico*. Madrid: Gredos, 1983.

Ramón Lacabe, María Luisa. *El estilo de José Luis Castillo-Puche en la Trilogía de la liberación*. Murcia: Universidad de Murcia, 1996.

B. Articles, Chapters or References in Books

Barrero Pérez, Oscar. *La novela existencial española de posguerra*. Madrid: Gredos, 1987.

Jiménez Madrid, Ramón. *Novelistas murcianos actuales*. Murcia: Alfonso X el Sabio, 1982. pp.85-116.

Roberts, Gemma. *Temas existenciales en la novela española de postguerra*. 2nd. ed. Madrid: Gredos, 1978. pp.236-261.

Sobejano, Gonzalo. *Novela española de nuestro tiempo*. 2nd. ed. Madrid: Prensa Española, 1975. pp.258-269.

C. Articles and Reviews appearing in Journals

Alborg, Concha. "Tres personajes de Castillo-Puche en busca de un camino." *Anales de Filología Hispánica* 2, (1986), 117-125.

Amell, Alma. "El seminarista en dos novelas de José Luis Castillo-Puche." *Horizontes* 62 (1988), 39-43.

Belchí Arévalo, Cecilia. ed. *Homenaje a José Luis Castillo-Puche. Monte Arabí* 18-19 (1994).

Blanco Amor, José. "Nuevos rumbos de la novela española." *La Nación* (Buenos Aires) 26 de febrero 1978.

Corbalán, Pablo. "Castillo-Puche entre la liberación y la fe." *Informaciones* 1 de julio 1971.

———. "Los demonios de J.L. Castillo-Puche." *Informaciones* 10 de noviembre 1977.

Del Amo, Javier. "La amarga necesidad de la sed." *El País* 22 de agosto 1979, 18.

Domingo, José. "Del seminario a la isla. Castillo-Puche. García Ramos." *Insula* 302 (1982), 6.

Fernández-Braso, Miguel. "Castillo-Puche a cuerpo limpio." *Pueblo* 7 de julio 1971.

256

González-Grano de Oro, Emilio. "Visión y sabor del poso de la nada." *Cuadernos Hispanoamericanos* 388 (1982), 201-205.

Peñuelas, Marcelino. "Denuncia y protesta. *El libro de las visiones y las apariciones* de J. L. Castillo-Puche." *Revista Iberoamericana* 47 (1981), 247-253.

Roberts, Gemma. "Con el pasado al hombro: *El amargo sabor de la retama* de José Luis Castillo-Puche." *Cuadernos Hispanoamericanos*, 361-362 (1980), 371-378.

———. "Memoria e identidad en *Conocerás el poso de la nada* de José Luis Castillo-Puche." *Revista Canadiense de Estudios Hispánicos* XII.1 (1987), 93-108.

Sobejano, Gonzalo. "La obra novelística de Castillo-Puche." *Monte Arabí* 21 (1995), 7-34.

Vázquez Zamora, Rafael. "José Luis Castillo-Puche: El cíngulo. Como ovejas al matadero." *Destino* 28 de agosto 1971, 45.

3.   Other Works

Abbott, Walter M. ed. *The Documents of Vatican II*. London: Geoffrey Chapman, 1966

Alborg, Juan Luis. *Hora actual de la novela española*. Vol. II, Madrid: Taurus, 1962.

Armstrong, Karen. *Through the Narrow Gate*. London: Pan, 1982.

———. *Beginning the World*. London: Pan, 1983.

Baroja, Pío. *Camino de perfección*. Madrid: Caro Raggio, 1974.

———. *El árbol de la ciencia*. Madrid: Alianza, 1967.

———. *Obras completas*. 2nd. ed. Madrid: Biblioteca Nueva, 1973.

Booth, Wayne C. *The Rhetoric of Fiction*. 2nd. ed. London: Penguin, 1991.

Bosch, Rafael. *La novela española del siglo XX*. New York: Las Americas, 1971.

Brenan, Gerald. *The Spanish Labyrinth*. 2nd. ed. Cambridge: CUP, 1962.

Brown, G.G. *A Literary History of Spain: The Twentieth Century*. London: Benn, 1972.

Chao Rego, J. *La iglesia en el franquismo*. Madrid: Ediciones Felmar, 1976.

Delibes, Miguel. *El camino*. Barcelona: Destino, 1980.

Douglas, J.D. *The New International Dictionary of the Christian Church*. Exeter: Paternoster Press, 1974.

Eliade, Mircea. *Mito y realidad*. translated by Luis Gil. Barcelona: Labor, 1968. - original title: *Aspects du Mythe*.

Enciclopedia universal ilustrada europea-americana. Madrid: Espasa-Calpe, 1958.

Escrivá, Jose María. *The Way*. Chicago: Scepter, 1965.

Ferreras, Juan Ignacio. *Tendencias de la novela española actual 1931-1969*. Paris: Ediciones Hispanoamericanas, 1970.

García Viñó, M. *Novela española actual*. Madrid: Ediciones Guadarrama, 1967.

Hooper, John. *The New Spaniards*. London: Penguin, 1995.

Jackson, Gabriel. *The Spanish Republic and the Civil War*. Princeton: PUP, 1965.

Lannon, Frances. *Privilege, Persecution and Prophecy: The Catholic Church in Spain 1875-1975*. Oxford: Clarendon, 1987.

Lodge, David. *Language of Fiction*. London: Routledge & Kegan Paul, 1966.

Martínez Ruiz, José. *Las confesiones de un pequeño filósofo*. 2nd. ed. Madrid: Austral-Espasa-Calpe, 1979.

——. *La voluntad*. Madrid: Biblioteca Nueva, 1970.

Nora, Eugenio G. *La novela española contemporánea*. Vol.III, 2nd. ed. Madrid: Gredos, 1971.

Ortuño Palao, Miguel. *Las calles de Yecla*. Yecla: La Levantina, 1982.

——. *El habla de Yecla*. Murcia: Sucesores de Nogués, 1987.

Payne, Stanley G. *The Spanish Revolution*. London: Weidenfeld & Nicolson, 1970.

——. *Spanish Catholicism: An Historical Overview*. London: University of Wisconsin Press, 1984.

Powell, John. *A reason to live! A reason to die!* Texas: Argus, 1972.

——. *Why am I afraid to tell you who I am?* Hong Kong: Fontana, 1975.

Preston, Paul. *The Spanish Civil War*. London: Weidenfeld & Nicolson, 1986.

Sender, Ramón J. *Réquiem por un campesino español*. Barcelona: Destino, 1974.

Shaw, Donald L. *The Generation of 1898 in Spain*. London: Benn, 1975.

The Jerusalem Bible. Popular Edition. London: Darton, Longman & Todd, 1974.

Index

Alborg, Concha 37-38
Amell, Alma 246
América de cabo a rabo 98
Armstrong, Karen 219-220

Baroja, Pío 95-97, 98, 233, 234, 235
Barrero Pérez, Oscar 13-14, 36, 45, 111-112, 141
Bienaventurados los que sueñan 1
Blanco Amor, José 139-140
Booth, Wayne 43-44, 45, 178
Brenan, Gerald 58, 163, 175-176

Camino de perfección 98
Chao Rego, José 61
Comillas 3, 5, 9, 11, 19, 42
Con la muerte al hombro 1, 13, 98, 109, 127-129, 229, 230
Corbalán, Pablo 50-51, 77-78, 117
Council of Elvira 182
Council of Trent 182

Del Amo, Javier 168
Domingo, José 79

El perro loco 98
El vengador 1, 98, 109
Escrivá, José María 5

Fernández-Braso, Miguel 65-66, 68, 87

Gil Robles, José María 106
González-Grano de Oro, Emilio 2

Hemingway, Ernest 95-96
Hicieron partes 1, 4
Hooper, John 56-57, 63, 76

Jeremías el anarquista 4-5, 98
Jiménez Madrid, Ramón 1, 127, 174-175, 194

La nave de los locos 96
La voluntad 98
Las calles de Yecla 99
Las confesiones de un pequeño filósofo 98
Lodge, David 97-98

Martínez Ruíz, José 98
Mosaico de Murcia 190
Murcia 2, 3, 5, 49, 102, 167, 189-191, 193, 202, 210, 233, 246

Oro blanco 98
Ortega y Gasset, José 96
Ortuño Palao, Miguel 99, 100, 105

Paralelo 40 1
Payne, Stanley 58, 166
Peñuelas, Marcelino 1, 117-118
Powell, John 29-32, 35, 223-226, 228, 234-235
Preston, Paul 166, 177-178

Réquiem por un campesino español 60
Roberts, Gemma 109, 111, 128-129, 157-158, 160-161, 180, 211, 215-216, 223

Second Vatican Council 5, 10, 56,
    57, 61, 64, 76, 182-183,
    218, 219, 246
Sender, Ramón 60, 248
Shaw, Donald 97
Sobejano, Gonzalo 1, 22, 42, 44,
    45-46, 76-77
Spanish Civil War 2, 22, 30, 34,
    42, 49, 57, 58, 60, 61, 98, 100,
    127, 156, 157, 165-166, 170,
    179, 193, 202, 203, 221, 229,
    235, 236-237, 238, 239, 240,
    241-242, 246, 247, 248, 250

T*he Spanish Civil War 1936-1939*
    166

Vázquez Zamora, Rafael 71

Yecla 2, 94, 98-99, 100, 101, 105
    106

STUDIES IN ART AND RELIGIOUS INTERPRETATION

1. Michael Sexson, **The Quest of Self in the Collected Poems of Wallace Stevens**

2. Lorine M. Getz, **Nature and Grace in Flannery O'Connor's Fiction**

3. Victoria Aarons, **Author as Character in the Works of Sholom Aleichem**

4. Ann T. Foster, **Theodore Roethke's Meditative Sequences: Contemplation and the Creative Process**

5. Charles B. Ketcham, **The Influence of Existentialism on Ingmar Bergman: An Analysis of the Theological Ideas Shaping A Filmmaker's Art**

6. James H. Evans, Jr., **Spiritual Empowerment in Afro-American Literature: Frederick Douglass, Rebecca Jackson, Booker T. Washington, Richard Wright, Toni Morrison**

7. Ben Kimpel, **Moral Philosophies in Shakespeare's Plays**

8. Donald Grayston (ed.), **Thomas Merton's Rewritings: The Five Versions of Seeds/New Seeds of Contemplation as a Key to the Development of His Thought**

9. Lewis J. Hutton, **The Christian Essence of Spanish Literature: An Historical Study**

10. Michael Ernest Travers, **The Devotional Experience in the Poetry of John Milton**

11. Richard E. Morton, **Anne Sexton's Poetry of Redemption: The Chronology of A Pilgrimage**

12. S. Carl King, **The Photographic Impressionists of Spain: A History of the Aesthetics and Technique of Pictorial Photography**

13. Daven Michael Kari, **T.S. Eliot's Dramatic Pilgrimage: A Progress in Craft as an Expression of Christian Perspective**

14. Caroline Phillips, **The Religious Quest in the Poetry of T.S. Eliot**

15. Edward R. Heidt, **The Image of the Church Minister in Literature**

16. Daven Michael Kari, **A Bibliography of Sources in Christianity and the Arts**

17. Nitzan Ben-Shaul, **Expressions of Siege in Israeli Films**

18. Giuseppe Di Scipio, **The Presence of Pauline Thought in the Works of Dante**

19. Charlotte Yeldham, **Margaret Gillies RWS, Unitarian Painter of Mind and Emotion (1803-1887)**

20. Raymond M. Herbenick, **Andy Warhol's Religious and Ethnic Roots: The Carpatho-Rusyn Influence on His Art**

21. Christian E. Hauer, Jr. (ed.), **Christopher Wren and the Many Sides of Genius: Proceedings of a Christopher Wren Symposium, with an Introduction and a Brief Biographical Essay**

22. Janet A. Anderson, **Pedro de Mena, Seventeenth-Century Spanish Sculptor**

23. Douglas Kenning, **Necessity, Freedom and Transcendence in the Romantic Poets: A Failed Religion**

24A. C.J.P. Lee, **The Metaphysics of Mass Art–Cultural Ontology**, Volume One: **Mysticism, Mexico and English Literature**

24B. C.J.P. Lee, **The Metaphysics of Mass Art–Cultural Ontology**, Volume Two: **'Madness' and the 'Savage': Indigenous Peoples of the Americas and the Psychology of the Observer in U.S. Film**

25. Michael Giffin, **Patrick White and the Religious Imagination: Arthur's Dream**

26. Martin Farrell, **The Search for the Religious Ideal in Selected Works of José Luis Castillo-Puche**

27. Michael Giffin, **Introduction to Religion in the English Novel**